Stately
Passions

Stately Passions

THE SCANDALS OF BRITAIN'S GREAT HOUSES

Jamie Douglas-Home

MICHAEL O'MARA BOOKS LIMITED

First published in Great Britain in 2006 by
Michael O'Mara Books Limited
9 Lion Yard, Tremadoc Road
London sw4 7nq

A CIP catalogue record for this book is available
from the British Library

Michael O'Mara Books edition:
ISBN (10 digit): 1-84317-154-6
ISBN (13 digit): 978-1-84317-154-6

Reader's Digest edition:
ISBN (10 digit): 1-84317-185-6
ISBN (13 digit): 978-1-84317-185-0

Print ⌐ss, Bath

Contents

Acknowledgements

I am grateful to my publishers, Michael O'Mara Books Limited, and in particular to Michael O'Mara and Toby Buchan, whose assistance and advice were invaluable; to my editors, Kate Gribble and Dominique Enright (who also made the index), and copy-editor, Hugh Morgan, and to Ariane Durkin for reading the proofs. Grateful thanks, too, to Judith Palmer and David Sinden for the illustrations for this book, to Button Group plc for the jacket designs, and to Martin Bristow for the design and layout of the text.

PICTURE ACKNOWLEDGEMENTS

Page 1: © Guildhall Art Gallery, Corporation of London, UK/ Bridgeman Art Library (*above*), Rischgitz, after the picture by R. Herdman (*below*)

Page 2: Illustrated London News Picture Library (*above*), Time Life Pictures/Getty Images (*below*)

Page 3: Getty Images

Page 4: PA/Empics (*above*), © Popperfoto/Alamy (*below*)

Page 5: Rischgitz, after Holbein (*above*), © Popperfoto/Alamy (*below*)

Page 6: TopFoto.co.uk (*above*), O. Lacour (from the original portrait at Penshurst) (*below*)

Page 7: Getty Images (*above*), TopFoto.co.uk (*below*)

Page 8: Getty Images

Page 9: TopFoto.co.uk (*above*), Mary Evans Picture Library/ Jeffrey Morgan Collection (*below*)

ACKNOWLEDGEMENTS

Page 10: Getty Images
Page 11: Getty Images (*above*), TopFoto.co.uk (*below*)
Page 12: Mary Evans Picture Library (*above*), Getty Images (*below*)
Page 13: Getty Images
Page 14: Getty Images
Page 15: Illustrated London News Picture Library (*above*),
   © Popperfoto/Alamy (*below*)
Page 16: TopFoto.co.uk (*above*), Getty Images (*below*)

Introduction

WHILE I WAS WRITING and researching *Stately Passions*, the irresponsibility and lack of accountability shown, over the centuries, by the British royal family and aristocracy made me gulp in amazement with increasing and worrying frequency. After all, the different generations of owners of these palaces and stately homes are merely custodians, one of whose duties it is to keep such houses and estates intact for their children, for their children's children, and, indeed, in royalty's case, for the country and their subjects.

Yet throughout history, their willingness to gamble away their inheritances, produce strings of illegitimate children and partake of a hedonistic lifestyle of drink- and, later, drug-fuelled decadence, without any regard for the consequences or even the faintest degree of contriteness, almost beggars belief. Didn't anybody in the opulent drawing rooms of these stately homes notice what was happening on the other side of the Channel during the French Revolution? Obviously not: indeed, the behaviour of Britain's royals and upper classes throughout the century that followed was arguably even more debauched than it had been before our Gallic neighbours decided to dispense with their dissolute monarchy.

Boredom, which a privileged and spoiled existence inevitably brings, was probably partly to blame for the propensity for bed-hopping with members of the same or the opposite sex; wife-swapping; betting staggering sums on the horses and the tables, like Georgiana, Duchess of Devonshire; and even, in Henry VIII's case, beheading an unfaithful spouse. But not entirely – even those who took their duties seriously and displayed some sort of social conscience, such as Prime Ministers Melbourne, Palmerston and Grey, were constantly involved in adulterous relationships and, actually or reputedly, fathered several bastard children. In their case, perhaps, the old adage that power is the greatest aphrodisiac is true.

In the end, however, it must be left to the reader to decide whether promiscuity and degeneracy occur with similar regularity in the less fortunate strata of society, or if this strange state of affairs can be put down to the simple fact that Britain's royalty and aristocracy were blessed, or fated, with oversized libidos, as well as often gargantuan appetites for drink or drugs – and occasionally both.

JAMIE DOUGLAS-HOME
January 2006

CHAPTER ONE

Royal Scots

The Palace of Holyroodhouse

THE RICH HISTORY OF THE PALACE OF HOLYROODHOUSE, which stands at the end of Edinburgh's famous Royal Mile under the city's prominent hillside landmark, Arthur's Seat, began in the dark twelfth century. Almost nine centuries ago, in 1128, Scotland's King David I was hunting on the outskirts of Edinburgh when he had a vision in which a cross, or rood, belonging to his mother, Queen Saint Margaret, appeared between the antlers of a stag that had turned on its pursuers. David was so moved by his religious experience that he ordered an Augustinian monastery to be built on the very spot where the attacking deer had stood. The apt symbol of the abbey – a stag's head, with its horns framing a cross – is used to this day.

When Edinburgh grew to be recognized as the Scottish capital, the country's monarchs chose to live at Holyroodhouse, surrounded by its tranquil parkland, rather than in cold and forbidding Edinburgh Castle, high on a windswept rock above the city. In 1501 James IV cleared the woodland close to the abbey and constructed a glorious palace where he could live with his new bride, Margaret Tudor, the daughter of England's King Henry VII. The centuries have taken their toll, however; today, all that remains there is a small piece of the gatehouse of James and Margaret's magnificent dwelling.

His successor, James V, added a huge tower between 1528 and 1532 and a new west front three years later. As James IV had built the palace to serve as a defensive stronghold, these renovations, which included an enormous amount of glasswork, made Holyroodhouse a far more comfortable place to inhabit for James's first wife, Madeleine, the daughter of Francis I of France, and his second wife, Mary of Guise, who was crowned in the abbey and was later to bear the King a daughter who would succeed him as Mary Queen of Scots.

Mary Queen of Scots, who returned to rule Scotland in 1561 after the death of her husband, Francis II of France, spent much of her short but dramatic life at Holyroodhouse and married each of her two other spouses, Lord Darnley and the Earl of Bothwell, in the abbey. But the palace fell into disrepair under her son, James VI of Scotland, and was not used as a royal residence after he moved to London following the death of Elizabeth I in 1603 to become England's king as well. When James returned to Edinburgh in 1617, the palace was smartened up, and further refurbishments were carried out when Charles I was crowned King of Scotland in 1633, having succeeded his father on the latter's death in 1625.

In the 1640s, during the Civil War, when it came under the occupation of Cromwell's soldiers, the palace suffered serious fire damage, but, after the restoration of the monarchy in 1660, Charles II ordered an extensive rebuilding programme following his crowning in Scotland. Although he never returned to see the results of his handiwork, 'Old Rowley'[1] certainly made the new palace more hospitable for its first occupant, his brother, the Duke of York, later to be James II (and VII of Scotland), and their descendants. He created a new royal apartment to the east and added the spacious upper floor, where the royal family's living quarters are now, to accommodate the court. Charles also commissioned the impressive classical façades that surround the central quadrangle, and transformed the old abbey church into the Chapel Royal.

After the English and Scottish Parliaments were united at the beginning of the eighteenth century, the palace began to be neglected by the royal family, whose apartments were then used as grace-and-favour dwellings for impecunious aristocrats. But royalty returned to Holyroodhouse in 1745 when the Young Pretender, Charles Edward Stuart or, to Jacobites, Bonnie Prince Charlie, held court there during his ill-fated attempt to claim the throne for his father, James the Old Pretender, the only son of James II. Ironically, the next royal resident was George II's soldier son, the Duke of Cumberland,[2] whose troops brought both the charismatic prince's rebellion and the flower of Scottish Jacobite youth to an untimely end at the bloody Battle of Culloden in 1746.

The abbey church's roof collapsed in 1765, ruining Charles II's Chapel Royal, but no further work was done on the palace until George IV's time. The King's state visit to Scotland on 15 August 1822 provided the impetus for his government to sanction the release of funds to give Holyroodhouse another fresh face. Queen Victoria, who succeeded William IV in 1837 and who liked to stay at the palace on her way to Balmoral, made further improvements, as well as re-establishing Holyroodhouse as Scotland's premier royal residence. Her grandson, George V, who initiated the tradition of holding garden parties when the sovereign is in residence, also visited often and modernized the palace extensively.

It is true to say, therefore, that many monarchs have left their mark on Holyroodhouse, but George IV must take the credit for safeguarding the location of the most nefarious and dramatic event in the ancient palace's chequered history. When he ordered that the apartment of Mary Queen of Scots should be 'preserved sacred from all alteration', the debauched old King cleverly ensured that

[13]

future generations would be able to absorb the chilling, even ghostly, atmosphere that still exists in Mary's bedchamber, and in the adjoining rooms at the top of the winding staircase that snakes up the palace's north-west corner tower. For it was here that the young and beautiful Scottish Queen, heavily pregnant with a future King of England and Scotland, witnessed the savage murder of her trusted secretary, David Rizzio, by a group of ruthless Scottish noblemen, headed by her insanely jealous husband, Lord Darnley.

Mary Queen of Scots was born at Linlithgow Palace in West Lothian on 8 December 1542. Her father, James V, who had already lost two infant sons, was a sick man and had been confined to his bed in Falkland Palace since a crushing defeat by the English at Solway Moss two weeks earlier. When he received the news of his daughter's birth, the Scottish King turned his head to the wall and, recalling that the Crown had descended to the Stuarts through Robert the Bruce's daughter, Marjorie, muttered: 'It came from a woman, and it will end with a woman.' Six days later, James was dead, and his baby daughter inherited the Scottish throne.

In March 1543 the Scottish Parliament appointed Mary's cousin and next in line of succession, the Earl of Arran, as regent until she reached her majority at the age of twelve. The by now excommunicated King of England, Henry VIII, thought it would be a good idea to arrange the marriage of his five-year-old son, Edward, to the tiny Mary to ensure that Scotland and England were united under his rule. Arran was willing to cooperate and, on 1 July, a treaty was signed at Greenwich confirming that Edward and Mary would eventually be wed.

The conditions of the agreement were that Mary should go to England when she was ten and be married the following year. But the Catholic faction, headed by Mary's mother, Mary of Guise, violently opposed the agreement. So she removed Mary from Arran's care, took her to Stirling Castle and had her crowned in its Chapel Royal on 9 December. A few days later, the Scottish Parliament repudiated Mary's betrothal to Edward and renewed the traditional alliance between Scotland and France.

Henry VIII was furious when he heard that his well-laid plans to bring Scotland, for so long a thorn in the flesh of its southern neighbour, to heel had been thwarted. So he sent an army over the border in retaliation. The brutal series of raids, known as the 'Rough Wooing', inflicted much damage on Lowland Scotland. Henry's troops burned the abbeys of Holyrood, where James V was buried, Melrose, Jedburgh and Dryburgh, and set fire to crops in the fertile Tweed valley. Henry persecuted the Scots until his death in 1547. The Duke of Somerset, the regent of the new boy king, Edward VI, pursued an identical policy, inflicting a terrible defeat on the Scots, who were under Arran's command, at Pinkie in September 1547.

As the English forces now occupied a large swath of the south-east part of the country, Arran appealed to the French for aid. As an incentive, he suggested to Henry II of France that Scotland's young Catholic Queen should be betrothed to Henry's eldest son, Francis. The French king, realizing that such a union would effectively mean that Scotland would become a satellite of France, liked Arran's idea.

In February 1548, after the Scottish Parliament consented to the marriage of Mary and the Dauphin, Henry II sent French troops to Scotland. They recaptured the strategically important town of Haddington, east of Edinburgh, from the English in June, and in July a treaty between France and Scotland was signed, formally agreeing to the marriage of Mary and Francis. On 7 August 1548 Mary, aged only five, said goodbye to her mother and her country and sailed for France. It would be thirteen years before she returned, as a widow of only eighteen years of age, to rule her native land.

Mary was brought up in the French court and, at the age of fifteen, married Francis, younger than her by a year. Only a year later the Dauphin's father was killed in a jousting accident, so his wife became Queen of France as well as Scotland (albeit under the regency of Francis's mother, Catherine de' Medici). This powerful union, however, did not last long, for Francis died of a brain tumour the following year. Although Mary was fond of her sickly husband, it is doubtful if her marriage to Francis, who reputedly had withered genitalia, was ever consummated. So when she came back to Scotland in August 1561, the young Queen was probably as inexperienced in the art of physical love as she was in the world of politics. Clearly, it was not going to be easy for the Catholic girl, who had been in France for so long, to rule the turbulent country that was now officially Protestant after religious reforms instigated by the fire-and-brimstone preacher, John Knox. In addition, the death of her mother, Mary of Guise, who had been Regent of Scotland since 1554, had left a highly unstable political situation.

Knox made many vicious attacks on Mary from the pulpit, denouncing her as a heretic, but the first year of her reign went relatively well. She was popular with her Protestant subjects, and her half-brother, the Earl of Moray, her principal adviser and the leader of Scotland's Protestant nobles, helped his sister to rule with calmness and moderation. But things changed in 1562, when Moray persuaded Mary to put down a rebellion in Scotland's Catholic north-west, led by the fourth Earl of Huntley.

It may seem odd that staunchly Catholic Mary agreed to repress those of the same religious persuasion so hard, but Moray had persuaded his sister that such action would make Elizabeth I look more favourably on Mary's claim to the English throne. Because Mary was the great-granddaughter of Henry VII, she arguably had a better claim than Elizabeth, who had effectively been made illegitimate by her father, Henry VIII, when he nullified his marriage to her mother, Anne Boleyn.[3] As it happened, Elizabeth refused to meet Mary, even though the rebellion had been crushed and Huntley was dead.[4] Consequently, Mary began to realize that Moray had deceived her in order to destroy a personal enemy and advance the Protestant cause. Her brother lost his sister's trust, and many Scottish nobles, who had been persuaded by Moray to ally themselves to the Protestant ranks, rejoined or turned to the Catholic fold.

Mary now began to follow her own judgement and decided to choose a husband who would advance her beloved Catholicism

[16]

and further her claim to the English throne. The candidate who best satisfied those criteria was her second cousin, Henry Stewart (or Stuart), Lord Darnley, who, like Mary, was a great-grandchild of Henry VII. It also helped that Darnley's father, the Earl of Lennox, was Scottish, while his mother was a prominent English Catholic.

The wedding took place on 29 July 1565 in Holyrood Abbey with Mary, being a widow, attired in a dignified black dress. There was riotous dancing and a great banquet after the nuptials. Then the young couple retired to bed. Mary presumably enjoyed this part of the ceremony, if John Knox's memories of the occasion are correct. 'During the space of three or four days,' the puritanical preacher wrote, 'there was nothing but balling, dancing and banqueting.'

Indeed, all the evidence suggests that Mary was deeply in love with the handsome Darnley before and immediately after her wedding. If not, she would never have ordered her heralds to announce, on 30 July, the day after her marriage, that her nineteen-year-old husband should henceforward be known as King Henry. There was even an unsubstantiated rumour that she had been so infatuated with her lover that she had gone through a secret marriage earlier in July so that the couple could consummate their relationship sooner.

Not everyone in Scotland, however, was as happy as Mary with her marriage. Moray and some of the Protestant lords soon rebelled, but were eventually driven south of the border by Mary's army, led by Darnley's father, Lennox, and James Hepburn, the Earl of Bothwell, who was a leading member of Mary's new and largely Catholic council. Yet Darnley's behaviour soon became of greater concern to Mary. Her once romantic suitor had become arrogant through pomp and position and, by the autumn, was spending less and less time with his adoring wife.

It seemed that he much preferred hawking and hunting to attending to his royal duties. There was also gossip that he was drinking heavily and consorting with prostitutes in the less savoury parts of Edinburgh and Glasgow. It was little wonder, then, that by the end of 1565 Mary was beginning to tire of Darnley's insensitive and inattentive behaviour. The great love she had felt for her husband began rapidly to fade. Darnley, however, had fulfilled one of his conjugal obligations before his eyes had strayed. He had made his young wife pregnant.

Conscious that there was increasing coolness between Mary and her husband, some Scottish Protestant nobles, who hated the Queen's Catholic inner circle of advisers, saw the easily led Darnley as the means to regain control of Scotland and engineer the return from exile of many of their peers. So one of their ringleaders, the Earl of Morton, told his cousin, Darnley, that David Rizzio, Mary's secretary from Savoy[5] and arguably her most trusted confidant, had too much influence at court. When Darnley questioned him further, Morton informed his gullible relation that the hunch-backed Rizzio was actually Mary's lover and therefore the likely father of the child she was carrying.

There was no evidence that Mary was having a sexual relationship with ugly little Rizzio, and the subsequent date of her child's birth shows that the talented Italian musician could not have been the father. But the jealous Darnley, whose judgement was probably also clouded by alcohol, stupidly chose to believe Morton and agreed to help the scheming Protestant lords commit a dreadful crime. The conspirators persuaded Darnley that Rizzio, who had apparently insulted his honour by having a torrid affair with Mary, should pay the ultimate penalty for such deceit.

On 9 March 1566, when Mary was hosting an intimate supper party, at which Rizzio was a guest, in her small apartment on the second floor of the Palace of Holyroodhouse, Darnley unexpectedly appeared on the narrow staircase that connected his rooms on the floor below to his wife's. A few moments later, a breathless Lord Ruthven joined him and said to Mary: 'Let it please Your Majesty that yonder man David come forth of your privy-chamber where he has been overlong.' Mary, not immediately clear about the purpose of this impromptu visit, replied that Rizzio was there at her invitation and enquired if Ruthven had taken leave of his senses.

The terrified Rizzio, realizing that he was in mortal danger, slunk back and hid in the large window at the end of the dining room. As Ruthven made a lunge towards the cowering Italian, Mary's guards moved forward. Ruthven then shouted: 'Lay not hands on me, for I will not be handled.' This was the signal for the rest of his band to enter. Andrew Ker of Fawdonside, Patrick Bellenden, George Douglas the Postulate, Thomas Scott and Henry Yair burst into the room, knocking over the dining table in the ensuing commotion. While Rizzio hung on to Mary's skirts like a terrified child, Ker and Bellenden produced their pistols and the other conspirators drew their daggers.

They tore the wretched Italian's fingers from Mary's dress and hauled their captive, screaming and kicking, out of the dining room and across the Queen's bedchamber into the small hall at the head of the staircase. There, the slight figure was butchered to death in a manner that could hardly have been more savage. George Douglas shrewdly administered the first wound with Darnley's dagger, thereby inextricably linking Mary's husband to the pernicious act. Incredibly, Rizzio was stabbed fifty-six times before the murderers threw his crumpled, bloodstained body down the winding staircase.

Bothwell and another of Mary's favourites, George Gordon, the fifth Earl of Huntley, were also targets of the conspirators that night. But when they heard the row in Mary's rooms, they sensed trouble and escaped by jumping out of one of the palace's rear windows. Mary, now parted from two of her closest allies, quickly realized that she could be in grave danger from the rampant Protestant lords. She knew that she would never be able to forgive Darnley for his role in Rizzio's demise or for endangering her unborn child, but she was certain that he now represented her only hope of survival.

Two nights later she went to his rooms and managed to convince him that the conspirators had been using him for their own designs. Before long Darnley was eating out of the palm of her hand and begging her forgiveness. The briefly reunited couple left

[19]

Holyroodhouse by the same staircase that Darnley and his fellow murderers had used and fled to Dunbar. There they met Bothwell, who was gathering the army that would later march on Edinburgh, restore Mary and force Rizzio's murderers to flee.

Mary was absolutely devastated by Rizzio's death. She scarcely stopped weeping, and refused to leave her chamber for days. Her worried aides heard her utter the same haunting refrain over and over again: 'I could wish to be dead.' Despite their apparent reconciliation, she hated Darnley with a passion for his part in the murder of her favourite, and the birth of their son James (later James VI of Scotland and I of England) in June 1566 did not change her feelings for her treacherous and unreliable husband in the least. Significantly, Mary was not alone in detesting Darnley. The nobles with whom he had conspired were infuriated that he had betrayed them two days after Rizzio's death. Bothwell, now the only man in Scotland Mary trusted, also wanted Darnley replaced as King. When Bothwell persuaded Mary to recall Moray and the other Protestant nobles from exile, more of Darnley's enemies came back to Scotland. The Queen's husband was rapidly running out of friends.

At Craigmillar Castle in November 1566, Bothwell convened a meeting of all the dissatisfied Catholic and Protestant nobles to discuss the issue of Darnley. They agreed upon two alternatives: divorce or assassination. Mary ruled out the former as it would make her son, James, illegitimate. She also told the nobles that they must do 'nothing against her honour', an ambiguous statement which they took to mean that she was happy to leave Darnley's fate in their hands. Immediately they left the Queen's presence, they are said to have signed a pact, known as the 'Craigmillar Bond', to murder her husband.[6]

In January 1567 Mary travelled to Glasgow to join Darnley, who believed he was safer from his enemies in Scotland's second city. On 1 February she persuaded her husband, who was seriously ill at the time, that he would recover quicker in Edinburgh. So Darnley, who may well have been suffering from syphilis, was installed for his convalescence in a small house, Kirk O'Field, about three-quarters of a mile from Holyroodhouse, just outside the city walls. Mary played the dutiful wife for several days and looked after her ailing spouse. On the evening of 9 February, she told Darnley that she must return to the palace at short notice to attend the wedding of a servant. As it turned out, it was fortunate that Mary chose to sleep at Holyroodhouse, for Bothwell and his accomplices had planned to murder Darnley in his bed that very night. They placed gunpowder below the house, but somehow Darnley survived the blast, only to be strangled as he tried to flee from his assassins.

Mary and Bothwell were quickly blamed for Darnley's murder. Soon, posters appeared all around Edinburgh depicting the Queen as Bothwell's whore and accusing the pair of the crime. Hearing that Moray and the Protestant exiles were behind the gossip, Bothwell, frightened for his and Mary's safety, abducted the Queen and rode to Dunbar Castle, where legend tells that he raped her before persuading her to be his wife. On 15 May, just over three months after Darnley's death, they were married in Holyrood Abbey. Exactly a month later, however, the Protestant lords defeated their troops at Carberry Hill, near Edinburgh. Mary agreed to give herself up provided Bothwell was allowed to go into exile. The newly married couple kissed passionately in front of both sides before Bothwell galloped away to try to raise another army in his wife's cause.

Two days later, Mary was imprisoned in Lochleven Castle, near Kinross, where she later miscarried Bothwell's twins. Next, she was forced to abdicate in favour of her infant son, James. Bothwell fled to Scandinavia, where he was arrested on a trumped-up charge and held prisoner until his death in Denmark ten years later, by which time he was insane. Mary eventually escaped from Lochleven in 1568, but her supporters were again routed at Langside. She then sought shelter in England, believing that Elizabeth would rally to her cause. Sadly, she was wrong; the Virgin Queen kept the cousin she believed to be seditious under house arrest (see pages 37–40). The English monarch was almost certainly right to be concerned,[7] and Mary was finally executed, for plotting against Elizabeth, at Fotheringhay Castle in Northamptonshire on 8 February 1587.

Historians have speculated for years whether it was mere coincidence that Mary left Kirk O'Field for Holyroodhouse on the night of Darnley's murder. They have also debated whether Bothwell really abducted Mary and raped her at Dunbar. Mary always denied prior knowledge of either event, but even her most fanatical supporters agree that it is hard to believe that she knew nothing about both of her third husband's plans, the assassination of Darnley and the flight to Dunbar.

It might be worth remembering, therefore, that in 1568 Mary's brother, Moray, who was now her son James's regent, accused his sister of playing golf with her French courtiers at Seton only days after Darnley's murder. He claimed, with some justification, that she must have been implicated in the plot if she was able to behave in such a disrespectful and unconcerned manner so soon after her husband's demise. Perhaps Moray was right that Mary was already Bothwell's lover and was complicit in the plan to eradicate Darnley from the moment of its conception at Craigmillar.

Of course, nobody will ever really know what was in the mind of the twenty-four-year-old Queen of Scots at the time. So perhaps it is better to give this enigmatic, if fascinating, historical figure the benefit of the doubt, and return a verdict permitted under Scottish law – not proven.

Balmoral Castle

Balmoral, the estate on Royal Deeside where Britain's sovereigns and their families spend their summer breaks, does not appear in the annals of Scottish history as early as its fellow royal residence, the Palace of Holyroodhouse.

The first mention in written records occurs in the early fifteenth century, when Balmoral is referred to as 'Bouchmorale'. In 1484, when it was leased to Sir Alexander Gordon of neighbouring Abergeldie Castle for the princely sum of £8.18s. per annum, its name had changed to 'Balmorain'. Sir Alexander's family built the first castle there, but by 1662 the Gordons were in such heavy debt that the Crown allowed the Farquharsons of Inverey to foreclose on the mortgaged Balmoral.

The Farquharsons themselves fell into financial trouble after supporting the Jacobite rebellions of 1715 and 1745, so James Duff, the second Earl of Fife, helped them out of a tricky situation by buying Balmoral for letting in 1798. The Earl, after a childless marriage, left his whole estate, including Balmoral, to an illegitimate son on his death in 1809, but a successful legal challenge to his will caused all his assets to be put under control of a body known as the Fife Trustees. They leased Balmoral, first to Captain James Cameron and then to a diplomat, Sir Robert

Gordon, who established a deer forest and made many alterations to the castle from 1834 to 1839.

Eight years later, at exactly the same time as Queen Victoria and her husband, Prince Albert, were visiting Scotland's rugged west coast in torrential rain, Balmoral, on the other side of the Cairngorms, was experiencing very different weather, to the delight of Sir Robert and his house guest, John Clark. The young man, who was convalescing in the castle after a serious illness, told his doctor father that Deeside was basking in perpetual sunshine and that the pure mountain air had improved his delicate health considerably.

Clark's father, Sir James, who was Victoria's physician, happened to mention his son's observations to the Queen, who was thinking of buying a property in Scotland. When Sir James, who was an expert on the effect of climate on health, added that Deeside, which traditionally receives a low amount of rainfall, might be a good place for the Queen to recover from her frequent bouts of rheumatism, the monarch became extremely interested.

As a direct result of Victoria's conversation with Sir James Clark, the Prince Consort commissioned a climatic report on Deeside, which confirmed that the area was one of the driest in Scotland. This information, and a love of sketches by the Aberdeen artist James Giles, who specialized in local landscapes, persuaded the royal couple that this beautiful and majestic part of eastern Scotland would be the perfect place in which to spend their annual autumn holiday.

Fate then intervened in an unexpected manner on 8 December 1847, when John Clark's host, Sir Robert Gordon, dropped dead while he was eating his breakfast. Knowing that the Queen was looking for a residence on Deeside, Sir Robert's brother, the fourth Earl of Aberdeen, suggested that Balmoral, which still had twenty years of its lease from the Fife Trustees to run, would suit the royal couple perfectly. As a result, Prince Albert dispatched Giles to Deeside to make some more sketches. When she saw the new drawings, Victoria was so delighted that she immediately agreed to take on the rest of the lease without having ever set foot on the Balmoral estate. The Fife Trustees assigned the lease to Albert on 20 May 1848, but Victoria and her husband had to wait until the autumn to see their new acquisition for the first time.

On 5 September 1848 the Royal Yacht *Victoria and Albert* moored off Aberdeen. After a civic reception and a luncheon at the Deeside town of Aboyne, a cannon welcomed the excited royal couple when they reached Ballater. At Crathie, another village close to Balmoral, they were greeted by a magnificent triumphal arch, inscribed with the message 'Welcome to your Highland home, Victoria and Albert'. At 2.45 p.m. Queen Victoria and Prince Albert arrived at Balmoral.

They were certainly more than pleased with their idyllic new home. Victoria later wrote in her *Leaves from the Journal of Our Life in the Highlands, from 1848 to 1861*: 'It is a pretty little castle in the old Scottish style. There is a picturesque tower and garden in front, with a high wooded hill; at the back there is wood down to the Dee; and the hills rise all around.' Albert was also delighted. After exploring the heathery hills surrounding the highest peak, Lochnagar, and the lovely glen that meanders down to Ballater, the happy Prince announced that the countryside around Balmoral was so like the mountains of eastern Saxony (from which, as Prince Albert of Saxe-Coburg and Gotha, he hailed) that it reminded him of home.

Albert steadily increased the royal property holdings on Deeside over the next few years. First, Birkhall, a house and 6,500-acre estate in Glen Muick, was bought to act as the future home of Albert Edward, the Prince of Wales (and later Edward VII), who was then eight years old. The Prince Consort also coveted the neighbouring fourteenth-century property of Abergeldie, but its owners, the Gordons, refused to sell and granted the Prince a forty-year lease instead. When she holidayed at Balmoral, Victoria's mother, the Duchess of Kent, lived at Abergeldie, which was finally purchased by the royal family for £100,000 in 1878, seventeen years after Albert's death.

The Prince made an offer for the Forest of Ballochbuie as well, but the Farquharsons were reluctant to do a deal. The members of that ancient Scottish family eventually changed their minds, however, and Victoria was able to add the huge tract of wooded hill to her expansive Deeside property portfolio in 1875. Last, but not least, Albert bought the Balmoral estate of 17,400 acres for 30,000 guineas (£31,500) in 1852. It was important to the Prince Consort that the property the royal family had leased for the past four years had now become their own.

As Victoria had intimated in her diaries when she saw Balmoral for the first time, the castle was relatively small. It was not long, therefore, before her husband decided to build a new and bigger dwelling for his large family and their guests.[8] The *schloss*, as the German-born prince used to describe his creation, would comprise two large rectangular residential blocks, built of local granite, united by an imposing square five-storey turreted tower. Victoria and Albert also decided that the whole interior, from the curtains to the doorknobs, would be made from or covered in a variety of tartans, so that their guests could not possibly forget that they were visiting the Highlands.

The construction of the new castle on a site about a hundred yards to the north of the old dwelling was a slow and expensive process. Victoria laid the foundation stone on 28 September 1853, but the royal family would not move into their new home until three years later. By 1859 all the renovations to the gardens and grounds, as well as new cottages for servants and other ancillary staff, were finished. With minute attention to detail, Albert even arranged for white poplars to be transported from his native Coburg to flank the new rose beds.

There were a number of reasons why Victoria and Albert loved Balmoral so much. First and foremost, though, it was the home they had created together and the estate that they themselves managed. They were happy that the ancient and often tiresome traditions that the royal household imposed on life at Buckingham Palace and Windsor Castle did not exist at the more relaxed and informal

Scottish hunting lodge. Albert could pursue his favourite hobby – stalking – and there were plenty of other recreations, like shooting, salmon fishing on the River Dee, walking and sightseeing by pony and trap, to keep family and guests amused.

Victoria's court and her government, however, were less enamoured of their Queen's new retreat which, inconveniently, was more than 500 miles from London. For example; the Prime Minister, the third Marquess of Salisbury, positively hated the place and, once there, could hardly wait to leave.[9] Following his example, prominent politicians and courtiers were reluctant to undertake the long and tedious journey to a place that did not interest them, although there was little enough they could do if ordered to attend upon their sovereign at her Highland retreat. That attitude, however, did not bother Albert and Victoria in the least. They were relieved to be so far away from the turgid ceremonial programme of the court in England, and enjoyed the break from Victoria's official constitutional duties.

Sadly, Albert was not able to enjoy the fruits of his labours on Deeside for very long. His errant eldest son, the Prince of Wales, had upset his mother and nearly aborted his engagement to Princess Alexandra of Denmark by embarking on a very public affair with an actress and courtesan, Nellie Clifden, in 1861. So Albert was dispatched on a cold and wet November day to reprimand his less than contrite son, who was then at Cambridge. He returned from this ordeal with a terrible chill.

By December, with the royal family at Windsor, the Prince Consort was growing weaker by the day. Suffering from typhoid, he began to drift in and out of consciousness and became delirious. It was clear that his death would not be long delayed. The end came on on Saturday, 14 December 1861 in the Blue Room at Windsor Castle, with a desolate Victoria clutching her beloved husband's hand. The Queen's grief was so consuming that she could not attend Albert's funeral. Thereafter she went into an extended period of mourning for the only man she had ever loved, which was to last until her own death forty years later.

[27]

John Brown, a hard-drinking, rough-and-ready gillie from Balmoral, was the unlikely individual who was destined to bring the forlorn, middle-aged widow out of her shell of grief and mourning. More controversially, their relationship would grow so close that gossips all over Victoria's kingdom would begin to air the scandalous theory that the bearded Highlander's role was much more than that of a devoted personal servant.

Brown, who was the son of a tenant farmer at nearby Crathienaird, started at Balmoral as a stable lad for Sir Robert Gordon in 1842. He is first mentioned in Victoria's *Journal* in 1849, when he helped to row a boat across a loch. He must have pleased his royal employer and the estate factor, as he was promoted to gillie later that year. In 1851 Prince Albert suggested that he should be appointed permanent leader of the pony the Queen liked to ride most days when she was at Balmoral. In 1858 Brown was promoted again to be the Prince's personal gillie. Brown travelled with Victoria and Albert on three long trips in Scotland in the years before Albert's death, and earned the monarch's praise for the help he gave her party when they were involved in a carriage accident near Balmoral in 1863.

In 1864 Victoria's second daughter, Princess Alice, was discussing with the Queen's Physician in Ordinary, William Jenner, and the Keeper of the Privy Seal, Sir Charles Phipps, the long and deep depression that was causing her mother to ignore most, if not all, her royal duties. Alice suggested that it might help to brighten the Queen's mood if John Brown were brought down from Balmoral, the Princess reasoning that the gillie might remind her mother of 'happier times'. Brown arrived at Osborne, on the Isle of Wight, in December 1864.[10] It was not long before Victoria became so dependent on her trusted Highland servant that she decided to give him a permanent position on her personal staff, and duly did so a year later.

Since Brown and the Queen were now hardly ever apart, it was unsurprising that rumours soon started to circulate in court circles about the propriety of their increasingly close relationship. Even

Victoria's daughters were often heard to refer cheekily to the tall gillie as 'Mama's lover'. But the situation became much more serious in July 1866, when the widely read satirical magazine *Punch* publicly sneered at Brown by running a mock Court Circular about his daily movements at Balmoral.

The gossip rose to a crescendo in 1867. Large crowds at the Royal Academy spring exhibition were amazed to see Victoria, in full mourning dress, mounted on a pony with a black-kilted Brown at its head, in a picture by Sir Edwin Landseer entitled *Her Majesty at Osborne in 1866*. Many spectators giggled, a few collapsed in outright laughter, and a fair proportion began to believe that Brown's appearance in an intimate family portrait, which included two of the royal princesses, meant the scurrilous talk they had heard about the Queen and her personal attendant was true.

The scandal was now becoming so widespread that the Prime Minister, the fourteenth Earl of Derby, suggested to Victoria that growing public disquiet might cause scenes of an 'unpleasant nature' if the Scotsman rode on the box of the Queen's carriage at the Review of the Troops in Hyde Park that summer. As it happened, the review was cancelled as a measure of respect for the recently executed Emperor Maximilian of Mexico, but Derby's concern shows that there were now severe worries in Westminster that there would soon be an embarrassing public demonstration about Victoria's unnatural closeness to her servant.

Brown, however, was unmoved by all the gossip he was inspiring and by all the newspaper space he was occupying. His employer must have felt the same, for she never made any attempt to lower his profile. If anything, 'Mrs Brown', as Victoria was now known by many of her subjects, grew even fonder of the gruff Scotsman over the ensuing years, rewarding him with regular salary increases and medals for devoted service. In 1876 the Queen also gave him a substantial cottage at Balmoral.

The sexual innuendo may have gradually decreased as Victoria grew older, but Brown remained very much part of the royal landscape. In fact, he could do no wrong in the Queen's eyes. He was often drunk on duty, and frequently rude to her family: for instance, the Prince of Wales, who had more than his fair share of run-ins with Brown, hated his mother's confidant with a passion. Brown was equally offhand with courtiers and politicians, with the notable exception of Benjamin Disraeli, with whom he got on exceptionally well. Indeed, he regularly sent salmon he had caught on the Dee down to Victoria's favourite Prime Minister in London.

Yet while Brown's enemies – and there were many in Victoria's court – may have longed for him to blot his copybook or fall from royal favour, they had to wait in vain. Brown's position grew stronger and stronger. He even took to sleeping in a room next to Victoria's bedchamber, causing an unnamed churchman to remark in horror to Lord Derby that such behaviour was 'contrary to etiquette and even decency'.

Brown died at Windsor on 27 March 1883 as a result of a heavy cold that induced a fatal high fever. Once more the Queen was beside herself with grief, and when observers read the inscription on the wreath she sent to his funeral at Balmoral on 5 April, the malicious tittle-tattle started all over again. The many visitors to Brown's graveside at Crathie churchyard began to wonder what the words 'A tribute of loving, grateful and everlasting friendship and affection from his truest, best and most faithful friend, Victoria R & I'" could possibly mean. Understandably, the general view was that it was strange, and certainly unconventional, for an employer to make such an intimate farewell to an employee, however loyal he had been.

Other heartfelt tributes from the Queen followed in the year after Brown's death. In February she published a second book, *More Leaves from the Journal of a Life in the Highlands*, which, to the fury of the Prince of Wales, contained many references to Brown. Eyebrows were also raised when the Queen ordered a plaque to be erected in Brown's honour in the royal mausoleum at Frogmore in Windsor Great Park. In March Victoria's courtiers, who were only just recovering from the embarrassing revelations in *More Leaves*, were appalled to hear that she was also considering publishing a memoir about her favourite servant, containing extracts from their correspondence and from his diary. Consequently, Brown's fellow Scot, Randall Davidson, the Dean of Windsor, cautioned the monarch that it would be foolish, and possibly damaging, to link her name so publicly with Brown's. Initially, Victoria was furious with the young cleric, but in the end she heeded his sound advice and the manuscript never saw the light of day.

Davidson and Victoria's other advisers were worried because the Brown memoir was reputed to include many fervent messages of devotion, which might easily be taken as the words a woman might use when writing to a lover. In a letter to Brown of October 1874, for instance, Victoria, by then in her mid-fifties, had penned the revealing phrase: 'I hope darling one that you will do this.' A handwritten note from the Queen to one of her ministers, the Conservative politician Lord Cranbrook, sent soon after Brown's unexpected death, also contained the emotive words: 'Perhaps never in history was there so strong an attachment, so warm and loving a friendship between the sovereign and servant.' Of course, none of these examples proves that Victoria and Brown had a sexual relationship, but Davidson was right in assuming that readers would have jumped to that conclusion if the memoir contained similar powerful expressions of affection.

The royal family certainly believed that Victoria's writings about Brown would be misinterpreted. In 1905, four years after her death, Edward VII bought more than 300 letters written by Victoria to Balmoral's factor, Alexander Profeit, which mentioned her relationship with the gillie. Sir James Reid, the courtier who arranged the transaction, recorded that the hoard contained explosive and compromising material with which Profeit's son, George, was effectively trying to blackmail the King. In addition, Princess Beatrice, the Queen's youngest daughter who was also her literary executor, deleted all references to Brown that might be misconstrued when she edited Victoria's enormous collection of personal papers and letters after the sovereign's death in 1901.

The royal family's nervous reaction to any affectionate mention of Brown in Victoria's correspondence does not confirm that the Queen and her servant were lovers, but it certainly adds fuel to the arguments of those who claim that the liaison was sexual. With good reason, believers that the relationship had a physical side are quick to ask the obvious question: if there was nothing to hide, why was Victoria's family so anxious to suppress the material?

Other stories concerning Victoria and Brown, most of them patently ridiculous, surfaced during her long reign. But nobody ever believed the assertions of the ardent Scottish republican Alexander Robertson, who claimed on one occasion that Brown was the Queen's morganatic husband, and, on another, that Victoria had actually given birth to the gillie's child. There were also widespread, albeit unconfirmed, rumours that Victoria used Brown at seances as a spiritual medium through whom she might contact the Prince Consort.

Victoria unwittingly ensured that the debate would continue long after she was gone. When she died, she left instructions that a lock of Brown's hair, a ring that had belonged to his mother, his photograph, a handkerchief and some letters should be placed in her coffin alongside mementos of her beloved husband, Prince Albert. No one will ever be able to say for certain whether Victoria had an affair with Brown or not, but perhaps the eccentric old Queen has the answer to that frequently asked question in the pile of secret letters that she insisted should be buried with her at Frogmore.

Balmoral has been used as the royal holiday home ever since. Just as in Victoria's time, not every member of the royal family likes to be out of circulation among its craggy mountains and tranquil glens. Indeed, the Earl of Snowdon, when he was married to Princess Margaret, used to dread his annual visits there. On the other hand, the Balmoral estate is certainly a favourite of the present Prince of Wales, and Birkhall, the adjacent property that he inherited from his grandmother, Queen Elizabeth, the Queen Mother, is probably his most loved house.

Prince Charles has fished the frothy River Muick, which tumbles through Birkhall's gardens, and painted watercolours of its wild and compelling woodland scenery. He has also stalked, shot and climbed on the nearby hills since he was a boy. He used Birkhall as a bolthole to escape from Gordonstoun, the Scottish public school he hated, and, more recently, from the misery of his collapsing marriage to Diana. Indeed, it was said at the time that he kept a photograph in a walnut frame on his bedside table of his mistress, the then Camilla Parker Bowles, smiling in the sunlight on a bench outside Birkhall. It was unsurprising, therefore, that in the Spring of 2005 he chose this very private residence for his honeymoon with Camilla, now created Duchess of Cornwall (and Duchess of Rothesay in Scotland). His affection for this unpretentious and friendly house, which still contains many memories of his grandmother, is great and long standing.

There was, however, a whiff of scandal when the Prince took Camilla on clandestine visits to Birkhall long before their marriage. Since those earlier trips took place when Charles's grandmother was still alive, there was speculation as to whether the Queen Mother condoned or even actively promoted the controversial affair. Of course, she would never have dreamed of discussing in public her role in such a private matter. Like her fellow Scotswoman, Mary Queen of Scots, and her husband's great-grandmother, Queen Victoria, the most popular royal of all chose to take her most intimate secrets to the grave.

CHAPTER TWO

Chatsworth

Sᴉʀ Wɪʟʟɪᴀᴍ Cᴀᴠᴇɴᴅɪsʜ ᴀɴᴅ ʜɪs ᴡɪғᴇ Eʟɪᴢᴀʙᴇᴛʜ, that redoubtable, almost legendary, figure of the Tudor era known universally as Bess of Hardwick, built the first house at Chatsworth, later to be the great stately home of the Dukes of Devonshire. They bought the manor of Chatsworth, not far from Chesterfield in Derbyshire, in 1549 and began constructing their home three years later. The famous Hunting Tower, which dates from the 1580s and still stands in splendid isolation on the hill behind the present house, is a tangible reminder of those distant days.

Sir William, who came from Cavendish in Suffolk, served Henry VIII well as a royal commissioner for the dissolution of the monasteries. Consequently, he was rewarded for his loyalty by the grateful monarch and granted lands once owned by the disbanded Church. When Bess married him, she persuaded her new husband to sell his holdings elsewhere and move to her native Derbyshire. The surrounding area was apt to flood, and access from the desolate moors to the east was poor, but the couple were not deterred and commissioned a large house on the square where the present Chatsworth stands. There is still a contemporary painting of the house, although no record remains of the Tudor interior.

By all accounts, Bess and Sir William, who was in fact her second husband and twenty-two years her senior, had a happy marriage.[1] They had eight children, of whom six survived infancy, including their second son, William, who would be ennobled as Baron Cavendish in 1605 and created Earl of Devonshire in 1618. This blissful and lucrative union came to an end when, on 25 October 1557, Sir William died. Bess, who came from a poor family and had started her working life as a servant at the age of twelve at Sir John Zouche's Derbyshire home at Condor Castle, owed a good deal of money, but through her late husbands she also owned a vast amount of property in Derbyshire and Nottinghamshire. It was not long, therefore, before this comely widow, who had by this time been appointed a lady-in-waiting to Queen Elizabeth I, found a rich new husband.

Elizabeth's court was the ideal place in which to attract a wealthy suitor. Before long, Bess had caught the eye of Sir William St Loe, a widower and an important figure in the royal household. They were married in 1559, and the second Sir William in Bess's life generously settled all her debts. Not all was sweetness and light, however, for Bess had the first of several brushes with the Queen during her brief marriage to St Loe. In 1561 the angry monarch sent her lady-in-waiting to the Tower[2] for seven months for concealing the fact that the heir to the childless Elizabeth's throne, Lady Catherine Grey,[3] had secretly married and become pregnant by the Earl of Hertford. Yet when Sir William St Loe died in 1565, Bess experienced a stroke of luck. As her husband had been at odds with his brother and heir, Edward, he left all his lands to his wife, whom he called his 'honest sweet Chatsworth', and her children.

After a decent period of mourning, Bess, now a widow for the third time, returned to take up her old position at court. Since her own lands had been bolstered by the substantial inheritance from her recently deceased spouse, she was now a most desirable catch for any nobleman in England. In 1567 she took arguably the richest of them all, George Talbot, sixth Earl of Shrewsbury, as her fourth husband. This union between two powerful families was further cemented by the marriages at the same time of Bess's children Henry, aged eighteen, and Mary, aged twelve, to Shrewsbury's daughter, Grace, and son, Gilbert. As her husband owned eight huge houses, including Sheffield Castle, Buxton Hall and Rufford Abbey, their combined land holdings in this enormous tract of the Midlands meant that rents from their tenants produced a vast income.

Nevertheless, money, power and property could not ensure that Bess's last marriage was happy or successful. When, in 1569, her husband was made guardian of Elizabeth I's cousin, Mary Queen of Scots, Bess was delighted.[4] Shrewsbury was paid only a meagre £2,000 a year to maintain the profligate Mary's vast and expensive household, but his wife rightly interpreted this prestigious appointment as proof that they were high on the list of Elizabeth's favourites.

Shrewsbury soon fell under the spell of his pretty ward and granted her as much liberty and comfort as possible during her long confinement at his and his wife's various houses. Yet after a while, because he spent so much time with the young Queen of Scots, Bess's delight in his important job quickly turned to jealousy. The Countess of Shrewsbury had nothing if not a practical turn of mind, so in order that she could keep a watchful eye on her husband she decided to get to know Mary better. The two women spent much time together, embroidering, sewing tapestries and talking, especially when Mary was living at Chatsworth in apartments set aside for her in the East Wing. They soon became intimate friends, and Bess's fears that her spouse was straying gradually subsided.

As his time as Mary's guardian grew longer and longer, Shrewsbury began to find his royal appointment an increasingly irksome chore. He carried out his duties with care, moving Mary from one of his houses to another, as the situation or his orders from Elizabeth required. He also foiled several plots to liberate Scotland's queen, and removed various spies and conspirators from her entourage. He had asked to be relieved from his position on occasion, but his requests had always been refused. By 1579 he was decidedly unhappy when he was informed that his already inadequate allowance had been reduced by a quarter, but the Earl was even more disgruntled by the terrible row that had developed during the previous four years between his formidably ambitious wife and his royal ward.

For Bess was now on the worst possible terms with Mary. The problem was that the Countess of Shrewsbury, anxious to bring her family closer to royalty, had arranged a marriage between her daughter, Elizabeth Cavendish, and Charles Stuart, the Earl of Lennox, a younger brother of Mary's murdered husband, Lord Darnley. Soon after the wedding in 1575, Elizabeth gave birth to a girl, Arabella, who, through her father, Lord Lennox, was a direct descendant of Henry VII, and the next heir to the English throne after Mary's son James. The baby therefore represented a serious threat to Mary's claim to the English throne, as well as to the security of Queen Elizabeth's own position. The latter sent Elizabeth Lennox to the Tower for a time for the questionable crime of bearing a child, but it was Mary's increasing resentment of the baby's grandmother for orchestrating the match that brought untold problems and embarrassment to the Shrewsbury household. Indeed, the subsequent moves of the angry Queen of Scots to discredit her once bosom friend could hardly have been more vindictive.

Mary determined to repay Bess for what she viewed as her treachery by making her life as unpleasant as possible. She wrote to Queen Elizabeth, passing on salacious details of what she had reputedly heard from the Countess's own, admittedly irreverent, lips. Bess had told her, she wrote, that the Queen had slept with the Duke of Anjou and with his envoy, Jehan de Simier, to whom Elizabeth had allegedly revealed state secrets during pillow talk. Mary continued by remarking that, again according to Bess, the respected courtier Sir Christopher Hatton had felt no alternative but to leave Elizabeth's court to avoid the monarch's uncontrollable and embarrassingly public fawning.

She also claimed that Bess had told her that Elizabeth's ladies-in-waiting hardly dared look her in the eye in case they dissolved in laughter at her delight in their flattery. The disloyal Countess, Mary further alleged, had suggested that Elizabeth's body was so ugly and deformed that no man would be able to consummate a marriage. The furious Queen of Scots ended by saying that the treacherous Bess had confided much more, which she would reveal at a future meeting with Elizabeth.

Luckily for Bess, Elizabeth probably did not read this potentially explosive letter, which was found among Lord Burghley's papers after his death.[5] But the Queen certainly heard the scandalous rumours being circulated by the Countess, her sons and her agent, Henry Beresford, that her husband, Lord Shrewsbury, with whom she was now on irretrievably bad terms, had been conducting an adulterous relationship with Mary Queen of Scots for years. Bess and her sons were summoned before the Privy Council, the highly influential, Crown-appointed body that advised (and still advises) the monarch. They admitted that they had repeated the allegations concerning Mary and Bess's husband, her sons' stepfather, but claimed that they did not believe a word of the slander. Queen Elizabeth, anxious to improve the rapidly deteriorating relationship between her faithful aide, Shrewsbury, and his wife, magnanimously agreed to act as a mediator.

Sadly, the Queen's intervention did not help the ailing marriage. When Bess discovered soon afterwards that her husband was engaged in a passionate affair with a nubile serving maid, the couple parted. Bess retired to Chatsworth and devoted the rest of her life and much of her great wealth to building other stately homes, including the magnificent Hardwick Hall in Derbyshire, where she died in 1608. Shrewsbury, who died in 1590, went to live with his mistress, and in 1585 was eventually allowed to relinquish his sixteen-year-long guardianship of Mary. When he handed over the position to Sir Ralph Sadler, the long-suffering Earl is reported to have remarked that he was relieved to have been delivered from 'those two demons' – Mary Queen of Scots and his formidable wife.

Two centuries later, in 1774, another ambitious gentlewoman, Lady Georgiana Spencer, became the chatelaine of Chatsworth on her marriage, at the tender age of seventeen, to Bess of Hardwick's descendant, the fifth Duke of Devonshire. Georgiana had had a privileged and aristocratic upbringing. She was the daughter of John, the first Earl Spencer, and his wife, the former Georgiana Poyntz. The new Duchess of Devonshire was therefore an ancestor of another renowned society beauty, Diana, Princess of Wales, and, like her modern-day kinswoman, was never to be far from scandalous gossip and rumour.

The fourth Earl of Devonshire, who was made the first Duke in 1694 for his help in bringing William of Orange to the throne six years earlier,[6] was a compulsive builder. His first project was to pull down the South Front, which he replaced with a new set of family rooms and an opulent suite of state apartments to cater for a royal visit from King William and his queen, Mary, the sister of the deposed King James II. Soon afterwards, he turned his attention to the East Front, constructing the famous Painted Hall and the Long Gallery, which is now the Library. He also rebuilt the West Front from 1699 to 1702 and then the remaining North Front. As well as completely altering the house, he made many changes to the outbuildings and created a huge formal garden and the spectacular waterfall, the Cascade.

Georgiana's father-in-law, the fourth Duke, decided that the house should be approached from the west, and therefore pulled down the existing stables and offices. He also demolished the cottages in the nearby village of Edensor so that his view from the house would not be impaired. In the early 1760s he built new stables to the north-west of the house, altered the course of the River Derwent and constructed a new bridge over it. His improvements did not end there, however, for he employed the great landscape gardener, Lancelot 'Capability' Brown, to get rid of the first Duke's formal garden and create a park typical of Brown's trademark natural look. As a result of all these changes, Georgiana's Chatsworth was very different from the house that had stood on the same spot in Bess of Hardwick's day.

The fourth Duke of Devonshire was an astute and competent Whig politician, but his son, William, who was nicknamed 'Canis' due to his love of dogs, did not inherit either his father's traits or his desire for public service. The shy fifth Duke was happiest when he was at home at Chatsworth, shooting in the company of his canine friends. His wife, on the other hand, favoured the bright lights of London. Her balls and parties at Devonshire House in Piccadilly, attended by royalty and the most famous statesmen of the day, were legendary, and invitations to them were highly sought after.

Georgiana may have been a leader of fashion and an inveterate social butterfly, but she also had a serious side. Unlike her husband, she was fascinated and intrigued by politics and politicians and was an avid fundraiser for the Whigs. In 1784 she became the first woman to campaign at an election when she publicly supported Charles James Fox, the great Whig politician, who was at that time Foreign Secretary (see also Chapter Eleven, note 5). She also secretly wrote a readable and thinly disguised autobiographical novel, *The Sylph*, which came out in 1780. Although the book was published anonymously as the work 'of a young lady', society soon guessed the identity of its author and clamoured for copies. *The Sylph*, which quickly ran through four editions, displayed a certain sexual licence as well as a degree of violence, and was considered very racy for its time.

Georgiana's life in many ways mirrors that of the heroine of *The Sylph*, Julia Stanley. Both women were involved in unhappy marriages, and both were plagued by financial worries. Georgiana, who had been married for six years by the time her novel was published, was often cripplingly depressed that she had not thus far been able to conceive, and especially to bear her husband a

[41]

son and heir. She was also worried by William's lack of affection towards her. Her addiction to gambling, which left her in virtually permanent debt, compounded her problems. Her betting was already out of hand, and she did not know how to stop. Indeed, the Duchess's latest financial embarrassment or the extent of her current debts were the subjects of constant rumour throughout her life.

She borrowed heavily from her friends, as well as from moneylenders, to fund her habit, but she never dared tell her husband the true extent of her losses. Once she asked the Duke's banker to advance her £5,000 – an enormous sum in the eighteenth century – in secret to settle her debts. Yet she kept only part of the loan and sent the rest to a bookmaker to lay bets on the Derby and the Oaks. She was just as reckless at cards, losing tidy sums to the faro dealers at the gambling tables that were a regular feature of parties at Chatsworth and Devonshire House. She even persuaded Thomas Coutts, of the famous bank that still bears his name, to lend her money by promising that she would introduce his daughter into society. One of her last letters sadly proves that she never learned her lesson. When she died in 1806, she left a note to her son, pleading that he should ensure that her husband honoured her debts, massive for the time, of £20,000.

If Georgiana's gambling was a permanent topic of conversation in all the smart London salons in the late eighteenth century, the bohemian state of her marriage caused society's tongues to wag even more. In 1782 the Duke and Duchess travelled to Bath to take the cure at the town's famous spa. It was hoped that the wholesome waters would relieve the Duke's gout and cure Georgiana of her misfortunes in pregnancy – she had suffered two miscarriages during the previous year. Her husband leased a house, reputed to be the finest in the town, from the Duke of Marlborough for the whole of the summer.

The couple had been in residence for only a week when they met Lady Elizabeth Foster, who was living with her sister, Lady Erne, in somewhat straitened circumstances in a less salubrious part of town. Both women, who were separated from their husbands, lodged with an aunt and subsisted on a meagre income provided by their miserly father, the fourth Earl of Bristol (see pages 211–13, 224–5). He was a clergyman who had risen through the Church's ranks to become the Bishop of Derry, before he unexpectedly inherited the earldom in 1779 following the deaths of his two childless elder brothers.

Elizabeth Foster, who was always known as Bess, and Georgiana took to each other immediately and soon became firm friends. Bess, already the mother of two sons, was the same age as the Duchess, but her physical opposite. She was thinner, less tall and frailer, with dark hair surrounding a small, delicate face. Edward Gibbon, who knew her well, said that her delicacy and charm made men determined to protect and possess her. 'No man could withstand her,' said the learned historian and chronicler of the decline and fall of the Roman Empire. 'If she chose to beckon the Chancellor from his Woolsack in full sight of the world, he could not resist obedience.' It was hardly surprising, therefore, that the Duke should warm to the attractive Bess as well.

The Duke and Duchess were also moved by the sad circumstances of Bess's marriage breakdown – her husband had apparently seduced her maid – and her financial position, but even so it was extraordinary how quickly she became an integral part of their life. Bess soon realized that for her to be at Georgiana's constant beck and call was an irresistible attraction to the latter. She was well aware that the Duke was lonely and that he, too, like his wife, required a confidante; she also recognized that he liked her both to flirt and to be submissive.

Georgiana's family and the majority of the Devonshires' friends thought that the couple were naive, in that it never occurred to them that Bess saw them as her way out of a life of poverty. They were also astonished that Georgiana did not realize that her new friend had designs on her husband.

Georgiana's mother, Lady Spencer, was well aware that Bess posed a threat to her daughter's marriage when she invited the

Duke and Duchess to stay with her at Hotwells in Bristol, not far from Bath, later that year. She politely added that Bess would not be welcome, claiming that her husband, Lord Spencer, was too ill to meet a stranger. Almost distraught at the thought of being separated from her new companion, Georgiana wrote to her mother, saying that there was no question that they would not bring Bess. At Hotwells, Lady Spencer saw her suspicions met when the Duke and Bess left early each morning to ride together and did not return until just before supper. Clearly, they were more than happy in each other's company, yet still Georgiana chose to ignore the omens. She was now so dependent on her new friend that she could not bear to be parted from her.

To Lady Spencer's relief, Bess went to Paris that Christmas on a wage of £300 per annum as governess to the Duke's illegitimate daughter, Charlotte Williams. Charlotte's mother, Charlotte Spencer, a former milliner (and no relation to Georgiana), had been the Duke's mistress before his marriage. The following year, 1783, the Duchess at last gave birth to her first child, Georgiana, or 'Little G' as she was known in the family, and the relationship between her husband and herself improved for a while. Georgiana, however, was still missing Bess. The two friends were in regular correspondence until Bess returned to England from the Continent in August 1784. She joined the Devonshires at Chatsworth, but none of the shrewd Lady Spencer's informants, such as her son, George, and his wife, Lavinia, was able to establish on their visits to Derbyshire whether she was conducting an affair with the Duke.

As it turned out, Bess and the Duke must have been very careful to conceal their intimacy. In February 1785 Bess, by now back in Paris and once again funded by the Duke, was three months pregnant with his child. Her mood turned to horror, however, when she received a letter from the unwitting Georgiana revealing that she, too, had become pregnant three months earlier. The appalled Bess quickly realized that their babies must have been conceived within days or even hours of each other. Her bizarre solution was to begin an affair, until her pregnancy began to show, with the notoriously libidinous Duke of Dorset, the then Ambassador Extraordinary in Paris (who, ironically, later had a liaison with Georgiana). Besides concealing her affair with William Devonshire, she reasoned that this would at least stop the salacious gossip in the French capital that she and Georgiana were involved in a 'Sapphic' – that is, lesbian – relationship.

On 1 September 1785 the newspapers announced that the Duchess of Devonshire had been safely delivered of a son; on the following day, however, a correction was published stating that the baby was, in fact, a girl, Harriet. The Duchess's lying-in room at Devonshire House was the height of comfort, decorated entirely in white satin, and her huge bed was covered in silver ribbons and paper flowers of all colours. The birth of the Duke's other child, however, could hardly have been in greater contrast. The need for secrecy was vital to avoid the scandal that Lady Elizabeth Foster was pregnant with an illegitimate child. Bess had therefore been constantly on the move, since her increasing waistline had made her pregnancy obvious. As a result she had been forced by her situation to give birth – to another girl, on 16 August – in a dingy hostel, which doubled as a brothel, in Vietri, a small town on Italy's Gulf of Salerno. The child, whom she named Caroline Rosalie, was lodged with a poor Italian family and was educated in Europe before joining her mother in England in 1790.

Bess stayed in Italy for a year, even though the Duke and Georgiana urged her to return home. She was reluctant to leave her child, but she also knew that there would be changes to her comfortable *ménage à trois* if Georgiana discovered that she was the mother of the Duke's latest bastard. Before she left France she attempted to cover her tracks, somehow persuading an elderly French count to accept paternity for her daughter, who took his surname of Saint-Jules and thereby officially became the illegitimate offspring of a foreign aristocrat and an unknown mother. Bess was never to admit publicly that the Duke was Caroline's real father until after his death in July 1811.

As it happened, Bess's fears of discovery proved to be groundless. When she returned to England, her relationship with the Duke and Duchess grew even stronger, and the eccentric aristocratic threesome continued to live happily together in all the Devonshires' homes. If anything, she and Georgiana became even greater friends and allies. She was the Duchess's constant companion, was party to all her inner secrets, and was the only person who ever knew the full extent of her gambling debts. Furthermore, although Bess took other lovers, she never lost the Duke's affection and respect. In fact, after Georgiana died in 1806, William was to repay his former mistress handsomely, for in October 1809 he took her as his second wife.

Before then, however, both Georgiana and Bess were to have other affairs, and both were to be embroiled in further scandals concerning children born out of wedlock. In 1788, in Rouen, Bess gave birth to another illegitimate child, Augustus William Clifford. There was some doubt as to whether the father was the elderly Duke of Richmond, with whom Bess was having the first of several affairs, or her established lover, the Duke of Devonshire. The latter was aware of her friendship with the former, although Bess had sworn that the relationship was purely platonic.

Bess assured Devonshire that the baby was not Richmond's, but his later indifference to the child suggests that he did not believe his mistress. Despite his doubts that he was the father, however, it seems that Bess wanted the world to think that her son was Devonshire's child. She called the boy by the Duke's Christian name, William, and also gave him a surname that was an ancient Cavendish title. This time, though, the Duke and Bess had sensibly decided to come clean and tell Georgiana immediately. They made the right decision, for the Duchess insisted on accompanying Bess to France to help with the birth.

These roles were to be reversed four years later when, also in France, Bess was at Georgiana's side as she gave birth to an illegitimate daughter, Eliza. Unlike Bess, the Duchess went to great lengths to disguise the identity of the father, the Whig Party's rising star, Charles Grey. Instead of offering a clue to the child's paternity, which was the usual practice at the time, she gave the little girl the surname Courtney, which related to her mother's family, the Poyntzes.

Grey had first caught Georgiana's eye at a Devonshire House party in 1787. He was only twenty-three years old, the son of a respected general from Northumberland.[7] His maiden speech in the House of Commons had been well received, and he was soon on the guest lists of all the leading society hostesses in London. Grey, who quickly developed a passion for Georgiana, was, surprisingly, the first to make the running. When he began initially to flirt with her and then to express his undying love, she was both frightened and flattered to have attracted the attentions of a man who was seven years younger than she. As she was the Duke of Dorset's lover at the time (as Bess Foster had been for a time in 1785), however, she at first kept her new admirer at arm's length. Yet Grey's persistence gradually began to pay off. By 1788 Georgiana had succumbed to his entreaties and taken the romantic politician to her bed. It seems that she preferred to know that she was Grey's only love, whereas the rakish Duke, as she knew only too well, was notorious for keeping several mistresses at once.

Georgiana was completely hypnotized by Grey. It was even rumoured that when the Prince of Wales called one day at Devonshire House, he was refused admittance. As his carriage drove away, he caught sight of Grey looking out of the window. Moreover, as their affair burgeoned, the lovers became less and less discreet. Grey would talk to nobody else at social functions and would rant and rave at Georgiana if he felt neglected by her. When she was pregnant with Eliza, Grey, knowing the Duke of Devonshire was away, injudiciously followed the Duchess to Bath, where she was making her customary annual visit to take the waters. He was often seen entering and leaving the house she had leased, and made no attempt to be discreet. In the end, Georgiana's scandal-conscious mother, Lady Spencer, realizing that the press might get wind of the affair, persuaded her daughter to send Grey back to London.

Between them, Lady Spencer and Bess managed to conceal Georgiana's pregnancy from the outside world and, more importantly, from the Duke. By October 1790, however, she was six months into her pregnancy, and her condition was becoming increasingly – if not glaringly – obvious. It was at this point that somebody in Bath must have put two and two together. Before plans could be made to whisk Georgiana away to the Continent on some invented pretext, the Duke arrived, unannounced, after a tip-off from a friend in London that he ought to see his wife.

Devonshire, some might say hypocritically as the recent father of an illegitimate child himself, was furious when he discovered his wife's condition. The Cavendish family lobbied for a separation, self-righteously wondering how Georgiana could have dared to repay her husband in so ungrateful a manner – for he had just settled a large proportion of her debts, against the advice of his agents and bankers. In the end the Duke ordered his wife to renounce Grey and have the baby adopted as soon as it was born. If she did not agree, he declared coldly, he would divorce her and she would never see her children again. Unhesitatingly, she accepted her husband's rigid ultimatum. For his part, Grey was devastated that she had agreed to the Duke's demands, and his replies to her explanatory letters were vicious and cruel.

When, on 20 February 1791, Georgiana gave birth to Eliza in a tiny shuttered room in a house she had taken near Montpellier, the infant was immediately removed from her mother's arms. She was nursed by a foster mother, and, once she was old enough to travel, was taken to England to be brought up in the guise of Grey's younger sister by his parents, Sir Charles and Lady (Elizabeth) Grey, at Fallodon in Northumberland.

Georgiana was never permitted to acknowledge that she was Eliza's mother, although it eventually became an open secret. In 1796 Lord Glenbervie, the leading social commentator of the day, recorded the following item in his diary: 'I heard yesterday a stray anecdote of a foundling left at Sir Charles Grey's under very mysterious circumstances. The Duchess of Devonshire was at that time abroad. Since her return about three years ago she has often visited the child, and been with it for hours at a time.'

Eliza, who became a ravishing beauty, grew up in complete ignorance of her two real parents. Georgiana did not live to see her reach adulthood, but Grey survived to see their daughter marry a soldier, Robert Ellice, who eventually rose to the rank of general. Three years after Eliza's birth, Grey wed Mary Ponsonby, by whom he fathered fifteen children. His political career reached its zenith in 1830 when, after twenty-four years on the Opposition benches, the by now second Earl Grey became Prime Minister at the venerable age of sixty-six. Having promised a government of 'peace, retrenchment and reform',[8] he was to be responsible for the Reform Act of 1832 and the Act that secured the abolition of slavery; however, in 1834 he resigned over the Irish Question. He died in 1845, nearly forty years after his former mistress, the mother of his illegitimate daughter. Today, he is probably chiefly remembered in the aromatic blend of China tea that was named after him.

Gossip, insidious and scurrilous, had also prevailed when, in Paris[9] two years earlier, in 1789, Georgiana had presented her relieved and grateful husband with a legitimate son and heir, the future sixth Duke of Devonshire. Once more Bess was at her side, but since the two women had decided to travel to France some time before the baby was born, rumour had it that the tiny Marquess of Hartington (the courtesy title of the eldest sons of the Dukes of Devonshire) was the love child of the Duke and Bess, and that the Duchess had not been pregnant at all.

It certainly seemed to be a strange time for a pregnant English-woman, especially an aristocrat, to travel without the protection of her husband, not least because France was at that time in the throes of massive political and social unrest with the coming of the Revolution in the spring of that year. Furthermore, when the scandalmongers heard that a Dr Croft, an unknown and inexperienced practitioner, had attended the Duchess during her lying-in period, they metaphorically rubbed their hands together with glee and asserted that she must have had something to hide, since otherwise a more established medical man would have been employed to deliver a baby as important as the sole male heir to a dukedom. It is unlikely that Hart, as the sixth Duke came to be known, was illegitimate, but the strange circumstances of his birth abroad continued to attract speculation until his death in 1858.

Chatsworth and its occupants continued to harbour the secret of the child of Charles Grey and Georgiana, Duchess of Devonshire, during the late eighteenth century and all of the nineteenth. It was, therefore, a case of history repeating itself when, more than 130 years later, another future Prime Minister, Harold Macmillan, and another member of the Cavendish family, his wife, Lady Dorothy, became embroiled in a scandal that the Devonshires and the cognoscenti did their best to keep away from the prying eyes and ears of the outside world.

The wedding of Macmillan, a rising Conservative politician and a member of the prominent publishing clan, to Lady Dorothy Cavendish at St Margaret's, Westminster, in 1920 was a highlight of the social season. Queen Alexandra (the widow of King Edward VII; see Chapter Twelve), the Duke of York (the future George VI) and the great novelist Thomas Hardy were among the guests. It was said that the bride's father, the ninth Duke, another of whose daughters had married a member of a brewing family, remarked of his former aide-de-camp,[10] 'Well, books is better than beer.'

Nine years later, in the same year as the Wall Street Crash, Macmillan experienced a double disaster. He lost his parliamentary seat at Stockton-on-Tees that he had won in 1924, and his wife, who had begun to tire of her predictable and unglamorous husband, took a lover. Dorothy, who had once taken part in a mock burglary at the home of a royal equerry, brandishing a toy pistol, loved excitement. It is not altogether surprising, therefore, that she chose as a lover a man who was in some ways almost the exact opposite of her staid husband – his political colleague, the dashing and reckless Robert Boothby. True, both men were at least partly Scottish, both had been educated at Eton and Oxford, both were Tory MPs, and both had won their parliamentary seats in the same year, but they were very different in character. Boothby, who was Macmillan's junior by six years, was a brilliant orator (something of which no one would have accused Macmillan) and a man with a taste for ostentation and high living; indeed, at the time he drove a flashy two-seater Bentley, a car that would have been anathema to the sober Macmillan.

In truth, the Cavendish family were not at all surprised that Dorothy had begun to look elsewhere. Macmillan had always been the butt of in-jokes at Chatsworth. The fun-loving Cavendish girls apparently used to plead not to sit next to the crofter's grandson at dinner. Boothby's biographer, Robert Rhodes James, wrote: 'He [Macmillan] was rated by them as the most stupendously boring man they had ever met, and they could not understand why the vivacious and attractive Dorothy had married him.'

The Macmillans had first met Boothby at his father's house in Scotland in 1928, when they played golf together. When, the following year, all three were guests at Bowood, the Marquess of Lansdowne's Wiltshire home, Dorothy and Boothby realized that they had much in common and laughed and joked together, comfortable in each other's company. Some weeks later, Boothby, in an attempt to console Macmillan after he had lost his seat at the recent general election, invited him to shoot on his father's moors and to bring his wife with him. Once on the grouse moor, Boothby asked Dorothy to accompany him in his butt, and, as he stood waiting for the birds to appear, was startled to feel his hand being squeezed. He turned round to see that the smiling Dorothy was the culprit. As Rhodes James succinctly commented: 'That was when it all began.'

The affair, which quickly became incredibly intense, provided benefits for both lovers. Boothby brought Dorothy the sexual excitement and fulfilment which whispers suggested Macmillan had failed to provide. 'She came all the way from Chatsworth to pursue me,' Boothby once wrote after a visit to Venice. Dorothy, on the other hand, gave the ambitious, social-climbing Boothby credibility and provided him with the access that he craved to high society and its glittering dinner tables. Between 1929 and 1935 they were constantly in each other's company and virtually lived together. The result, it was rumoured, was Dorothy's daughter, Sarah Macmillan, born in 1930 and widely thought to be Boothby's child.

Dorothy did not attempt to hide anything from her husband. Boothby's letters were not secreted in some locked dressing-table drawer; on the contrary, they were left lying openly around the Macmillan family home. The affair soon became known in Westminster and in fashionable circles, but in an age when the press barons tended to protect their own (and when there was in general a good deal more 'respect' – if not sycophancy – shown both to the upper classes and to politicians) it did not become public knowledge until after Dorothy's death in 1966. King George V, anxious to avoid a scandal, reputedly advised his ministers to 'Keep it quiet'. Macmillan sought guidance from his mother, Nellie, who advised against divorce. She was probably right. As her son had won his Stockton seat back in 1931, talk of his wife's adultery would have had a detrimental effect on his career, not least by scandalizing his constituents.

The liaison certainly affected two of the protagonists, the notable exception being Dorothy who, Boothby later remembered, 'never suffered a pang of remorse'. In stark contrast, the proud Macmillan was devastated by his wife's blatant unfaithfulness. In 1931 he suffered a nervous collapse and was sent to recuperate in a Munich sanatorium. The official cause was the flaring-up of an old war wound in his thigh received at the Battle of the Somme in 1916, but it is likely that his illness was a mental breakdown, brought on by feelings of betrayal, hurt pride, jealousy and embarrassment at his wife's less than discreet affair. It was reported that on one occasion he had been seen banging his head against the partition of a railway carriage compartment, and an old family retainer even later claimed that the MP had made a suicide attempt. To his credit, however, the severely wronged Macmillan stayed loyal to his beloved wife.

Boothby, too, was put under severe pressure by the passionate relationship. In 1935 he proposed to a young woman, the Hon. Diana Cavendish (interestingly, a distant kinswoman of Dorothy's), over dinner. When he woke up the next day, however, slightly the worse for wear, he realized that he had made a mistake. To his horror, he learned that his mother had already announced the engagement. It was too late to repair the damage. In consequence, Boothby drank too much and became inordinately depressed during the days before his marriage. Unsurprisingly, the union did not last long. Boothby was back in Dorothy's arms after his divorce two years later.

Sarah also suffered terribly. She only found out in her teens that Boothby, rather than Macmillan, was her real father. When she later married, she discovered that she was unable to have children, the effects of an abortion she had had at a very young age. Her mother had forced her to have the termination, saying that a child born out of wedlock would have ruined Macmillan's career. Boothby was in no doubt that Dorothy's callous attitude caused Sarah's early and untimely death in 1970, aged forty. He later said: 'It is the one thing I could never quite forgive Dorothy: the one wicked thing she did . . . I think it was part of her guilty conscience, but it definitely killed Sarah.'

For her part, Dorothy continued to juggle husband and lover for the rest of her life. She travelled at home and abroad with Boothby and telephoned him every day. Yet she also ran Macmillan's house at Birch Grove in Sussex and acted as a willing consort in his burgeoning political career. Boothby and Macmillan were always civil to each other in public, and both always embraced the same Conservative political philosophy. Yet during the ensuing years up to Dorothy's death in 1966, the two men were party to contrasting fortunes. Some said that the affair gave Macmillan the grit and motivation he needed to succeed in politics, and it seems probable that such an analysis is correct.

He held his first government posts during the Second World War, joining the Cabinet in 1942, and after spells as Minister of Defence, Foreign Secretary and Chancellor of the Exchequer he fought his way up the ladder to become Prime Minister on the resignation of Sir Anthony Eden in 1957. The highlight of his premiership was the Conservative victory in the 1959 election with a massive majority of a hundred seats. He resigned in 1963 after a series of setbacks, which included the damaging Profumo scandal (see pages 142–57), but, having accepted a hereditary earldom – he took the title of Earl of Stockton[11] – he became the epitome of the knowledgeable and respected elder statesman in the House of Lords in his later years. He died, full of honours, in 1986, aged ninety-one, twenty years after his faithless, if charming, wife.

Boothby, however, failed to prosper, despite becoming an outstanding commentator on public affairs on both radio and television. Macmillan, when he was Prime Minister, generously rewarded the man who had cuckolded him for so long with a peerage in 1958 (he had been knighted in 1953), but the new peer's declining years were besmirched by a sex scandal of a somewhat different orientation.

On 11 July 1964, the *Sunday Mirror* went on sale with the sensational headline: 'Peer and a Gangster: Yard Probe Public Men at Seaside Parties.' The article accompanying the headline stated that Scotland Yard was investigating a homosexual relationship between an unnamed leading politician and important member of the House of Lords, and a gangster, again nameless, who was head of the biggest protection racket London had ever seen. A week later, the same paper ran a similar story, claiming that it possessed a picture of the thug and the peer, which it dared not print. The identity of the two men was common knowledge in Westminster, but when the German magazine *Stern*, with scant regard for British libel law, exposed the crime boss as Ronnie Kray and the peer as Bob Boothby, the world and his wife knew whom the *Sunday Mirror* was describing.

In a letter to *The Times,* Boothby refuted any close connection with Ronnie Kray and denied the inference that he was having an affair with the homosexual gang leader. He explained that he had been to Kray's flat to discuss a business plan, concerning his possible investment in a housing and factory development in Nigeria, in which the notorious Kray twins were involved at the time. He added that he had declined to participate in the scheme but had agreed to be photographed with Ronnie Kray, who idolized famous people. Boothby went on to reveal that the result was the wholly innocent snapshot of which the *Mirror* claimed to have a copy.

Having seen this letter, the *Sunday Mirror* lost its nerve and backtracked. The paper acknowledged that there was no truth in the allegations or the sexual innuendo and sacked its editor, Reginald Taylor. Boothby received from the newspaper a full and frank apology, as well as a compensation payment of the then substantial sum of £40,000.

Yet while the peer may have emerged from the scandal with a handsome payout, his reputation was irretrievably damaged. There was talk at the time that a cat burglar, Leslie Holt, had introduced the peer to Ronnie Kray after the latter had served three years in prison for grievous bodily harm. Some gossips even claimed that Holt was Boothby's homosexual lover, and that Kray had supplied the politician with rent boys at the series of dissolute seaside parties to which the *Sunday Mirror* had alluded.

Furthermore, it seemed that there might be more than a grain of truth in the *Mirror*'s subsequently withdrawn allegations, when another strange story began to do the rounds. Apparently, some years earlier, the police had arrested a drunken youth after he had been found in a London street, waving a bottle of champagne around and carrying a gold watch engraved with Boothby's name. Taken before magistrates when he had sobered up, the youth was conditionally discharged and put on a train back to his native

Scotland. Reporters traced the boy and found that he hailed from Boothby's former constituency, Aberdeenshire East. (Boothby had had to give up his seat on being elevated to the House of Lords in 1958.) He told the newsmen that he had travelled to London at Boothby's suggestion and had then been taken to a Soho restaurant, Quo Vadis, where he had been wined and dined. The young Scotsman told the reporters that he had later gone back to the politician's flat, where the two men had sex. He swore that Boothby had given him the gold watch as payment for services rendered.

Was Boothby, who had such a long and passionate heterosexual relationship with Lady Dorothy Macmillan, also an active homosexual who had promiscuous affairs with rent boys and hardened criminals? The defence will say that there is no proof that he had homosexual leanings. They will agree with the subsequent Labour leader, Michael Foot, who described Boothby as a 'non-playing captain' when he championed in the press the then taboo subject of homosexual law reform. The prosecution, on the other hand, will reply that there is no smoke without fire, and that the colourful peer who once stole a future Prime Minister's wife was fortunate to persuade the *Sunday Mirror* to retract its allegations that he was also a practising homosexual. As far as Boothby's sexuality is concerned, it might be fairer to use another legal phrase and say that the jury is still out.

The great house at Chatsworth is still owned and lived in by the Cavendish family, now presided over by the twelfth Duke of Devonshire, who succeeded to the title on his father's death in 2004. Remodelled frequently over the centuries, there is today little of the house, except perhaps its magnificent setting, that Bess of Hardwick would recognize, though rather more that would be familiar to the wife of the fifth Duke, Georgiana. Seeing it, anyone with a feeling for history might be forgiven for believing that, despite the changes, one might still catch a fleeting sense of Mary Queen of Scots, or a half-glimpse of the fifth Duke riding in the park with Lady Elizabeth Foster, or an echo of the laughter of Lady Dorothy Macmillan.

CHAPTER THREE

Hampton Court

THE FIRST RECORDED BUILDINGS at Hampton Court, known the world over as Henry VIII's favourite royal palace, were owned by a religious order, the Knights Hospitaller of the Order of St John of Jerusalem, which was founded in the early twelfth century to protect the Holy Land from the infidel Saracens. In 1236 the Knights acquired the manor of Hampton, which is only twenty miles up the River Thames from the centre of London. It seems that they used the present palace site as a place of storage for the produce of their surrounding agricultural holdings. Excavations, as well as documents of the time, suggest that the building on the brethren's property was a large barn or hall, with a stone room attached that was used as a sort of medieval estate office.

Archaeological findings also indicate that, by the fifteenth century, there was some new residential accommodation in the area of the present-day Clock Court. So it is likely that the order's abbots were then using Hampton as a pleasant rural riverside

[57]

retreat from the crowded and unhealthy capital. The dwelling must have been quite large and comfortable, for in 1503 the abbot of the day entertained Henry VII and his wife, Elizabeth of York, who was pregnant with her seventh and last child. Two years later, the King's Lord Chamberlain, Sir Giles Daubeney, obtained a ninety-nine-year lease from the Knights. But Sir Giles died in 1508, and six years later the order entered into a similar leasing arrangement with the powerful Thomas Wolsey, the Archbishop of York and right-hand man of the new monarch, Henry VIII.

Henry and his first queen, Catherine of Aragon, visited Hampton in March 1514, probably to view the property that their leading political and religious adviser wished to acquire. Cardinal Wolsey gained possession the following June and immediately began the extensive construction project which, in the space of just six years, would convert the old manor house that Sir Giles Daubeney had leased into a magnificent palace. Work on the new residence must have been reasonably well advanced even by 1516, as Wolsey was able to receive the King and Queen for dinner that May. But the Cardinal did not consider that the palace was ready for entertaining on a lavish scale until he returned from helping Henry successfully negotiate with the French King, Francis I, at the famous summit meeting between the two often warring countries known as the Field of the Cloth of Gold, in 1520.

No design drawings or contemporary paintings of Wolsey's opulent dwelling survive, but building accounts mention a Base Court, a Great Chamber and a King's Dining Room. Recent scientific evidence, however, indicates that the Cardinal's Hampton Court was the first great Renaissance palace in Britain, with a fabulous towering Great Hall, a vast central courtyard with sculpted medallions of Roman emperors set into its walls, and substantial kitchens.

Wolsey, however, was not able to enjoy the splendours of his new home for more than a decade. The King's most trusted adviser's influence gradually began to fade after he failed to persuade Pope Clement VII to grant Henry a divorce from

Catherine of Aragon. The Cardinal was sacked as Lord Chancellor, and eventually disappeared from Henry's court in 1529. All his wealth, lands and houses became the property of the King. But even the transfer of these substantial assets, which included the lease on Hampton Court, failed to sate the King's displeasure, for Henry next ordered the arrest of his once favourite minister for high treason. Wolsey, now broken and suffering from ill health, died, three weeks later, on 29 November 1530, on the way to London for his trial.

Presumably, Henry, who was notoriously difficult to please, was not overly impressed by the Cardinal's magnificent residence. Indeed, he completely transformed Hampton Court during the next decade, spending the then enormous sum of £62,000 rebuilding and extending the palace. By the time the King's renovations were completed in the early 1540s, there were real-tennis courts, bowling alleys, glorious pleasure gardens, a huge 1,100-acre hunting park, kitchens covering 36,000 square feet, an ornate chapel, a vast communal dining room, the Great Hall, and, last but not least, a giant lavatory, accurately known as the Great House of Easement, which could seat twenty-eight people at a time. Fresh spring water was even piped three miles from Coombe Hill in Kingston through a sophisticated network of lead pipes.

So when Henry's new palace was finished, it was an exemplar of style and modernity. It proved to be rather more than that, however. During a short spell of less than fifteen years, Hampton Court also played host to all six of the King's wives. Moreover, it is no exaggeration to say that Henry's rapid turnover of spouses was responsible for some of the greatest and juiciest scandals in the British royal family's colourful history.

Anne Boleyn, who had spent some years at the French court in her youth and was the sister of Henry's mistress, Mary, the wife of a courtier named William Carey, reputedly caught Henry's eye in 1522. He had taken other lovers when it was clear that Catherine of Aragon was growing too old to produce the male heir he so desired.[1] But by 1525 it was obvious that Anne, who had dark eyes and hair and an olive complexion, and who, not being fair-haired and blue-eyed, certainly did not conform to the Tudors' ideal of beauty, was the girl he, surprisingly, desired above all others.

Soon the King began secretly courting the twenty-three-year-old Anne, the daughter of Sir Thomas Boleyn, later first Earl of Wiltshire, and Lady Elizabeth Howard, the eldest daughter of the second Duke of Norfolk. Henry made it known in mid-1527 that he was determined to divorce Catherine. He also made it abundantly clear that he had resolved to make Anne Boleyn his second wife, despite Wolsey's warnings that she would not make a suitable consort. The soon to be disgraced Cardinal's protestations failed to change the King's mind, and he continued wooing his new love with the ardour of a love-struck youth. As just one example, Anne spent the Christmas of 1530 with Henry at Hampton Court, and received the considerable sum of £100 as a gift from her by now besotted suitor.

Anne had probably had some sexual experience during her teenage years. In fact, there was some argument at the time that she had once been pre-contracted (an undertaking by both parties to marry) to Henry, Lord Percy, heir to the fifth Earl of Northumberland.[2] Rumours that she had indulged in a heavy affair, which probably stopped just short of full intercourse, with Lord Percy were rife around Henry's court. But she showed mature judgement for one so young and, even if she was not a virgin, yet managed to behave just as one should. There is no doubt that she made the King far keener by coyly refusing his advances for five long years.

The streetwise Anne gave in and consented to sleep with the King only in late 1532, when she was sure that he was well and truly hooked. Soon she was pregnant, a citcumstance that forced Henry and his advisers to move fast. The couple wed secretly either in Whitehall or Westminster on 25 January 1533. At Easter the marriage was made public, and in May the recently appointed Archbishop of Canterbury, Thomas Cranmer, declared Henry's first marriage null and void, and his second to be valid.[3] When

Anne was crowned at a magnificent ceremony on 1 June that year, the new Queen of England was six months pregnant.

In July Anne came to Hampton Court, where a series of splendid celebrations took place in her honour. There was hunting, dancing, gambling, archery and much musical entertainment. Henry even decided to build a complete set of rooms for his young bride on the same floor as his own apartments. It seems that the 'Queen's Old Lodgynges', on the floor below, were simply not smart enough for the apple of his eye. New formal gardens, with flower beds edged with freshly painted railings in the Tudor colours of green and white, were also constructed to stretch down from the palace to the banks of the peacefully lapping Thames. As the new and pregnant Queen walked among the fragrant rosebeds with hardly a care in the world during that idyllic summer, it did not seem possible that she would not live to occupy the splendid new suite her loving husband had commissioned.

Henry was initially disappointed when, in September 1533, Anne gave birth to a girl. None the less, there were still great rejoicings at Princess Elizabeth's birth; after all, Anne had proved that she was fertile. There was no reason, therefore, why she should not provide Henry with a son sooner rather than later. That was why the miscarriage that ended her next pregnancy in 1534, a month or so before the baby was due, was such a sharp blow. She was now in her mid-thirties, and her striking dark beauty was beginning to fade. Yet loss of looks would not matter if she could give the King the thing he wanted above all else: a healthy male heir.

From the autumn of 1534 and through the first nine months of 1535, Anne tried hard to become pregnant for the third time, but by now she was finding it difficult to conceive. She confided to her sister-in-law, Jane, Viscountess Rochford, that the problem lay with the King's periodic bouts of impotence. More dangerously, she also told Lady Rochford that Henry had neither the skill nor the virility to satisfy a woman. However, her husband must have briefly recovered his sexual prowess in the autumn because, by New Year 1536, Anne was enthusiastically joining in the festivities at Hampton Court, happy in the knowledge that she was three months pregnant. Two other reasons also contributed to her good humour. Anne was aware that Catherine of Aragon was dying, and thus that even those who did not acknowledge Henry's divorce would soon have to recognize her as his legal and only wife. She was also confident that the attention that her husband was paying to one of her pretty young ladies-in-waiting, Jane Seymour, would come to nothing if she could give birth to that elusive son and heir.

Catherine died on 7 January, but Anne's improved situation was destined to be short-lived. At the end of the month she miscarried a 'man child'. The King was unsympathetic when he visited his grief-stricken wife. According to one of Anne's biographers, George Wyatt, Henry's last words as he left her chamber were distinctly ominous. The disappointed monarch decreed that 'he would have no more boys by her'. From that defining moment, Anne Boleyn's fate was effectively sealed.

Henry moved quickly to replace Anne with the nubile Jane Seymour. First, on 12 May 1536, Mark Smeaton, Sir Francis Weston, Sir Henry Norris and William Brereton were convicted of various crimes against the King, which included, in two of their cases, committing adultery with the Queen. The four men, who were almost certainly innocent, were condemned to die at Tyburn,[4] by being part hanged, cut down alive, disembowelled, castrated and finally quartered limb by limb. Three days later, the trial for treason of Anne and her brother George, Viscount Rochford, once one of Henry's greatest friends, took place in the Great Hall of the Tower of London.

Anne's jury consisted of twenty-six peers headed by her uncle, the Duke of Norfolk. The result was a foregone conclusion, however, as the men with whom she had reputedly had sexual relations had already been condemned. Some of the other charges, such as the claims that she had committed incest with her brother and indulged in witchcraft, were farcical. Nevertheless, and despite the lack of concrete evidence, Anne was found guilty. Lord

Rochford's case followed, and he too was judged to have committed a series of equally unlikely crimes.

Henry then decreed that Rochford should join the four who had been convicted at the earlier trial at the Tower of London, where all five were executed on 17 May. (Apparently, Smeaton, Weston, Norris and Brereton had been saved from a more grisly end at Tyburn by the late intervention of their sympathetic King.) It was also up to her husband whether Anne lived or died. She did not have to wait long to hear the bad news. Henry delayed his decision only until Cranmer had nullified his marriage to Anne on extremely doubtful grounds. The King then gave the order that the woman who believed she was his second wife should be beheaded on Tower Green on 19 May.

When Henry first brought Anne to Hampton Court as his bride in July 1533, the entrance that the couple used was rechristened Anne Boleyn's Gateway. Stonemasons and woodcutters also carved her family crest of a falcon, as well as the initials 'H' and 'A' entwined in a lover's knot, into the ceilings in several parts of the palace in honour of the King and Queen's recent marriage. But after Anne was executed, Henry hurriedly ordered the royal workforce to remove her crests and replace the letter 'A' in the lover's knot with a 'J' – for his new wife, Jane Seymour. In the rush to complete their task, the craftsmen unfortunately missed some of the emblems. For example, a falcon crest high in the roof of the Great Hall escaped alteration, and an 'A' was left in the carving on the Clock Tower's archway. So Henry, hard though he tried, never quite managed to rid his beloved Hampton Court of reminders of the Queen he had grown to hate.

It is sometimes said that Henry was playing real tennis[5] at Hampton Court when news arrived that Anne was dead. He is reputed to have stopped the game and rushed through the palace to Jane Seymour's bedchamber, where he immediately consummated a previously chaste relationship. It is a good story, but it is much more likely that Henry was hunting at nearby Richmond when he received word of Anne's death.

Actually, Jane had been discreetly moved away from the palace at a much earlier date. It is known that she was lodging with Henry's trusted friend, Sir Nicholas Carew, at Croydon in the week before Anne's death. However, she had moved to a house on the river near London[6] by 15 May. At six o'clock on the morning after Anne's execution she was transported from there by barge to Hampton Court, where she and Henry were betrothed in front of a select band of courtiers. It is often stated erroneously that they were married at the palace that spring morning, but in fact the wedding took place in Whitehall ten days later.

It is not known if Henry waited until marriage to have full sexual relations with his virginal bride, but the impotence that had troubled him in the past was clearly not a problem. Perhaps Jane's legendary innocence reassured and restored the unconfident and, now, extremely corpulent forty-five-year-old monarch. Unlike her predecessor, his new wife presumably had nobody else with whom she could compare her husband. Indeed, if proof positive was needed of the revived King's virility, it was provided in January 1537, when the good news was announced at Greenwich that Jane was pregnant.

In September that year Jane, heavy with child, occupied the new Queen's Apartments at Hampton Court, which had originally been built for Anne Boleyn, to await the birth. Henry could hardly contain his joy when Jane produced a baby boy, later to be Edward VI, in her chamber in the south-east corner of the Clock Court at two o'clock in the morning on Friday, 12 October 1537. The new prince was christened on the following Monday in the palace's chapel, but there were dark clouds on the horizon. Only twelve days after being delivered of her son, just before midnight, Jane died of septicaemia brought on by puerperal fever, then the most common killer of women who had recently given birth. Poignantly, at her funeral at Windsor on 9 November a distraught Henry wore traditional mourning dress. She was the only one of his queens so honoured. Nor did his love for Jane ever weaken. On his death in 1547, it was found that his will stated that he wished to be buried by her side.

Over the years, an apparition, clothed in white and carrying a lighted taper, has been seen walking from Jane's old Hampton Court apartments, which are close to the Silver Stick Gallery, on the anniversary of Edward VI's birth. The sad but friendly ghost is reputed to be that of Henry's most loved queen. Another famous Hampton Court phantom also has a close connection to Henry's third wife. A woman named Sibell Penn fostered Edward after his mother's death, and years later treated Elizabeth I through an attack of smallpox in 1562. When the long-serving and faithful royal nurse died after herself catching the dreaded disease from the Queen, she was buried in Hampton church and a life-size marble effigy was constructed over her tomb.

In 1829, however, the ancient church was demolished. Sibell's grave was disturbed, and her remains were dispersed. Immediately, strange and unaccountable sounds, resembling those of a person spinning thread, were heard in the south-west wing of the palace. A wall was removed and an old spinning wheel was discovered in a previously hidden room, whose oak floorboards had been worn thin by the feet that had worked the wheel's treadle. Nineteenth-century romantics fervently believed that, after her tomb was desecrated, Sibell had returned in desperation to the room where she had worked in Tudor times. A palace sentry first viewed her ghost in the 1890s. Since then, Sibell's shadowy figure, clothed in a flowing hooded gown, which is eerily similar to the image of the effigy on her tomb, has been seen on numerous occasions.

As for Henry VIII, devastated by his tragic loss he seems to have been reluctant to stay at the palace where Jane had died for some time to come. He appears to have used Hampton Court as a glorified nursery for his son, Edward, in the care of his devoted nurse, Sibell Penn. However, the King returned there in November 1539 to await the arrival of his fourth wife, Anne of Cleves. Sadly, the court painter Hans Holbein had radically overused his artistic licence when he was dispatched to the Continent by Henry to paint a portrait of the twenty-four-year-old German princess the King intended to marry. Consequently, the excited King, who had never seen Anne in the flesh, was expecting a beautiful and flirtatious girl rather than the dowdy and plain woman he met at Canterbury on New Year's Day 1540. 'You have brought me a Flanders mare,' he is said to have complained in private.

Given the difficult circumstances of their first meeting, it was no surprise that Henry's perennial problem of impotence should resurface, five days later, on his wedding night. It also did not help that his wife, as well as being unattractive, knew virtually nothing of the facts of life. In fact, the King later told one of his courtiers that 'he could never in her company be provoked and steered to know her carnally'.

After that first disaster, it was perhaps inevitable that Anne and Henry never really lived together. Even so, the Queen was initially amazed to receive a deputation from her husband on 25 June, declaring that her marriage was invalid, though she soon recovered from the shock. In fact, she was in residence at Hampton Court when she heard the news that she was to receive an extremely generous settlement from Henry, and in due course did so when they eventually divorced in July 1540. Safe in the knowledge that she would be well looked after, Anne was happy to depart gracefully; indeed, Henry and his fourth wife remained on good terms for the rest of the King's life. Although she was present at the coronation of her stepdaughter, Mary, in October 1553, Anne preferred to live quietly at Hever Castle in Kent until her death in 1557.

Henry may have found it impossible to consummate his marriage with Anne of Cleves, but he had no trouble finding sexual satisfaction with his fifth wife, the delightful Catherine Howard,[7] whom he christened 'his rose without a thorn'. When the happy royal couple, who had married with indecent haste at Oatlands[8] on 28 July, stayed at Hampton Court during the New Year of 1541, the ageing King could hardly keep his hands off his pretty twenty-one-year-old bride. His courtiers observed that he gave Catherine many expensive presents, including a fabulous necklace of diamonds and rubies. But in March the King, who was already suffering from leg ulcers, succumbed to a high fever. Although Henry was confined to his bed for some ten to twelve days, it was noted that the young Queen was not present to attend to her sick husband.

It is likely that, during Henry's illness, Catherine, who was understandably tiring of her obese and much older husband's attentions, had started to look elsewhere for her sexual pleasure. Stupidly and recklessly, the Queen began to consort with one of her old flames, the good-looking but unreliable courtier (and Catherine's distant kinsman) Thomas Culpeper, who in his misspent youth had escaped prosecution for raping the young wife of a park keeper. Catherine soon wished to see more of Culpeper and began to grant him 'great favours'. It was, however, the letter that she wrote to her lover in April that was eventually to cause her downfall. 'I heard that you were sick and never longed so much for anything as to see you. It makes my heart die to think I cannot be always in your company' were incriminating words, to say the least, and hardly smacked of the sentences a woman would write to a man who was merely a close acquaintance.

When Catherine's fall came, it was fast and unexpected. In an instant, she went from being a beloved wife, one who had just completed a long and tiring tour of the royal domains with her doting husband, to *persona non grata* and a despised scarlet woman. A certain John Lascelles came to visit Cranmer with salacious details of Catherine's sexual antics when she was a girl at the Dowager Duchess of Norfolk's house in Lambeth.[9] The shrewd Archbishop immediately realized, with horror, that the Queen had a far from blameless past. On All Souls' Day, 2 November, during a Mass at Hampton Court, Cranmer slipped a scrap of paper cataloguing Lascelles's accusations into the praying Henry's hand.

At first, the King refused to believe the charges against his innocent rose. But when Catherine's secretary, Francis Dereham, was identified as one of several men to whom she had granted sexual favours in her Lambeth days, the Queen was in dire trouble. Her situation grew worse when Dereham, after he had been removed to the Tower and tortured, revealed that Culpeper had followed him as Catherine's lover in the carefree days of her youth.

[67]

Naturally, Culpeper was also soon whisked away to the Tower and tortured. It was, therefore, only a matter of time before Catherine's more recent indiscretions, including the letter she had written to Culpeper in April, emerged.

When Cranmer confronted her with the evidence, Catherine pleaded guilty to loose behaviour in her youth but resolutely denied that she had ever been unfaithful to the King. But Henry had already washed his hands of his irreverent wife. On 5 November he left Hampton Court and did not return until the 14th, by which time the recently arrested Catherine had been taken away to Syon House.[10] On 24 November 1541 Catherine was indicted for 'behaving like a common harlot with divers persons', such as Culpeper and Dereham. The severed heads of her executed lovers eventually ended up impaled on spikes on London Bridge. The Queen, still pleading that she had never cuckolded the King, was to suffer a similar fate. On 13 February 1542, at the Tower of London, Catherine gained the unwelcome distinction of becoming the second of Henry's wives to die on the scaffold.

Legend tells that Catherine, as she was being transported from Hampton Court to Syon, escaped from her guards and ran, screaming, down the corridor, now known as the Haunted Gallery, to the chapel where Henry was hearing Mass. She managed to reach the chapel door before she was recaptured. As she was roughly dragged away by her escorts, her husband refused to be moved by her desperate cries for mercy. The problem with this compelling tale is that sound historical evidence confirms that Catherine was not informed of the charges against her before Henry left the palace on 5 November. That slight flaw, however, has not prevented several sightings of a wailing spectre, dressed entirely in white, in the vicinity of the chapel. The female figure, which is believed to be Catherine, reputedly approaches the spot where Henry kneeled and then turns away, distraught, to continue its bitter, never-ending lament.

Elizabeth I used Hampton Court sparingly during her long reign, often making only an annual visit. When the vain so-called

Virgin Queen was in residence, however, the principal source of court gossip, as it was at all her other palaces, was usually her complicated love life. It is also fair to say that most of the rumours concerned Elizabeth's enigmatic relationship with her greatest favourite, Robert Dudley, Earl of Leicester, who had been given the then extremely important position of Master of the Horse on her accession in 1558. That much-coveted role ensured that Dudley, who was in charge of the Queen's stables, transport and hunting, was nearly always at Elizabeth's side.

Dudley, the fifth son of John Dudley, the first Duke of Northumberland,[11] was tall, long-legged, dark-complexioned and extremely handsome. He had known the Queen since they were children, when for a time both had been imprisoned in the Tower. So it was certainly not strange that the flirtatious twenty-five-year-old Queen should burn a candle for the glamorous figure, who was reputed to be the most skilful horseman in her kingdom. Elizabeth soon lavished further appointments, honours and lands on Dudley, with the almost inevitable result that questions began to arise about the propriety of their relationship. When Dudley's wife, Amy, died in suspicious circumstances at Cumnor Place in Oxfordshire in 1560, a jury ruled her death to have been accidental. Even so, idle talk that Dudley had arranged the killing with Elizabeth so that the pair could wed persisted for months after the event.

Dudley and the Queen were certainly on very familiar terms, as is clear from the following story, told by the courtier and memoirist Sir Thomas Randolph in a letter to Sir William Throckmorton. One day, Elizabeth was sitting in the open gallery at the end of the real-tennis court at Hampton Court, watching a game between Dudley and the Duke of Norfolk. When the match ended, Dudley approached the Queen and whipped a napkin from her hand to wipe his sweating brow. Norfolk, appalled by such a display of cheeky intimacy, reprimanded Dudley, warning that he 'would laye his racket upon his face', whereupon the Queen, furious at the admonishment of her favourite, 'offendid sorely with the Duke'.

Of course, such demonstrations of affection do not mean that Dudley and Elizabeth were lovers, but they certainly added fuel to the fire of those courtiers who believed they were. Furthermore, there were many other instances to suggest that their liaison was less than innocent. There were quarrels that could be interpreted as lovers' tiffs. For example, in the autumn of 1565 Dudley made Elizabeth jealous when he paid too much attention to Lettice Knollys, one of the Queen's ladies-in-waiting. There were cross words and a series of angry exchanges, although Elizabeth's fury did not last long. By the winter, Dudley was back in favour, and it was said at court that they spent the whole of New Year's Day entwined in each other's arms. In 1566 they were caught kissing on the open road in London, and Dudley was even seen in the monarch's bedchamber at Greenwich, handing her a shift as she rose enticingly from her bed.

When she was only fourteen, Elizabeth was known to have indulged in a form of sexual horseplay with her stepmother Catherine Parr's second husband,[12] Thomas, Lord Seymour of Sudeley. Indeed, Catherine, who was then pregnant, stopped Elizabeth lodging at her Chelsea home after catching the red-haired Princess in an amorous embrace with her thirty-six-year-old husband. Since Elizabeth had clearly not been averse to experimenting with the opposite sex in her teenage years, it is likely that she was as keen in her twenties and early thirties. It is possible, therefore – and, indeed, probable – that, even if they did not have full sexual intercourse, she and Dudley indulged in a serious and very physical sexual relationship.

There were other close confidants, men like Sir Walter Ralegh, Sir Christopher Hatton and the seventeenth Earl of Oxford, but all the evidence suggests that their friendships with the Queen were entirely platonic. The same is probably true of her last favourite, Robert Devereux, Earl of Essex. The rash and arrogant Essex certainly took great liberties with the Queen. Indeed, he amazed the court by rushing, uninvited, into her bedroom on his return from commanding her army in the disastrous Irish campaign of

1599. By then, however, the Queen was in her late sixties, so it is probable that her love for Essex was predominately maternal.

There were many other rumours about Elizabeth's allegedly voracious sexual habits during her long life, although the vast majority were so ridiculous as to be almost beyond belief. She was said to be as lustful as her mother, Anne Boleyn, and to force her courtiers to sleep with her on pain of death. The Venetian Ambassador to Spain was even told that she had borne thirteen natural children.

The most unlikely story of all, however, surfaced long after the Queen's death, when a man, conveniently called Arthur Dudley, appeared in Madrid claiming to be the son of Elizabeth and the Earl of Leicester. He said that he had been born to the Queen at Hampton Court in 1562 but had been taken from the palace, as a small baby, by a servant to the house of a miller and his wife in the nearby village of East Molesey. The kindly miller brought up the child, Arthur, as if he was his own son, but on his deathbed the old man revealed the 'truth' about the boy's parentage. The youth was astounded. He had always believed that a servant named Robert Sotheron was his natural father, and that his mother was a prominent lady in Elizabeth's court who had embarked on an illicit below-stairs relationship. With so little evidence, however, this curious tale remains just a rumour.

Like Henry VIII, James I loved Hampton Court for the wonderful hunting, and visited the palace many times. He presided over the famous Hampton Court Conference of 1604, which resulted in the Authorized (or King James) Version of the Bible being published seven years later; however, his behaviour with a string of male favourites would have been regarded as distinctly unholy. James fathered eight children, although only three survived, by his wife, Anne of Denmark, but the monarch, who became King of England in addition to that of Scotland at the age of thirty-six, was actually much more interested in men.

James was only fourteen when he first fell in love with the elegant Esme Stuart at his Scottish court.[13] It seems, too, that the young Scottish king was quite promiscuous, for he also had an affair with Alexander Lindsay, Lord Spynie, and caused a great scandal by passionately kissing Francis Hepburn, Earl of Bothwell, in public in the 1580s.

By the time James came to England after Elizabeth's death in 1603, his two most influential favourites were Robert Carr and George Villiers. Both men were well looked after by their royal lover. The handsome, loose-limbed Carr, who originally came from the Scottish Borders, became James's latest conquest after he fell off his horse at a London tournament in 1607. To the amazement of the spectators, James rushed towards Carr's crumpled figure and cradled his former pageboy in his arms. Carr was eventually made Earl of Somerset, but proved both treacherous and incompetent when he tried to interfere with the government of the realm, for which he and his wife were imprisoned in the Tower, although they escaped execution.

James had tired of the unintelligent Carr by the time he was introduced to Villiers, the blue-eyed son of a penniless Leicestershire squire, in 1613. Their first sexual tryst is believed to have occurred at Farnham Castle in Surrey in August 1615. Villiers, whose luxuriant chestnut hair was constantly fondled by James at court, did not have to wait long before he gained his reward for gratifying the King. Like Somerset and others of the King's favourites, he was soon elevated to the peerage as Viscount Villiers in 1616, and was created Earl of Buckingham the following year. James told his ministerial council in 1617: 'You may be sure that I love the Earl of Buckingham more than anyone else, and more than you who are here assembled.' It was little wonder, therefore, that all the senior politicians and courtiers hated the ruthlessly ambitious favourite for the enormous influence he exerted over the King. Yet he could do no wrong in James's eyes, and his endless flattery again paid dividends when he was made Duke of Buckingham in 1623.

Buckingham and Somerset often joined James on his regular hunting trips to Hampton Court. It is possible that his long-suffering queen was thinking of her husband ostentatiously caressing his latest male lover in public when she shot a dog with an arrow while hunting in the royal palace's grounds. It has always been assumed that the Queen, who died at Hampton Court in 1619, mistook the King's hound, Jewel, for a stag. James raged at his wife's unfortunate mistake, but it may be that Anne, well aware that it was his favourite hunting dog, was simply paying her husband back for the huge embarrassment his very open and scandalous homosexual affairs had caused her.

Charles I used Hampton Court frequently in the early part of his reign, and received the Grand Remonstrance – the list of grievances of the people against the King – from the Long Parliament there in 1641, shortly after the outbreak of the Civil War. In 1647, when he was deposed by Parliament, he was also imprisoned there. His guards, however, could never keep tabs on the King, as he was permitted to wander through the palace's 1,500 rooms at will, with the result that it was almost inevitable that Charles would manage to escape. Sure enough, after three months in captivity, he walked out of Hampton Court's gate at nine o'clock on the evening of 11 November 1647 and crossed the Thames by ferry. Loyal friends met him on the other side of the river, and the party rode away to the Isle of Wight.

Hampton Court was actually sold in 1652, three years after the execution of Charles I, by the Parliamentarians, but when Oliver Cromwell became Lord Protector in 1654 the palace was repurchased for his use. He may have been anti-royalist and a man of puritanical tastes, but Cromwell apparently loved living in such comfortable and regal surroundings, as did his wife, Elizabeth. In 1660, when the monarchy was restored, the palace returned to royal hands. Charles II preferred to live at Windsor, but scandal was never far away when the charismatic and lustful sovereign, whom his subjects liked to call 'Old Rowley', visited Hampton Court to play tennis or hunt in the park.

Charles had many mistresses during his reign, including the Duke of Monmouth's mother, Lucy Walter, and the actress and, supposedly, orange-seller, Nell Gwyn. But Barbara Palmer, who became the Countess of Castlemaine when her husband Roger was granted an earldom, commanded the royal attentions for more years than her rivals. She had many other lovers, ranging from the playwright William Wycherley to the Earl of Mulgrave, but always seemed to return to the King, who never tired of her considerable charms.

Barbara, who reputedly bore the King five illegitimate children during their long, if intermittent, relationship, was the instrument of a huge uproar when Charles insisted on presenting her not only to his entire court, but also to his new wife, the Portuguese Princess Catherine of Braganza, during their honeymoon at Hampton Court in June 1662. The Queen fainted, and at first absolutely refused to see her husband's mistress. In retaliation, an angry Charles sent her large band of attendants away and told her, untruthfully, that her dowry, the cities of Bombay and Tangier, had not been signed over. The Portuguese Ambassador was also so insulted that 'he left Hampton Court and retired to his own house in the city'. Eventually, however, Catherine gave way to her insensitive husband's demands, and even, rather inappropriately, consented to make Charles's lover a Lady of the Bedchamber.

Charles also built a set of apartments at the south-east corner of Hampton Court for Barbara, who was later created Duchess of Cleveland for services rendered. Her rooms were very different in style from the Tudor architecture that was still predominant in the rest of the palace, and were the forerunners of the style favoured by the subsequent Stuart monarchs, William III and his queen, Mary II.

The 'Merry Monarch' usually had his way, as far as pretty women were concerned, but the glamorous Frances Stuart, who, with helmet, shield and spear (later a trident), was to appear as Britannia on the United Kingdom's penny coins until decimalization in 1971, was notable for turning down his advances. When she was fourteen, the Scottish girl had travelled to Portugal to be a maid of honour to Charles's future bride.[14] Frances accompanied Catherine to England for her marriage, and Charles immediately fell in love with his wife's attendant, whom Samuel Pepys claimed was 'the greatest beauty I ever saw'.

Hard though he tried, the King could not entice the flirtatious Frances into his bed, even though his distant kinswoman laughed at his jokes and encouraged him with kisses. Nevertheless, the court, inevitably, began to speculate as to whether Charles and Frances had physically consummated their relationship. When the Queen fell ill with a fever in 1663, there were further rumours that the King and Frances would wed if Catherine did not survive her illness. Frances, however, still refused to sleep with Charles, even though it was he who chose her as the model for Britannia, whose image appeared on medals given to sailors in 1664 during the war against the Dutch that broke out that year (three years later the image appeared on the country's coinage). The Great Plague struck London in 1665, so Frances moved with the rest of the royal retinue to Hampton Court, where Sir Peter Lely painted the famous picture that portrays her, aptly, as the chaste goddess Diana, the huntress.

When London was free of infection and the court returned to the capital, the King continued to press Frances to become his mistress, offering her wealth and land, but she still declined. He was, of course, furious when she eloped with the third Duke of Richmond[15] in 1667, but when, two years later, he heard that she was suffering from smallpox, he rushed to her bedside and forgave her for marrying without his consent. She recovered, but, since Charles had now fallen for Nell Gwyn, his great love for Frances, which remained unrequited, came to an end.

Frances also had a close, if somewhat odd, relationship with Barbara Castlemaine. She and the King's mistress used to dress up as a bride and groom, with Frances playing the male part. Furthermore, because the two women often shared a bed in Barbara's Hampton Court apartments, there was understandable speculation in Charles's court that they might be having a lesbian relationship. Barbara also used to summon the King to her bedroom so that they could gaze in wonderment at the gorgeous Frances while she

[75]

slept. Perhaps the lascivious monarch and his voluptuous mistress found that voyeurism added spice to their sex life.

After William and Mary came to the throne in 1689, the royal couple commissioned Sir Christopher Wren, the architect of St Paul's Cathedral and prime mover in the rebuilding of much of London following the Great Fire of 1666, to rebuild Hampton Court. William did not like the principal royal residence, Whitehall Palace, and much preferred to spend his time in the country, hunting. So Hampton Court, which was chosen as a suitable substitute, was deemed to be in need of a massive facelift. Wren originally decided to pull down the whole Tudor palace except for the Great Hall, but in the end time and money dictated that the King's and Queen's main apartments on the south and east sides of the palace, on the site of the old Tudor lodgings, were the only parts to be replaced.

Wren began the work in May 1689. Because William wanted his renovations finished fast, huge sums were made available. The Tudor courtyard was the first to go, and a new one soon constructed in its place. In December tragedy struck when two workmen were killed and eleven injured after a large section of the South Wing collapsed; when work resumed, it proceeded with more care and less haste. Accounts from the period reveal that between April 1689 and March 1694 an astonishing £113,000 was spent on the new royal apartments. Then, in late 1694, the Queen died from smallpox, and a devastated William lost interest in the project. Consequently, work ceased, leaving the new buildings as a brick shell with bare floors and walls.

No further work was done until William returned from fighting in Europe in 1697. In 1698, however, when his bête noire, Whitehall Palace, burned down, the King travelled to Hampton Court and asked Wren for an estimate to complete the interiors. Wren's tender was £6,800. The King, who was notorious for his parsimony, thought that figure excessive and accepted a lower estimate from Wren's deputy, William Talman, who eventually completed the allotted task, under budget, for £5,200.

Late payment of accounts and the constant interference of the King, who insisted on numerous minute alterations, often hindered Wren's long stint at Hampton Court. The great architect, however, was not the only one who was left out of pocket by the mean Dutchman. The French designer Jean Tijou, who produced a set of twelve beautiful screens, many gates and the Grand Staircase balustrades for Hampton Court, was still petitioning to be paid ten years after his work was completed. In the end, the disgusted Tijou gave up and returned to France, having extracted only a nominal sum.

William, who commissioned more building at Hampton Court than any other monarch and gave the palace its world-famous maze, did not live to see the completion of a construction project that finally cost some £131,000 – several million pounds in today's money. Towards the end of his reign he suffered from dropsy (oedema), which led his doctors to suggest that he should cut down on his beloved hunting. But the obstinate monarch ignored their pleas and rode to hounds even harder, insisting that the exercise reduced the pain and the swelling in his legs.

William's dogs were in hot pursuit of a stag in Hampton Court's Home Park on 21 February 1702 when he fell heavily from his horse, Sorrel, and broke his collarbone. It seemed strange that the King's horse had stumbled on level ground, but closer examination of the site revealed that Sorrel had put his foot into a mole run. The King's surgeon, who was luckily at Hampton Court, immediately set William's fracture, but the King again ignored his doctors' advice and travelled back to London. His injury seemed straightforward at first, but complications later arose and he died on 8 March at Kensington Palace. When his bitter enemies, the Jacobites, heard of the fanatically Protestant Dutchman's demise, they raised their whisky glasses to the mole that had dug the fatal hole and, long into the night, drank toasts to 'the little gentleman in black velvet'.

It has always been widely debated whether William, who never remarried but maintained a long-standing mistress, Elizabeth Villiers (later Countess of Orkney), was also homosexually inclined. Certainly he surrounded himself with handsome male favourites, both before and after his wife's death. Also, like his predecessor, James I, he rewarded his attentive young men more than generously for their loyalty. While it may not prove that he was the King's lover, the suspicious tale of the rise and fall of the first of his close confidants, Hans William Bentinck, is interesting, to say the least.

William first met Bentinck, the son of a Dutch nobleman, in Holland when he was fourteen. When they were young men, William would have died from smallpox if Bentinck had not slept next to him for sixteen days and reputedly absorbed some of the fever into his own body. The Prince of Orange, as he then was,[16] never forgot his debt to his friend, who later became his personal envoy and negotiated his marriage to Mary. Bentinck came to England when William became King in 1689 as his most trusted adviser, and was immediately created first Earl of Portland.

Bentinck's huge influence suddenly and dramatically decreased, however, when he became extremely jealous of all the attention William was paying to his good-looking former pageboy, Arnold Joost van Keppel. William's affection for Bentinck must have faded fast, for his previously inseparable companion was sent to Paris as the Ambassador to France in 1698. Bentinck seems to have enjoyed the favour of the French King, Louis XIV, but, strangely, he was soon recalled to England. Then, in May 1699, without any warning, he resigned all his offices, including his position as First Gentleman of the Bedchamber, and went back to Holland.

No public explanation was given for his swift and sudden departure, but rumours abounded that Bentinck had been implicated in a serious homosexual scandal in London. Intriguingly, the originator of the slanderous gossip was none other than his successor as William's favourite, Arnold van Keppel. It certainly paid van Keppel to get rid of his rival, for he was created Earl of Albemarle in 1697. The scheming Dutchman was thus an ancestor of the Hon. George Keppel, whose wife, Alice, was Edward VII's last mistress (see Chapter Twelve). Nor does the royal connection stop there. Alice Keppel was the great-grandmother of the Duchess of Cornwall, the wife of the current Prince of Wales.

William's successor to the throne, his sister-in-law Queen Anne, refitted the Chapel Royal and decorated the Queen's Drawing Room, but the Queen's Apartments, which had been started in the Dutch monarch's time, were not completed until 1718, during the reign of George I.[17] At that point Sir Christopher Wren, who had worked tirelessly on Hampton Court from his small office in the Fountain Court for five monarchs, was scandalously dismissed as the Surveyor-General to please the King's Hanoverian favourites. His replacement was William Benson, who had played a significant part in Wren's dismissal for allegedly doctoring accounts. Wren retired to his house on Hampton Court Green, but did not have to wait long to be proved innocent. In less than a year, the dishonest Benson was exposed as a fraud and sacked. So the doyen of English architecture was a contented and vindicated man when, in 1723, he died in his armchair, snoozing after a delicious dinner, at the ripe old age of ninety-one.

George II's reign saw the Queen's state and private apartments refurbished, and new lodgings, designed by the great English architect, interior decorator and landscaper, William Kent, for the King's second son, William Augustus, Duke of Cumberland (see pages 81–3), were added on the east side of Clock Court. As it turned out, they were the last set of rooms ever constructed for a member of the royal family at Hampton Court.

In the summer of 1737 a monstrous quarrel broke out between the King and his heir, Frederick, Prince of Wales. George and his wife, Queen Caroline, did not like their son and were furious when his spouse, Augusta, became pregnant. Caroline was convinced that Frederick was incapable of fathering a normal healthy child, and therefore asked to be present at the birth in case a changeling was substituted for a weak and sickly royal heir.

Frederick refused to allow his doubting mother near his wife. When Augusta went into premature labour at Hampton Court on 31 July, the Prince of Wales ordered a carriage to meet them at the palace's west door. Despite his wife's pleas to be left in her bed, Frederick dragged Augusta down the aptly named Prince of Wales Staircase and bundled her into the waiting coach. Forbidding the watching servants to tell his parents of their rushed departure, he ordered the amazed coachman to drive as fast as he could to St James's Palace. Somehow, the royal baby and her mother survived the bumpy and dangerous journey to London, and a girl, also to be called Augusta, was born three hours later.

When, next day, the King and Queen heard about their granddaughter's birth, they were both annoyed and suspicious. So the Queen travelled from Hampton Court to London to examine the tiny Augusta. When she saw the baby, Caroline cruelly exclaimed: 'If instead of this ugly she-mouse there had been a large, fat, jolly boy I should not have been cured of my suspicions that there had been some juggle.' Frederick and his family were immediately banished from St James's Palace[18] by the furious King, and sent to live at Kew in disgrace. George also informed his son that he would never be forgiven for having engineered such a defiant and undutiful act of deception. There was, however, a tragic sequel to this bitter family squabble. Queen Caroline died later in the year, without ever seeing her son again; poor 'Fred' as he was known, was himself to die in 1751, aged forty-four (see Chapter Four, note 1). The 'ugly she-mouse', on the other hand, was destined for a brighter future. No doubt her grandmother would have been extremely surprised that she grew up to become the renowned society beauty, the Duchess of Brunswick.

George II never visited Hampton Court with a full court retinue after his wife's death. Indeed, 1737 turned out to be the last year in which the entire palace, which had played such an important part in the monarchy's history for so many centuries, was used by the royal family. It may be mere coincidence, but scandal, sexual and otherwise, has been notable for its absence from Hampton Court ever since.

CHAPTER FOUR

Fort Belvedere

HIS ROYAL HIGHNESS WILLIAM AUGUSTUS, Duke of Cumberland, commissioned the original building at Fort Belvedere in Windsor Great Park in around 1750. The three-turreted triangular folly was secluded in the woods close to Cumberland Lodge, the home of the second surviving son of King George II.[1] No doubt the Duke had Fort Belvedere built so that he could climb to the summit of its tall towers and, as the name implies, gaze out over the trees at the surrounding scenery (the word 'belvedere', meaning 'fair sight', comes from the Italian *bel*, meaning 'beautiful', and *vedere*, 'to see'). It must indeed have been a beautiful vista, especially when the rhododendrons, which thrive in this part of Berkshire, were in flower. The fort's architect was almost certainly Henry Flitcroft, who was employed by the Duke from the 1730s and received substantial payments for work in the Great Park in the latter years of the next decade.

Cumberland, who had been appointed Ranger of Windsor Forest in July 1746, three months after his crushing victory over an army of Scots Jacobites at Culloden in Invernessshire, transformed the Great Park during his nineteen-year stewardship. He created the famous lake, Virginia Water, from an insignificant brook, and bred thoroughbred racehorses at his stud at Cranbourne Lodge. He also revived Ascot racecourse, which had been founded by Queen Anne in 1711 but had closed due to lack of patronage in 1744. The Duke reputedly suffered heavy gambling losses on the turf, but he will go down in history as the breeder of two of the most influential horses ever produced in Britain, the successful stallion Herod and the great Eclipse, who was never beaten in eighteen races and later sired three Derby winners.

When he was not racing or discharging his duties as Windsor's Ranger, Cumberland was a professional soldier. He commanded the British forces and their allies in the War of the Austrian Succession (1740–8) and the Seven Years War (1756–63), suffering heavy defeats by the French at Fontenoy in 1745 and at Hastenbeck in 1757, after which he was forced to surrender; he then retired from military ventures. But he is best remembered and, incidentally, hated throughout Scotland, for his victory over the Jacobite army of the Young Pretender, Prince Charles Edward Stuart, at Culloden, near Inverness, on 16 April 1746, and his subsequent cruel repression of the Highlands.

Over a thousand Scottish soldiers were killed on that boggy moor on that dank and misty spring morning, but Cumberland refused to have mercy on Bonnie Prince Charlie's retreating forces. After the battle was over, he was engaged in a game of cards when his officers arrived to ask for new orders. 'No quarter,' wrote their commander on the back of the nine of diamonds, one of the cards he was holding in his hand. Cumberland was as good as his word. He stayed in Scotland for three months, during which time he rounded up more than 3,500 men; quite apart from the casualties at Culloden, more than 120 clansmen were executed for their part in the failed rebellion. Hundreds more were imprisoned, and draconian laws were enforced in the Highlands for many years to come, including those that banned the wearing of the kilt and the playing of bagpipes.

As a result of his ruthless action, the bloodthirsty Cumberland earned the unwelcome sobriquet of 'Butcher'. In England a fragrant flower, sweet william, was named after the Duke to celebrate his victory, but north of the border a weed, the common ragwort, rejoices in the less genteel name of 'stinking billy'. The nine of diamonds, the card on which Cumberland penned his unforgiving instruction, is still known as the 'curse of Scotland' to this day.

The profligate Cumberland, who became very corpulent in middle age, died young, at forty-four, in 1765, but no alterations were made to Fort Belvedere until King George IV was on the throne. In 1827 the dissolute monarch, whose pursuit of pleasure as Prince Regent was legendary, asked his favourite architect, Sir Jeffrey Wyattville (who also remodelled parts of Chatsworth), to transform the folly into a castellated house. The work was finished in 1829. Exactly a century later, another future king with a love of the good life, Edward, Prince of Wales, moved in.

Edward had surprised his father, George V, when, in 1929, he asked if he could have the rather gloomy Fort Belvedere as his country retreat. 'What could you possibly want that queer old place for?' the gruff old monarch had asked in his guttural German accent. 'Those damn weekends, I suppose.' Edward certainly wanted a house in which to entertain his friends and, indeed, his mistress – at that time the pert and pretty Freda Dudley Ward – but he also needed a home of his own, which he had never had until then. It might have looked like a grown-up version of a child's model fortress, but Edward always said that he loved Belvedere more than any other material thing.

Edward attacked his new dwelling with relish. He completely redesigned the interior, which had previously been rather dull and austere. He added more bedrooms and bathrooms to accommodate large house parties, for he loved entertaining his friends, and built a swimming pool and tennis court for his more energetic guests. But working in the garden and the surrounding grounds gave him his greatest pleasure. He had inherited a run-down, tangled maze of rhododendrons, laurels and silver birches, and therefore decided to fell many of the trees and shrubs and to clear the undergrowth to open up the grounds and bring more light to the house. Whenever he could, Edward would vanish into the undergrowth with axe, saw or scythe. He would sometimes tell a footman to bring him an apple and a cup of tea for a light lunch. The servant would whistle on arrival, and Edward would whistle back to reveal his exact location in the jungle of brambles and nettles. He often worked until dusk, creating wide avenues to provide the glorious views for which his ancestor, 'Butcher' Cumberland, had originally constructed, and named, Fort Belvedere.

Life at Fort Belvedere was the opposite of the stuffier and much more formal atmosphere at Windsor Castle, the residence of Edward's parents, King George V and Queen Mary. Edward even flew the less official flag of the Duchy of Cornwall rather than the more regal Prince of Wales's standard. Meals were relaxed, and guests were not required to wear evening dress. There was dancing after dinner to gramophone records of the latest tunes, and parlour games were played deep into the night. Knowing that the racket would bother nobody in that distant, hidden corner of Windsor Great Park, Edward also practised his favourite instrument, the bagpipes, which he had first taken up at university at Oxford, but had neglected since. When he was at Fort Belvedere, he felt all the responsibilities and expectations of his birthright fall from his shoulders, and his early years there were almost certainly the happiest and most carefree of his life.

When Edward had entered his teens, George V and his advisers had begun to look for a wife for him; this was, after all, the Prince of Wales, the most important member of the royal family after the King. Of course, the search had become a good deal narrower than had once been the case, for many possible brides from the great royal houses of Europe were now classed as undesirable aliens because their countries had fought on the enemy side in the

First World War. By the end of the 1920s, therefore, when, aged thirty-five, he took possession of Fort Belvedere, there was some concern at court that the heir to the throne, who was by then in his mid-thirties, was still a bachelor with no suitable prospective wife on the horizon.

In consequence, when he gave his eldest son the keys to his new home, the King probably hoped that Edward would soon woo and win his future wife there. However, the ageing monarch, who would live only another six years, could never, in his wildest dreams, have imagined that the woman whom Edward would often entertain at Fort Belvedere, and would eventually choose as his bride, would be so far from ideal that she would spawn one of the greatest constitutional crises in British history.

Edward's unwavering determination to marry an American divorcee, Wallis Simpson, which caused his abdication from the British throne in December 1936 after a reign of less than twelve months, has fascinated historians and commentators ever since. They have always been intrigued as to why he sacrificed everything for a foreign commoner who was relatively plain, had already been married twice and, at forty years of age, was hardly in the first flush of youth. Yet a glance at Edward's amorous exploits before he met Mrs Simpson in 1934 provides some clues to his deep-rooted and overwhelming infatuation with this ambitious and domineering daughter of an unsuccessful American businessman.

Partly by breeding and partly by upbringing, Edward (who was usually known as 'David' to his family and close friends) was a slow-maturing type. As a young man, therefore, he had never been bothered by his own dilatoriness in finding a wife. In fact, he did not lose his virginity until he was twenty-two years old. Towards the end of 1916, when he was serving with the army in France, two of his equerries, Claud Hamilton and Piers 'Joey' Legh, decided that it was time their charge experienced the joys of lovemaking. So they took the Prince to Amiens, gave him a good dinner with plenty of wine, and then handed him over to an experienced French prostitute named Paulette. Paulette was obviously very skilful at her job for, from that moment, sex became an extremely important item on Edward's agenda.

There was another *fille de joie*, Maggy, with whom he spent three days in Paris in 1917, but he was not so naive as to believe that these liaisons depended upon anything but lust (on his part, at least; presumably the women were motivated to some extent by financial considerations, and possibly even by dreams of social advancement). He did not feel that they were remotely connected with love, either. His first experience of the latter emotion, though it was almost certainly unrequited, was with Marion, the wife of the Earl of Leicester's heir, Viscount Coke. (Born Marion Trefusis, she was also a first cousin of Denys, husband of Violet Trefusis – see Chapter Six.) He soon fell head over heels in love with Lady Coke, who was twelve years older, but she was far too canny to accept an invitation to join him in Paris. She knew that Edward did not truly expect her to become his lover and mistress. What he craved and required over all other things in a woman was to be mothered and comforted, and Marion Coke was happy to fulfil that vital role. Significantly, Wallis Simpson was prepared to play a similar part nearly twenty years later. There is no doubt that her ability to take charge of, and indeed run, Edward's life completely was one of the main reasons why, as King in 1936, he felt he could not live without her.

Lady Coke had a rival for Edward's affections in the Hon. Sybil Cadogan, known as Portia to her family and friends. Portia, a granddaughter of the fifth Earl Cadogan, was large and ungainly, but she certainly attracted Edward, and it is even possible that the couple discussed marriage. Whether she despaired of Edward ever proposing, or simply tired of her royal suitor, is not clear, but the romance was definitely over by 17 June, when she announced her engagement to an old Oxford friend of the Prince's, Edward, Lord Stanley, son of the seventeenth Earl of Derby. There was another brief fling that winter with Lady Rosemary Leveson-Gower, the daughter of the fourth Duke of Sutherland, but when Edward met Freda Dudley Ward his affections for every other woman in his life so far, including Viscountess Coke, faded into insignificance.

They first encountered one another in February 1918 (the final year of the First World War) when Mrs Dudley Ward and her escort took shelter in a doorway in Berkeley Square after an air-raid warning had sounded. They were invited into the safer interior of the house, where a dance was in progress.[2] Edward, who was the guest of honour, was immediately attracted to the newcomer and danced with her for the rest of the evening. The next day the smitten Prince invited himself to tea with his new friend, and so began his association with the first of the two great loves of his life. It was destined to last until Wallis Simpson arrived on the scene fifteen years later.

Winifred 'Freda' Dudley Ward was petite, elegant and exceptionally pretty, but, more important for the mistress of a future king, she was the epitome of discretion. She was almost the same age as Edward and a keen golfer, tennis player and dancer, which meant that they had plenty in common. She was not from aristocratic stock – her father, Colonel Charles Birkin,[3] was a successful manufacturer of lace from Nottinghamshire – but when she was nineteen she had married a kinsman of the Earl of Dudley, William Dudley Ward, who was a Liberal Member of Parliament. As he was sixteen years older than Freda, by whom he had two daughters, and as the couple were, by this time, leading separate lives, Dudley Ward was quite prepared to give his blessing to an affair with the heir to the throne, provided it was conducted with propriety. Indeed, 'Duddie', as the MP was affectionately known, probably condoned, and may have even privately approved of, his wife's 'arrangement'.

There was not much chance for the relationship to become more than an occasional flirtation until Edward returned permanently to London in early 1919 (he had been with the Canadian Corps in France in 1918, and had then visited the USA and Canada), but the affair positively raged for the next four years. Edward could think of nothing else, and seems to have written to Freda virtually every day throughout 1921 and 1922. His notes have a constant theme, declaring his undying love but also bemoaning his own position. Indeed, he expresses similar sentiments to those he revealed during what came to be called the 'Abdication Crisis' fourteen years later. He wallows in self-pity, and declares how unfair it is that he is unable to spend every moment of every day with the woman he loves.

It must have been hard for Freda to put up with his black moods, but she had an enviable knack of being able to bring Edward out of his blackest depressions. She constantly urged him to perform the duties that his position required, and encouraged him to smoke and drink less. She was therefore good in many ways for the Prince, who had a self-destructive streak. Unsurprisingly, however, the King and Queen were not enamoured of their eldest son's new love.

George V never met Freda, but he made it known that he felt it to be inappropriate that a woman with her social background should have such a close relationship with his eldest son. Queen Mary was also quick to reprimand Edward if she thought he was spending more time on his mistress than on his royal duties. Clearly, his mother and father were worried. They were well aware that the easily distracted Edward would not be looking for a suitable wife as long as Freda was on the scene.

When, in 1922, there was talk that William Dudley Ward and his wife might divorce,[4] Edward, who was on official business in the Far East, became worried that his relationship with Freda would not survive such an upheaval. If she were free of the constraints of marriage, he thought, Freda, knowing the unlikelihood, if not impossibility, of her ever marrying the Prince of Wales, might marry another admirer, Michael Herbert, who had been a rival for her affections for some time. By the time he reached Japan and heard that there was to be no divorce, however, the Prince had persuaded himself that the affair would continue as before. But when he got back to England, he was horrified to hear from Freda that she thought they ought to see less of each other. Her excuse was that the reputation of her daughters was suffering; in reality, her ardour for the Prince, which had been powerful in the first few years, was cooling rapidly.

Edward was devastated when he realized that Freda was trying to put their affair on to a more platonic level, and plunged into a spree of heavy drinking and chasing other women, such as Audrey Coats. Yet those flings meant nothing to him. Indeed, he always reported every amatory escapade to Freda, and she remained his greatest friend and most trusted confidante. His devotion to Freda persisted throughout the 1920s and the early 1930s, but in truth the relationship was extremely unsatisfactory. It was too distant to bring him contentment, and yet close enough to preclude serious involvement with any other woman. In fact, the passing of a dozen years or so had not changed the situation at all. Edward still knew, as his parents did, that there would never be a Princess of Wales as long as Freda Dudley Ward continued to figure in all his dreams.

Edward was writing to Freda, still declaring his love, up until 1931, and he continued to seek her advice and approval for another three years; indeed, she helped him choose the designs when he renovated and extended the interior of Fort Belvedere. By now, however, he had begun to crave a less temporary relationship that would satisfy his sexual needs. In fact, he wanted a permanent mistress although, crucially, not a wife. As it happened, he did not have to wait too long. Edward found that the American-born socialite Thelma Furness,[5] the pretty twin sister of Gloria Vanderbilt,[6] and the wife of the first Viscount Furness, was more than happy to fulfil the exact role he had in mind.

Lady Furness, who was kind and frivolous, had a pretty racy past. Born Thelma Morgan, the daughter of an American diplomat, when she was only sixteen she had eloped with a bounder, a divorcee named James Vail Converse who was at least ten years older. She quickly divorced him and then married Lord Furness, who was even older but, importantly, was a rich shipping heir. Thelma had tired of 'Dukie' (he had been christened Marmaduke), her rather stupid and bad-tempered husband, by 1931 and was clearly on the lookout for an extramarital affair when she first met Edward at an agricultural show in Leicestershire. The relationship that Thelma and the Prince embarked on was easy-going and undemanding. She had no wish to make him her exclusive property, but, unlike Freda, she made no attempt to curb his more indulgent traits. As a result, many of his friends believed that Thelma was a bad influence. In fact, Henry 'Chips' Channon was convinced that she had modernized and Americanized Edward, making him both more irresponsible and dangerously over-democratic. 'Hers is the true blame for this drama,' the perceptive diarist later wrote of the Abdication Crisis.[7]

That may have been a little unfair on Lady Furness, but she was certainly the woman who started the whole business. On 10 January 1931 she introduced Wallis Simpson and her husband Ernest to the Prince of Wales at her country house, Burrough Court, near Melton Mowbray. Wallis does not appear to have made much of an impression on the heir to the throne at that initial meeting, and they did not meet again until the following May. In January 1932 the Simpsons invited Edward to dinner at their London flat in Bryanston Square. The Prince must have enjoyed himself, as he stayed until four o'clock in the morning. At the end of the month, he paid the Simpsons back by inviting them to spend the weekend at Fort Belvedere. By 3 May 1933 Wallis was able to write to her aunt, Mrs Bessie Merryman, that she had stayed the weekend at the fort on several occasions, and on the previous two evenings had danced with Edward at the nightspot of the day, the Embassy Club in London. Furthermore, since she confided to her trusted older relation that 'Thelma was still the Princess of Wales,' it is likely that Wallis was already thinking of herself as the new pretender to her fellow countrywoman's crown.

Wallis soon had the opportunity to make her move. In January 1934 the by now divorced Thelma set sail for her native land. In her memoirs she revealed that she had asked Wallis to 'look after him [Edward] while I'm away. See that he doesn't get into any mischief.' Whether she was anxious to keep Edward, or was merely indicating to her friend that she was fed up with her lover, is a matter of debate. But it is abundantly clear that Thelma did her best to leave the way clear for her rival by conducting a very public flirtation with the licentious Aly Khan,[8] which soon became the talk of fashionable New York.

Of course, Edward heard of his mistress's latest dalliance. He invited Thelma to Fort Belvedere for the weekend not long after her return from the United States, where she soon learned that their liaison was already doomed. When she saw Wallis playfully slapping Edward's hand at dinner she gave her friend a disapproving glare, only to receive a much sharper look in return. She later recalled: 'That one cold, defiant glance had told me the entire story.' On the following day Thelma Furness, realizing her position had been usurped, packed her bags and relinquished her role to the determined Mrs Ernest Simpson.

It is well worth examining Wallis's earlier life at this juncture. It undoubtedly reveals the ambitious streak that caused her to set her cap at the Prince of Wales, but it also shows why she did not possess the right credentials to be the wife of a British king.

Bessie Wallis Warfield was born on 19 June 1896, two years after Edward, in Baltimore, Maryland. The Warfields and her mother's family, the Montagues, came from the upper reaches of southern East Coast society and Wallis was brought up as a member of the Baltimore aristocracy, albeit an impoverished one. Her father, Teakle Warfield, had no money, and in any case died of tuberculosis when Wallis was only five months old. As a result, her mother was forced to let out rooms in their apartment and otherwise to depend on the charity of richer family members. All Wallis's friends had smarter dresses and bigger houses, so the shrewd little girl, who made up for her lack of beauty with a quick wit and a good memory, set her heart on improving her fortunes and getting out of parochial Baltimore as quickly as possible.

Wallis seized the first opportunity or, more accurately, the first eligible husband, that came along. Her marriage to Earl Winfield ('Win') Spencer, a good-looking United States Navy officer, in November 1916, may have removed her from Baltimore, but it proved to be an unmitigated disaster. Spencer, who had seemed to have excellent prospects of promotion, turned out to be an ill-tempered alcoholic with an unwelcome habit of resorting to violence. Wallis left him, and for six years lived by herself in

Washington, where she had a passionate affair with an Argentinian diplomat. She then rejoined Spencer, who by now was stationed in the Far East. She quickly discovered that he had not changed, however, and left him a second time. Yet she relented once again, and spent another year in China, trying to repair her ailing marriage. Ultimately, Wallis realized that the task was hopeless, and in 1925 returned to Baltimore to sue for divorce.

Anxious to put the difficulties of the past ten years behind her, Wallis chose as her next husband a man who was the opposite of her first. Ernest Simpson, who worked in his family's shipping business, was respectable, prosperous, reliable, and uninspired. Born to an English father and an American mother, he had even served briefly in the Coldstream Guards. He and Wallis married in July 1928 and settled in London, where they enjoyed an active social life, Wallis soon gaining a reputation as an excellent hostess who served her guests delicious food and the finest drink. Their friends were mostly fellow Americans making their living in London. One of these was the First Secretary at the United States Embassy, Benjamin Thaw, whose wife Consuelo was nothing less than a sister of Thelma Furness.

In the eyes of the Establishment, and of many other people as well, Wallis's divorce, her social standing and her adulterous affair in Washington made her an eminently unsuitable applicant for the post of future queen, but her earlier life revealed a ruthless side of her character, which also emerged at the beginning of her affair with Edward. She had disposed of her first husband and of her rival, Thelma Furness, without a qualm. Now, determined to eliminate the only other obstacle in her path, she relentlessly set her sights on blacking out the memory of Freda Dudley Ward.

In mid-1934 Freda, who had been preoccupied with the illness of her eldest daughter for some time, telephoned Edward when the crisis seemed to be over. She was surprised when the embarrassed operator announced that she had been instructed not to put Lady Dudley Ward through to her employer. Wallis had clearly told Edward that all communication with Freda must cease, though, typically, he had been too frightened to break the news to his former mistress himself. The fact that the Prince was quite prepared to cut Freda and her daughters entirely out of his life after a friendship of sixteen years shows the extent to which he was already dominated by the forceful Mrs Simpson.

Wallis quickly stamped her indelible mark on Fort Belvedere as well. A footman whom Thelma Furness had recommended was sacked, and the cook soon followed. She infuriated Edward's staff by visiting the kitchen at dead of night to make bacon and eggs, leaving a terrible mess of dirty pots and pans in her wake. Jack Crisp, Edward's valet, later claimed that she would break the points of all the pencils in the house so the staff would have to sharpen them again.

At this stage Ernest Simpson was always in attendance, for it seems that he was quite happy in the company of his wife's royal conquest. There is no doubt that Ernest was a snob, but he also knew that, at that time, Wallis valued the security their marriage provided. He therefore viewed Edward as an enjoyable diversion for his spouse rather than a threat. Wallis was of the same opinion, and often maintained, perfectly truthfully, that the curious three-some all got on extremely well, however strange that may seem.

In August 1934, however, the situation changed when Simpson was not included in a party Edward took to Biarritz for a cruise on a yacht. This holiday elicited the first mention of Edward's burgeoning affair in the press, when the American magazine *Time* informed its large readership of the fun the Prince of Wales was having at Cannes with the 'beautiful' Mrs Simpson. In November that year Edward included Wallis's name on a list of people he wanted to invite to Buckingham Palace for a party to celebrate the marriage of his brother, the Duke of Kent.[9] The King scratched her name out straight away, but a furious Edward somehow managed to smuggle her into the palace. When George V, an irascible man at the best of times, saw her, he exploded with rage. 'That woman in my own house!' roared the monarch to one of his aides.

The King's alarm that Wallis was exerting an unhealthy hold on his heir was confirmed when she was invited, again without her husband, for a skiing holiday in Austria in February 1935. Not long afterwards, the King's banning of Wallis from appearing at court, which upset Edward greatly, caused the Prince to swear to his father that the American was not his mistress. None of the King's advisers believed that Edward was telling anything but a blatant lie, but his father, strangely, chose to take his son at his word. As a result, the King reluctantly lifted the ban and Wallis was allowed to take her place as Edward's guest at the next court ball. This move, however, did not indicate any sort of acceptance of Wallis by Edward's family or friends. Indeed, the Duchess of York[10] openly said that she would not meet her brother-in-law's mistress, and the Duchess of Kent was said to be reluctant to be associated with a woman she considered to be a dangerous adventuress.

Yet the displeasure of Edward's family and their open hostility towards Wallis did not in the least dissipate his love for his mistress. He took her on holiday to the South of France in the summer of 1935, although his exasperated father, now thoroughly fed up with all the gossip, only sanctioned the outing if, for reasons of respectability, Wallis and her luggage did not pass through Customs at the same time as his son. During the following autumn and winter, Edward and Wallis attended parties together, and the relationship waxed rather than waned. In January 1936 Harold Nicolson (see Chapter Six), after joining Edward for a trip to the theatre, wrote: 'I have an uneasy feeling that Mrs S . . . is getting him out of touch with the sort of people he ought to frequent.' Then, on 20 January, only a few days after Nicolson had made this entry in his diary, George V died and, although they did not know it, the new King and his mistress began to head into a far more treacherous situation.

At first, Edward took his duties as monarch very seriously, scanning the official red boxes diligently and reading all that he was sent, but this burst of duty and hard work was destined not to last. His devotion to Wallis and his desire to be with her meant that he was soon leaving the boxes unopened and cancelling or turning up late to official engagements. His cavalier attitude to government papers certainly began to worry his personal staff. His Private Secretary, the Hon. Alec Hardinge (later the second Baron Hardinge of Penshurst), was appalled when Edward asked an air attaché from the United States Embassy (in other words, a foreign national), who was staying at Fort Belvedere, to deliver the official boxes to Buckingham Palace. As early as February 1936, worried senior civil servants were telling the Prime Minister, Stanley Baldwin, that Edward was showing state papers to his mistress.

Edward's lack of interest in his official role as king and his besotted attitude towards Wallis were a cause of concern to Whitehall's mandarins and his own aides. Nevertheless, these were early days in his reign, and so they hoped that the new monarch would soon learn to live up to his responsibilities, and begin to realize that affairs of state must take precedence over his mistress. Such optimism, however, turned out to be misplaced. In May, Edward invited Ernest and Wallis Simpson to a dinner at York Place at which Stanley Baldwin and his wife were also guests. 'It's got to be done,' he told Wallis. 'Sooner or later my Prime Minister must meet my future wife.' By June, Wallis was a regular feature in Court Circulars, and had even travelled in one of the carriages at Royal Ascot. 'The people of this country,' Ramsay MacDonald told Harold Nicolson, 'do not mind fornication but they loathe adultery.'

Perhaps the Labour leader was exaggerating, since few people outside an informed circle were even aware of Wallis's existence or her role in Edward's life. That situation changed, however, when Edward's summer vacation in the Mediterranean on the millionairess Lady Yule's steam yacht *Nahlin*, with Wallis as his companion, was extensively reported in the European and American press.[11] This produced a bizarre situation. The rest of the world knew of the firm link between the King and Mrs Simpson, but few members of the public in Britain were aware of their liaison.

As early as July the possibility that Ernest and Wallis would divorce was being openly discussed, and politicians, among them Winston Churchill, were begging Edward's principal adviser, Walter

Monckton,[12] to put a stop to the process, since it was sure to lead to a public scandal. Monckton agreed with Churchill, but was inclined to think that the affair would blow over, not least because Wallis had repeatedly assured him that she had no intention of marrying the King. Ernest had already 'done the decent thing' and committed the 'adulterous act' then required by law for his wife to be granted an unopposed divorce, so the latter's solicitor, Theodore Goddard, arranged for the proceedings to be heard at Ipswich Assizes in October.

News that Wallis would soon be a free woman caused panic in Whitehall, and rumours quickly spread that Edward was contemplating a morganatic marriage as soon as the divorce came through. Baldwin, who had previously been reluctant to press Edward on his intentions, realized that the time had come to confront the King, and to that end travelled from London to Fort Belvedere on 17 October. The meeting between the two men started unpromisingly. The Prime Minister, tired from the drive, asked for a whisky and soda. Raising his glass, he said to the monarch: 'Well, Sir, whatever happens, my Mrs and I wish you every happiness from the depths of our souls.' Edward immediately burst into tears, and the emotional Baldwin found himself weeping as well. The King and his Prime Minister soon recovered their composure, however, and then the serious talking started.

Baldwin told Edward that the number of letters he received about the affair was growing larger every day, and that public disquiet was increasing by the hour. He asked the King to conduct the relationship with more discretion, to which the other replied: 'The lady is my friend, and I do not wish to let her in by the back door.' The Prime Minister then ventured to ask whether Edward could exert his influence to put a stop to the divorce. 'That is the lady's private business,' was the curt reply. Baldwin then suggested that perhaps Mrs Simpson might leave the country for six months. The King did not deign to give an answer.

Baldwin's intervention might have failed to change Edward's mind, and the Simpsons' imminent divorce seemed sure to bring

ABOVE: *The Murder of Rizzio*, by John Opie. Mary, Queen of Scots, is distraught as her husband, Lord Darnley, and a group of Scottish noblemen butcher her loyal secretary before her eyes.

BELOW: The Tragic End to a Tragic Life: Mary, Queen of Scots, faces her executioners, an inevitability after Queen Elizabeth I reluctantly signed her cousin's death warrant. It took two blows from the executioner's axe before her head was severed.

Queen Victoria in 1900 (*right*).
After the death of her beloved
husband Albert in 1861,
scandal surrounded her close
relationship with her gillie,
John Brown (holding her
pony, *below*), a servant at her
Scottish home of Balmoral.

Georgiana, Duchess of Devonshire, born a Spencer and an ancestor of the late Diana, Princess of Wales. Two centuries after the irrepressible Bess of Hardwick, who built the first house at Chatsworth in 1551, Georgiana and her husband scandalized eighteenth-century society when they embarked on a curious *ménage a trois* with Lady Elizabeth Foster, as well as several other affairs.

ABOVE: The future Prime Minister, Harold Macmillan, weds Lady Dorothy Cavendish in 1920. Their happiness did not last long: Dorothy embarked on a passionate and unapologetic affair with another MP, Robert Boothby (*right*), in 1929, which lasted until her death in 1966. Even so, Boothby and Macmillan remained friends.

RIGHT: The infamous Henry VIII, King of England 1509–47. His favourite royal palace was Hampton Court.

LEFT: Henry VIII's second wife, Anne Boleyn. Hampton Court was remodelled in her honour, but her inability to provide a male heir sealed her fate, and she was executed for 'treason' on 19 May 1536.

LEFT: Henry's third and favourite wife, Jane Seymour, with Hampton Court behind. She died at the palace twelve days after bearing the future Edward VI. Her spirit is said to haunt the palace to this day.

RIGHT: Henry VIII's daughter by Anne Boleyn, the so-called 'Virgin Queen', Elizabeth I. Her complicated love life was the source of much court gossip throughout her reign, many of the rumours concerning her enigmatic relationship with her greatest favourite, Robert Dudley, Earl of Leicester.

ABOVE: He Did It For Love: The former King Edward VIII, later titled the Duke of Windsor, smiles at the woman for whom he gave up a kingdom, the American divorcée Wallis Simpson. Their affair and subsequent marriage rocked the monarchy and the country, and led to Edward's abdication.

RIGHT: Edward's former mistress Thelma, Lady Furness. The indomitable American introduced her fellow countrywoman, Mrs Simpson, to the then Prince of Wales in January 1931.

Margaret, Duchess of Argyll. In her scandalous divorce case from the eleventh
Duke in 1963, the judge described her as 'a completely promiscuous woman whose
sexual appetite could only be satisfied by a number of men'. She is pictured here
wearing her infamous string of pearls; in a shocking photograph used in evidence
in the divorce case, the pearls were all she was wearing as she illicitly pleasured
an unidentified 'headless' man.

the scandal into the public eye, but, even at this late stage, few people in high places, including members of the royal family, thought that the King would ever dare to marry his mistress. Naturally, it should be added that Edward and Wallis had good reason to propagate this line of thought. They knew very well that Wallis's case would fall apart if the judge in the divorce hearing were to learn that the plaintiff was romantically involved with another man.

As it happened, the judge, Mr Justice Hawke, did indeed make it known that he was not happy with the proceedings when he heard the case on 27 October 1936. None the less, he was obliged to grant a decree nisi when he was presented with the evidence that Ernest had spent the night with another woman in a hotel in Bray, Berkshire. The Ipswich court was bursting to the seams with the British press, but, strangely, only the briefest of references appeared in the papers. This was largely thanks to the powerful owner of the *Daily Express* (and other papers), Lord Beaverbrook, who persuaded his fellow British newspaper proprietors not to cover the case in detail. Edward had somehow managed to convince the press baron, during a meeting at Buckingham Palace on 16 October, that he had no intention of marrying Wallis.

The British people may still have been in the dark, but the American press made sure their readers knew every sensational detail, true or otherwise, about the Simpson case.[13] One magazine even announced, on 26 October, that Edward and Wallis would wed eight months after the decree absolute was granted. The Canadian papers were, like their British counterparts, more reticent, but the Canadian people were shocked and alarmed when rumours rapidly filtered across the border that the allegations were largely true.

On the same day the editor of *The Times*, Geoffrey Dawson, told the King's Private Secretary, Alec Hardinge, that he thought it was only a matter of weeks, or perhaps days, before the British public discovered all the facts and expressed their utmost displeasure. Two weeks later, when a question was asked in the House of Commons regarding the date of the impending coronation, planned for May 1937, John McGovern, an Independent Labour MP from Glasgow, rose and shouted: 'Why bother, in view of the gambling at Lloyd's that there will not be one?' There were cries of 'Shame! Shame!' from the floor, but it did not stop McGovern from calling out: 'Yes, Mrs Simpson.' Dawson's dire forecast was proving to be right. The circle of those who knew about the King and Wallis was rapidly growing wider and wider, and Edward's position was undeniably weakening. There were dark days ahead.

On 11 November Edward went to Portland to inspect the Home Fleet for two days. He returned to Fort Belvedere, delighted that the trip had gone so well. But his good mood soon turned to despair when he read a letter from Hardinge, warning that the government was becoming alarmed about his relationship with Wallis. The Private Secretary added that an approach would soon be made asking Edward to curtail the affair and, if it was rejected, the government might well resign. He went on to say that the silence of the press could not be guaranteed to last for more than a few days, and ended by asking that Wallis should leave the country within the week.

Hardinge's uncompromising (and now famous) letter to his employer was, with the benefit of hindsight, not entirely accurate, but it certainly spurred Edward into action. Matters now began to move at an increasingly rapid pace. On 16 November he sent for Baldwin and told the Prime Minister that he wanted to marry Wallis. Baldwin replied that whoever married the King would automatically become Queen, and that he doubted that the British public would accept Mrs Simpson in that role. Edward, knowing that he was being asked to choose between his kingdom and his mistress, decided to put the pressure on Baldwin, stating adamantly that he would abdicate if the government opposed his marriage.

Nine days later, Edward sent for Baldwin again. This time he tried the Prime Minister with a watered-down proposal, saying that he would be prepared to accept a morganatic marriage with Wallis as his consort, not his queen. Baldwin answered that such a move would require new parliamentary legislation in Britain and in the Dominions. He added that he doubted that Parliament would

[98]

sanction such a change to the law. Edward told him to raise the proposal with his Cabinet. Two days later, Baldwin raised the issue of a morganatic marriage in Cabinet, where it was rejected out of hand. The Prime Minister also canvassed the views of his counterparts in the Dominions, who also rejected the King's proposal.[14]

On 2 December Baldwin told Edward that none of his (that is, the King's) governments anywhere in the world was willing to consent to a morganatic marriage. He gave the now desperate monarch three stark choices: to end his affair with Wallis; to marry her, against the counsel of his ministers, who would then be forced to resign; or to abdicate. The next day the floodgates opened when the British press finally broke the full story. Edward knew it was time to get Wallis out of the country. Luckily, she had moved down to Fort Belvedere from London to escape the furore before a baying, stone-throwing mob, infuriated by what its members had read in the papers, gathered outside her Regent's Park home.

Dinner at Fort Belvedere on the night of 3 December 1936 was a melancholy affair. Lord Brownlow, whom Edward had asked to travel with his mistress to the Continent, wrote that the King 'was dreading Wallis's departure, almost like a small boy being left behind at school for the first time' (Brownlow was the King's Lord-in-Waiting, and a close friend). When the moment to leave finally arrived, Wallis walked through Edward's bedroom to the lawn without so much as a goodbye to the staff. 'Well, that's the end of that,' a footman whispered to Edward's loyal butler, Osborne. 'Don't be too sure,' the wise retainer replied; 'we'll keep our fingers crossed.' As Brownlow and Wallis climbed into the car, Edward, with tears streaming down his face, leaned across to obtain one last touch of her hand. Then the car drove off, and the woman who had brought the great institution of the British monarchy to its knees left Fort Belvedere for the last time.

A week later, on the morning of 10 December, after Walter Monckton had brought the draft down from London in the early hours, Edward and his three brothers assembled at Fort Belvedere to sign the historic Instrument of Abdication. The Duke of Kent arrived half an hour after his brothers, the Dukes of York and Gloucester, giving Edward a welcome opportunity to relieve the tension by remarking with a laugh: 'George would be late.'[15] The solemn signing, however, began immediately, and in a few moments the reign of the first British sovereign to resign the Crown voluntarily had ended. Baldwin, in dignified fashion, announced the sad news to the Commons that afternoon. The next day, Parliament endorsed the abdication, and Edward gave his famous broadcast to the nation from Windsor Castle. On 12 December Edward's brother Bertie (Prince Albert of York)was proclaimed King George VI, and the new Duke of Windsor left his native land for Austria. He married Wallis Simpson in France on 3 June 1937, but did not return to England until 1952, when he attended the funeral of the brother who had so reluctantly succeeded him as King.

Over the years a multitude of reasons have been advanced to explain the extraordinary hold Wallis Simpson exerted over the man who became, albeit briefly, King Edward VIII. Some emanate in the realms of fantasy, but others may contain more than a grain of truth. The celebrated psychologist Dr William Brown believed that Edward's sex life had been unsatisfactory before he met Wallis, and that the Prince viewed her as some sort of saviour because she had relieved him of his inhibitions. Significantly, one of his mistresses, Thelma Furness, who presumably would have known, also claimed that Edward suffered from impotence. It is perfectly possible, therefore, that he was sexually defective in one way or another. The idea, often advanced, that Wallis perfected the art of lovemaking and learned exotic techniques in a Chinese brothel, during her marriage to her first husband, is almost certainly a fabrication. Yet there is no doubt that she was able to generate tremendous sexual thrills, which may even have been partly sadomasochistic, in the earlier stages of her relationship with Edward.

It is, however, also important to remember that sex was only a part of her allure. Edward's all-consuming love for Wallis was evident until the end of his days in 1972. He would fret if she was away from him for any length of time, his eyes would never leave her, and he would crane across a dinner table to hear what she was saying. He might have been frightened of her, but, crucially, he enjoyed that sensation. The long-serving courtier Ulick (later Sir Ulick) Alexander described Edward as being possessed by 'the sexual perversion of self-abasement'. That may have been true as well, but his slavish devotion to Wallis also made him content.

Whether or not Wallis loved Edward is a more difficult question to answer. She certainly liked to protect him, enjoyed his dependence upon her, and strove to make him happy. Yet the famous aristocratic beauty and socialite, Lady Diana Cooper, who often observed the couple at close quarters, said 'she [Wallis] is hard as nails and she doesn't love him'. As harsh as it is, such a comment is probably close to the mark. Throughout her life, love never entered the equation when Wallis was pursuing a man.

Scurrilous rumours continued to follow Wallis around until her death in 1986, and even beyond it. Most of the stories were ridiculous, but the odd one had its basis in fact. Talk that she was illegitimate, a lesbian, a nymphomaniac, and had a child by Count Ciano – Mussolini's son-in-law and Italy's Foreign Minister during much of the Second World War – should be treated with the contempt it deserves. Another claim that she spied for the Nazis and passed sensitive information to their foreign minister, Joachim von Ribbentrop, in 1940 has never been confirmed by official documents. There is no evidence either that a so-called 'China Dossier', a report about Wallis's time in the Far East, supposedly commissioned by Baldwin for George V, ever existed. Furthermore, the allegation that she conducted an affair with von Ribbentrop while he was serving as the German Ambassador in London during the Abdication Crisis in 1936, is another piece of gossip with no foundation whatsoever. Sadly, the wonderful tale that Wallis received seventeen carnations from the lusting envoy to remind her of the number of times they had slept together is yet another myth.[16]

It is probable, however, that Wallis did have a secret liaison with a married London car salesman, Guy Trundle, only a year before the abdication, something that only came to light with the release of formerly classified documents years after her death. A report filed by the Metropolitan Police, which had Wallis under close surveillance in early July 1935, opens with the following startling words: 'The identity of Mrs Simpson's secret lover has now been definitely ascertained. He is Guy Marcus Trundle, now living at 19 Bruton Street.' The report went on to reveal that 'Trundle is a motor engineer and a salesman and is said to be employed by the Ford Motor Company. It is not known what salary he gets . . . Trundle claims to have met POW [Edward] through Mrs Simpson. He is said to boast that every woman falls for him. He meets Mrs Simpson at informal social gatherings as a personal friend, but secret meetings are made where intimate relationships take place.' It is tempting to ask if the course of history would have changed if Edward had been made aware of this information. On the other hand, since his infatuation with Wallis was so strong at the time, it is perfectly possible that he would have been quite prepared to ignore his mistress's indiscretion.

Fort Belvedere ceased to be a royal residence when Edward left these shores in 1936. But when a new book, *Philip and Elizabeth*, was published in 2004, the Duke of Windsor's favourite house appeared briefly in the news again. In the book, which examines the long marriage of the Queen and the Duke of Edinburgh, the author, Gyles Brandreth, extensively quotes the Duchess of Abercorn, a great friend and confidante of Prince Philip. In her interview with Brandreth, the Duchess categorically laid to rest the age-old rumours that she had for many years enjoyed a rather more than close platonic relationship with the Queen's husband. This denial of any impropriety, however, did not prevent the emergence of an old photograph, taken in the 1980s, showing Prince Philip, clad only in a towel, with his arm around the Duchess, who is wearing a swimsuit, which was duly published in several tabloids. Intriguingly, the place where this happy snapshot was taken is widely believed to be the British home in Windsor Great Park of the Canadian food tycoon and friend of the royal family, Galen Weston. The house is Fort Belvedere.

CHAPTER FIVE

Inveraray Castle

INVERARAY CASTLE, the home of the Dukes of Argyll and headquarters of the Campbell clan, could hardly have a more beautiful or a more romantic location. It stands in splendid isolation, high on the wooded hills above the windswept northern shores of Loch Fyne on Scotland's wild western coast. When Archibald Campbell, third Duke of Argyll, inherited the dukedom in 1743, he instigated one of the most imaginative construction projects ever undertaken in the Highlands. He decided to replace the old fifteenth-century fortified tower house with the magnificent turreted castle which stands there now, and to rebuild the town of Inveraray on the shores of the loch below. The famous London architect Roger Morris designed the new castle with help from Scotland's William Adam, who acted in a supervisory role. Both Morris and Adam died in 1748, and the latter's sons, John and Robert, completed the work for the fifth Duke in 1789.

The interior, which was completed between 1770 and 1789, is as majestic as the outside of the building and its surrounding scenery. The Armoury Hall, the walls of which are covered in displays of pole-arms, Brown Bess muskets, Lochaber axes and Scottish broadswords, provides an apt reminder of the Campbells' warlike and often violent past, while the Tapestry Drawing Room, by contrast, is more serene and graceful and contains the original Beauvais tapestries, which were commissioned in the 1780s. All in all, Inveraray breathes history from every stone.

The Campbells had always been great builders. They had moved their clan base from their traditional home on the shores of Loch Awe to the vicinity of Loch Fyne some years earlier, but Colin Campbell, who was created first Earl of Argyll in 1457, constructed the first castle on the site at Inveraray in around 1450. Archibald, the second Earl, was killed at Flodden Field in 1513, but he left four sons and seven daughters to protect the family fortunes. But it is his third son, Sir John Campbell of Lorne, who is remembered best as the perpetrator of arguably the boldest abduction in Scotland's colourful folklore. Accounts, needless to say, vary considerably.

John Campbell was riding with a band of clansmen in the vicinity of Cawdor (or Calder) Castle, near Nairn, the home of Sir John Calder, Thane of Cawdor, when he saw a small girl playing in the fields with no protector other than her nurse. Recognizing the child as the Thane's heiress, Muriella, he resolved to kidnap her. As they approached, the nurse, realizing that the little girl was their target, and anxious to put a permanent, identifiable mark on the young heiress's body to ensure that should she die the Campbells could never substitute another girl as Cawdor's heiress, seized the child's hand and bit off the end joint of one of her little fingers. Muriella was seized and rushed away from her family lands by part of the band, while the rest remained to thwart any pursuit by Cawdor's men. However, they stupidly allowed the child's nurse to escape, and she fled back to Cawdor Castle to raise the alarm. Soon, a large posse was riding after the kidnappers to rescue their chieftain's daughter.[1]

Not long after, the Cawdor pursuers caught up with the abductors, who were celebrating the ease of their capture with a few drams around a campfire. The Campbells were taken by surprise, but it took them no more than a few seconds to concoct a bold and innovative plan. As the Thane's men approached, Sir John jumped on to his horse, the child in his arms, and, with a few of his men retreated rapidly towards Inveraray. Meanwhile, his uncle, Campbell of Inverliver, ordered his seven sons to overturn a large kettle, which had been boiling on the fire, and gather round it to persuade the rescuers that Muriella was hidden underneath.[2]

Under the misapprehension that the girl was under the great pot, the Thane's posse dismounted and a desperate fight developed. Old Inverliver and his strong sons were hopelessly outnumbered, but they put up a commendable defence. Their opponents, however, proved too powerful. One by one, the eight valiant Campbells were bludgeoned to death. With a triumphant cry, the Cawdors charged forward to release their chieftain's daughter, but their great joy turned at once to despair when they discovered that they had been deceived by the Campbells' clever ruse. Further pursuit was obviously hopeless, as the young heiress and her captors were now many miles down the road to Inveraray.

Muriella, after the drama and bloodshed of her abduction, had a good life in the end. Sir John carefully educated and looked after her until adulthood, and she grew into one of the greatest beauties in the Highlands, renowned for her glorious mane of auburn hair. Eventually they were married, their union producing a substantial benefit to Sir John and his family, as it added the fortune and fertile lands of Cawdor to the already enormous Campbell holdings.

If many Scottish people viewed Sir John's abduction of Muriella as immoral and barbaric, the Campbell name was blackened further by one of the most discreditable and controversial events in Scottish history, which occurred around a hundred and fifty years later, on a cold and snowy morning in February 1692. The terrible Massacre of Glen Coe, when a detachment of government troops – Scots soldiers, indeed – cold-bloodedly killed or caused the deaths of seventy-eight unsuspecting members of the Macdonald clan, still causes rancour in the Highlands. The Campbells played an integral part in this cruel instance of mass murder, which to this day arouses strong emotions.

At the end of August 1691, William III published a proclamation, offering an amnesty to all Highlanders who had fought for James II, the Catholic Stuart king whom William had deposed.[3] Their chieftains were required to swear allegiance to the Crown before 1 January 1692, with military execution the harsh penalty for any clan leader who failed to take the oath by that date. Apart from the fact that it wounded the pride of the chieftains to have to submit to the English Crown (and a Dutch king, at that), all Jacobites had sworn allegiance to James II, who was now in exile in France, and they needed him to release them from their obligation before they could pledge their loyalty to his successor.

Envoys were dispatched to the Continent to await James's decision, but the exiled monarch did not grant his permission until 12 December 1691, only nineteen days before the amnesty was due to expire. It then took over a week for the ambassadors to travel back to Edinburgh, and several more days before the messengers brought the news to each chieftain, who would then have to journey to the appointed authority to swear the oath of allegiance. For Alexander Macdonald of Glen Coe, known to all as MacIain, the clan chief of the Macdonalds of Glen Coe, time and the bitter weather were not the only obstacles in his way: when MacIain arrived at Fort William in the early hours of New Year's Eve, the last day by which he had to swear allegiance, he learned from the Governor, Colonel John Hill, that only the chief magistrate could administer the oath. When MacIain protested that it would be impossible to reach the magistrate in time, Hill advised him to travel to Inveraray, and gave him a letter to present to Sir Colin Campbell, urging the latter, as the district's senior legal official, to receive the clan chief's oath because he had arrived at Fort William before the amnesty deadline.

MacIain left Fort William immediately. But his long and tiring journey of seventy-four miles to Inveraray was fraught with difficulty, for he had to negotiate snow-clad mountains that were all but impassable at such an inhospitable time of year. He had completed about half of his journey when he was captured by a group of grenadiers and imprisoned for a day, despite having a letter of protection from Colonel Hill. He eventually reached Inveraray on 2 January, but was horrified to be informed that Sir Colin had yet to return from a Hogmanay party.

The latter did not arrive back at Inveraray until 5 January and at first refused to administer the oath, since the deadline granted in the proclamation had expired. Eventually, in the light of Colonel Hill's letter, Campbell accepted MacIain's oath on 6 January. The leader of the Macdonalds of Glen Coe returned, relieved, to his home.

Historical evidence indicates that Sir Colin Campbell had never wanted MacIain to be found guilty of an offence that actually amounted to little more than a technicality. He wrote to Colonel Hill: 'I am sending to Edinburgh that Glen Coe [MacIain], though he was mistaken in coming to you to take the oath of allegiance, might yet be welcome. Take care that he and his followers do not suffer till the King and Council's pleasure be known.' He then sent Colonel Hill's letter and other documents to his clerk, also called Colin Campbell, in Edinburgh with orders to show these documents to the Scottish Privy Council (the Scottish Parliament continued in existence until the twin Acts of Union in 1707).

Sadly for MacIain, the clerk was less fair-minded than his namesake. He also hated the Macdonald clan with a passion, for Campbells and Macdonalds had been at odds, usually over such matters as cattle raids, for many years. So once it emerged, unofficially, that a majority of the Privy Council might give MacIain the benefit of the doubt, he erased the chief's name from the certificate listing the clan leaders who had taken the oath of allegiance. The clerk, like many of his clansmen, may have loathed the Macdonalds, but he also clearly wanted to curry favour with his superior, King William's Secretary of State for Scotland, Sir John Dalrymple, the Master of Stair.

It was no secret that the Master of Stair, a Lowlander from near Stranraer with no love of the Highlander, was keen to make an example of troublesome and rebellious clans. Troops were already marshalled at Fort William and Inverness with orders to march on Keppoch, Glen Garry, Lochiel, Appin and Glen Coe, and he was severely annoyed to learn that known Jacobite clans were prepared to swear allegiance to King William. When, thanks to Campbell the clerk, he received apparently official confirmation that MacIain had not taken the oath, he was delighted at the prospect of being able to make an example of a clan he especially disliked. A quick and brutal assault on the Macdonalds of Glen Coe would serve to remind the other clan chiefs not to renege on the oath of loyalty to the King. From London, orders bearing the date 16 January, signed and countersigned by King William, were quickly dispatched to Dalrymple. On reading the crucial sentence 'If MacIain of Glen Coe, and that tribe, can be well separated from the rest, it will be a proper vindication of the public justice to extirpate that set of thieves,' he could scarcely contain his satisfaction. He now had permission to enact terrible retribution upon the Macdonalds of Glen Coe. When Dalrymple forwarded the orders to the Commander-in-Chief of the King's forces in Scotland, Lieutenant-General Sir Thomas Livingstone, the Macdonalds' fate was effectively sealed.

Livingstone, having received his instructions from Dalrymple, wrote, not to Colonel Hill, but to Lieutenant-Colonel James Hamilton, Hill's deputy at Fort William, pointing out that the proposed raid on the Macdonalds would provide a good opportunity for the garrison to show that it served a useful purpose. Hamilton's orders from Livingstone were crystal clear. He should start with MacIain, and spare nothing that belonged to the errant chieftain. Livingstone concluded with the ominous and now famous suggestion that one of the main objectives of the operation was 'not to trouble the government with prisoners'.

It was Dalrymple, however, not Livingstone, who chose two companies, numbering 120 men, of the Earl of Argyll's foot regiment from Inveraray to carry out the planned operation in Glen Coe. The Secretary of State, well aware of the ancient blood feud between the Macdonalds and the Campbells, presumably thought this unit of regular soldiers, raised from among the Earl's tenants, as likely to be highly motivated when it came to teaching MacIain and his family a harsh lesson. Dalrymple's choice of commander was also interesting. He picked Captain Robert Campbell of Glen Lyon, a man of sixty with a deep personal grudge against the Macdonalds of Glen Coe who, returning from battle less than two years before, had caused terrible destruction to his estate. It is worth noting that Captain Campbell's niece, Sarah, was married to MacIain's younger son, Sandy.

Dalrymple's scheme required Campbell and his soldiers to arrive in Glen Coe on 1 February 1692 and remain there, awaiting further instruction. Campbell, still unaware of the full horror of the ultimate task he was to be set by Dalrymple, was to tell the Macdonalds that the reason for his force's presence was purely to collect tax arrears in the surrounding area, and that Glen Coe seemed the perfect place in which to be based. He carried bogus papers, signed by Governor Hill, to prove that this was the sole purpose of his assignment. The Macdonalds swallowed this explanation and gave Campbell and his men food, drink and free accommodation in the villages throughout the glen. For twelve days the Macdonalds' guests ate, drank and made merry among their generous hosts. Indeed, Campbell visited his niece, Sarah, almost every day and shared a dram with her young husband.

On 12 February Colonel Hill, after direct intervention from Dalrymple, reluctantly told his deputy, James Hamilton, to execute the orders which Livingstone had already sent him. A simultaneous attack on various locations along Glen Coe was to take place at seven o'clock the next morning, and Hamilton was to lead his men from Fort William to a key point in Glen Coe, to assist Campbell's troops in their grim work. The final instructions were brutal and uncompromising: 'You are hereby ordered to fall upon the rebels, the Macdonalds of Glen Coe, and put all to the sword under seventy. You are to have a special care that the old fox and his sons do upon no account escape your hands. You are to secure all avenues that no man escape.'

[109]

These orders were communicated to Campbell of Glen Lyon, who was then told that the time of the assault had been moved forward to five o'clock. That evening, now with full knowledge of the murderous acts he was to perpetrate the next morning, Campbell continued to play his role as the Macdonalds' trusted friend. He played cards with MacIain's sons, John and Sandy, that night and even accepted an invitation from the old chieftain to dine the following day.

Early on the morning of Saturday, 13 February the killings began simultaneously in three villages in the glen. At five o'clock exactly at his base in Inveriggan, Campbell consigned nine Macdonalds, who had been tied up and gagged for the past few hours, to their deaths. These men included the laird. MacIain's sons, however, had managed to escape, thanks to an old retainer's suspicions, and were now with their families and servants high above Inveriggan, their footprints mercifully erased by the thickly falling snow.

In villages throughout the glen, the butchery continued. Macdonalds were dragged from their beds and murdered by Campbell's soldiers, who torched all the houses, causing the surviving inhabitants to flee from their burning homes. Women and children ran towards the mountains through the relentless blizzard, most of them without proper outdoor clothing or shoes, so that many died from exhaustion and exposure before they reached any form of shelter from the bitter snow and gales. Thirty-eight men of this small but close-knit branch of the Macdonald clan were murdered, and a further forty of their womenfolk and children perished in this orgy of destruction.

News of the atrocity was greeted with indignation throughout Scotland. Even the court of King William III received the account of the massacre with horror. Over the next three years, the nation's disgust and sense of injustice increased, so that by 1695 the King and his ministers had become alarmed at the people's anger.

In an attempt to pacify his subjects, William dismissed Dalrymple from office and appointed a Commission of Inquiry to examine all that had occurred at Glen Coe. The commission declared, untruthfully, given that the verb 'extirpate' means to destroy completely, that there had been nothing in the King's instructions that warranted such wholesale slaughter. Having thus exonerated William, the body then went on to lay the blame fully on Dalrymple's shoulders, though he and the other participants in the murders avoided retribution because it was clear that, if made to answer for the crime, they would argue that they had merely obeyed their sovereign's written instructions – a watertight defence.

Having got their master off the hook, William's advisers began to spread the fiction that the massacre was simply the result of a long and bitter feud between the Campbells and the Macdonalds. This clever ruse may have caused the Establishment's part in the Massacre of Glen Coe gradually to fade out of public consciousness, but there is also a certain amount of truth in the assertion that a Campbell conceived the original idea, namely that the Macdonalds of Glen Coe should be used as the example to warn those clans who were still thinking of defying the Crown.

During the year before the massacre, John Campbell of Glenorchy, the first Earl of Breadalbane (of a different branch of the Campbell clan from the Argyll branch based at Inveraray), was the chief architect of the peace initiative in the Highlands. There is evidence that MacIain was prepared to sign the oath of allegiance to the King as early as June 1691, but Breadalbane, who had had some cattle stolen by the Macdonalds of Glen Coe, introduced this personal grievance into the negotiations. MacIain refused to recompense Breadalbane for the cattle, and the opportunity to bring the chieftain into the fold was lost. Furious that he had failed to gain satisfaction over his missing stock, Breadalbane decided to teach MacIain a lesson, and therefore recommended to Dalrymple that the Macdonalds of Glen Coe should be singled out for an unwelcome dose of the King's justice.

For want of evidence, 'Grey John', as Breadalbane was known, was never brought to court for his role. Dalrymple soon recovered from the affair; nor were Robert Campbell of Glen Lyon and his accomplices at Glen Coe ever brought to justice.

The Massacre of Glen Coe occurred more than 300 years ago, but many Macdonalds have never forgiven the Campbells for the cold-blooded slaughter of their ancestors. Apart from the implication of the King and his ministers and the fact that the perpetrators escaped justice, what has made the incident so infamous was the repeated breaching of trust: the order to kill that was given in spite of the chief's oath, and the betrayal of the tacit laws of hospitality, particularly strongly felt in Highland society: Campbell and his men had been guests of the Macdonalds, drinking and dining with them for nearly two weeks, before they rose early in the morning, when all defences were down, and murdered their hosts. Still today, Campbells are not welcomed as guests in many places – the Clachaig Inn in Glen Coe, for instance, has a sign above its door inscribed with the words: 'No hawkers or Campbells welcome'.

Memories are long in the Highlands, and bitter events such as the Massacre of Glen Coe are not quickly forgotten, much less forgiven. In 1940, No. 1 Combined Operations Invasion Training Centre was established in and around Inveraray, and it was here that many commandos underwent their initial training. At the end of one course, the men were paraded and reviewed by a general, who, since some training took place on his land, invited the then Duke of Argyll to take part. When the parade ended the men were stood easy and addressed by the general, who concluded his remarks by thanking the Duke for the use of his estate, and suggesting that the assembled troops should give three hearty cheers in appreciation. As a warrant officer bellowed 'Three cheers for His Grace the Duke of Argyll', a voice growled from deep within the ranks of one of the Scottish Commandos, 'Stand fast the Macdonalds!' (Ironically, though, it is the Campbells whose motto is 'Ne obliviscaris': 'Do not forget'.)

The reputation of the Campbells may have suffered because they stood by William of Orange in the late seventeenth century, but this also had its rewards: the tenth Earl of Argyll – he whose soldiers carried out the Glen Coe killings – was awarded the title of Duke of Argyll and Marquess of Lorne and Kintyre[4] by King

William in 1701 in recognition of his support. Over the centuries they remained loyal to the Crown, which, combined with some shrewd marriages, extended their power and their lands, and by the nineteenth century their properties included forty estates covering nearly 1.25 million acres, mostly owned by the clan chief, the Duke of Argyll.[5] There was the odd black sheep, however: the fourth and fifth Dukes, honourable soldiers both, were followed by the dissipated playboy figure of the sixth Duke, Sir George William Campbell (1768–1839), a companion of the Regency dandy Beau Brummell, who sold the lands and buildings of Castle Campbell in Clackmannanshire in an attempt to pay off his debts. He is known to have had at least one illegitimate child, but, although married – to Lady Caroline Elizabeth Villiers, daughter of the fourth Earl of Jersey – he had no legitimate heir. On his death the title went to his brother John, who more or less restored the family's fortunes.

Ties with the royal family were taken further when, on 21 March 1871, the eighth Duke of Argyll's heir, the Marquess of Lorne, was married to Princess Louise, the artistic and bohemian fourth daughter of Queen Victoria. As Lorne, who became Governor-General of Canada when he was only thirty-three years of age, was almost certainly homosexual, it is probably no surprise that he fathered no children during his long marriage to the Princess.

In his youth, Lorne had been a regular guest at all-male parties at the house of his uncle, Lord Ronald Gower (see also page 251), who made little secret of the fact that he was attracted to members of his own sex. There was also a scurrilous rumour doing the rounds that Princess Louise had been forced to brick up the garden door that led directly from their London apartment in Kensington Palace into Hyde Park to prevent her husband escaping at night to pick up soliciting guardsmen from the nearby barracks.

On his father's death in 1900 Lorne, at the age of fifty-four, inherited the dukedom, becoming the ninth Duke of Argyll. And in 1907 he was indirectly implicated in another homosexual scandal, this one concerning the robbery of the Irish Crown Jewels from their resting place in Dublin Castle in the same year. As the jewels vanished on the eve of an official visit by King Edward VII to Ireland, a Royal Commission was appointed to look into the theft. It was adjourned and, significantly, never sat again after it discovered the embarrassing fact that the King's brother-in-law, the Duke of Argyll, was a close confidant of one of the prime suspects, Frank Shackleton. Shackleton, the brother of the great Antarctic explorer, Sir Ernest, was known to be a promiscuous homosexual, and had severe money problems at the time. So far as is known, the jewels have never been recovered.

The ninth Duke survived the Irish Crown Jewels scandal and managed to keep his secret life under wraps, but in the 1880s his youngest brother, Lord Colin Campbell, was embroiled in a long and bitter divorce case. Within three days of meeting her he had become engaged to the beautiful, intelligent and accomplished Gertrude Elizabeth Blood, and they married the following year, in 1881. It is said that he had syphilis at the time of their marriage. The union soon fell apart – a precursor to that of another Lord Colin Campbell less than a century later. In 1884 Lady Colin obtained a judicial separation from her husband on the grounds of cruelty, and in 1886 she petitioned for divorce. It was a long and acrimonious case, with Lady Colin accusing her husband of adultery and cruelty, while he made counter-accusations of adultery with four co-respondents. The divorce case over, Lady Colin Campbell created a new life for herself as a writer and journalist; she became a friend of Burne-Jones, Whistler and George Bernard Shaw, and even exchanged insults with Oscar Wilde. Her ex-husband left the country, and died in Bombay in 1895.

It was to be less than a century before a Campbell was embroiled in another highly public scandal. This time the protagonists were the eleventh Duke of Argyll and his wife, Margaret, whose lurid sexual habits and numerous adulterous liaisons were plastered across the front pages of every newspaper in a sensational divorce case in 1963.

Ethel Margaret, the only daughter of the Scottish millionaire George Hay Whigham, was born in 1912. After being educated privately in New York, London and Paris, she came to London as a teenager and quickly became the life and soul of every society party. The rich and beautiful Margaret attracted plenty of aristocratic suitors, and even announced her engagement to Charles Greville, the seventh Earl of Warwick, although the wedding never took place. There was also talk of romances with the playboy Prince Aly Khan, with Lord Beaverbrook's son, the Hon. Max Aitken, and with George, Duke of Kent, but it was Charles Sweeny, a handsome and wealthy American amateur golfer, who eventually won the pretty young heiress's heart.

The glamorous couple were married in style in February 1933. They lived happily for some time and Margaret produced two children, a daughter, Frances, later to become the Duchess of Rutland, in 1937, and a son, Brian, in 1940. Charles and Margaret gradually drifted apart, however, and were divorced in 1947. Four years later, she became the third wife of Ian Douglas Campbell, the eleventh Duke of Argyll. Inveraray and the Campbells celebrated the arrival of the latest Duchess and hoped that their clan leader, who had not been blessed with happy marriages previously, had found the right woman at last.

The new chatelaine of Inveraray apparently shared the same sentiments as her husband's family and clansmen. Margaret later wrote in her rather sanitized autobiography, *Forget Not* (a translation of the Campbell motto): 'I had wealth. I had good looks. As a young woman I had been constantly photographed, written about, flattered, admired, included in the list of the Ten Best-Dressed Women in the World and mentioned by Cole Porter in the words of his hit song, "You're the Top". The top was what I was supposed to be. I had become a duchess and mistress of an historic castle. My daughter had married a duke. Life was apparently roses all the way.' (The reference to her in the song was in fact dropped, because it rhymed 'Mrs Sweeny' with 'Mussolini'.)

As Margaret intimated in her memoirs, life at Inveraray was idyllic at the beginning. The land-rich but cash-strapped Duke was able to renovate Inveraray, which had been damaged by fire, with

Whigham money, and Margaret rejoiced in the title she had always desired. But as the years passed by it seems that her eyes began to stray. She started to spend much of her time in London in her house in Upper Grosvenor Street, while the Duke preferred to stay in Scotland at Inveraray.

Her relationship with the Duke grew progressively worse, until they eventually became involved in a prolonged and acrimonious divorce that began in 1959. At one stage, the Duchess even cross-petitioned her husband, claiming he had committed adultery with her stepmother, Jane, who was a year younger than she. In 1963, when the case was finally heard in the Edinburgh courts, there were gasps of incredulity when the Duke's counsel gave the court a list of eighty-eight men, including three members of the royal family and two government ministers, who his client believed had enjoyed amorous physical relations with his wife. The presiding judge, Lord Wheatley, quickly made it known that he had never seen such a disgusting catalogue of sexual licence.

The incredulity turned to sheer amazement when the puritanical Lord Wheatley was shown a series of black-and-white Polaroid photographs of the Duchess, wearing nothing but her famous three-strand pearl necklace, administering oral sex to a naked man. As the snapshots, which had been taken in the mirrored bathroom of her London home, exhibited the man's genitalia and body but excluded his face, the aroused subject understandably became known as the 'headless man'. Speculation was rife that the mystery figure was a member of the Cabinet. Already racked by one crisis, Harold Macmillan's Conservative government invited a senior judge, Lord Denning, who was already investigating the scandal concerning another Cabinet minister, John Profumo (see pages 142–57), to track down the man in the photographs.

The photographs bore captions which were presumed to have been written by the headless man himself, so Denning thought up a ruse to compare the handwriting of the five leading suspects – Duncan Sandys, then the Minister of Defence and a former son-in-law of Winston Churchill, Douglas Fairbanks Junior, the Hollywood film star, Jock Cohane, a prominent American businessman, Peter Combe, a homosexual press officer at the Savoy Hotel, and Sigismund von Braun, the brother of Werner, the German space scientist – with the captions. Denning asked the five men to meet him at the Treasury at different times, knowing that they would have to sign their names at the door to gain entry to the government department. It was later claimed that this process of elimination revealed beyond doubt that Fairbanks was the mystery man. It should be added, however, that the actor repeatedly denied the allegation until his death in 2000, and Denning himself (who died in 1999, aged 100) never confirmed the headless man's identity.

The painstaking Denning also went to great lengths to save Sandys's skin, even persuading the unfortunate politician to visit a Harley Street consultant, whose task was to compare the minister's penis to the one in the photographs! The distinguished judge's eccentric tactics appear to have exonerated Sandys, and his political career survived the scandal. But some time afterwards, when the Duchess let slip that the only Polaroid camera in Britain at that time had been lent to the Ministry of Defence, there was further speculation that there were, in fact, two headless men.

Fortune did not favour Margaret, Duchess of Argyll, after Lord Wheatley granted her husband the divorce. As the dour Scottish judge decreed in his summing-up that all the evidence at his disposal established that she was 'a completely promiscuous woman whose sexual appetite could only be satisfied by a number of men', it was probably unlikely that she would find herself another husband. The Duke, on the other hand, was luckier; soon after his divorce was granted, he married, for the fourth time, Mathilda Mortimer. He died of a stroke in 1973, aged sixty-nine.

Margaret survived her ex-husband by twenty years, but she had dissipated her father's vast fortune by the time of her death in a Pimlico nursing home in 1993. In death, it seems she may have found peace at last. She was buried in the same grave as her first husband, Charles Sweeny. Money was in short supply towards the end of her colourful life, but, to her credit, the Duchess was never tempted by financial gain to reveal the name of the enthusiastic lover in those pornographic Polaroid camera shots.

Hardly more than a decade later, the younger son of the unlucky eleventh Duke was embroiled in an extraordinary, and acrimonious, divorce case.

In 1974, after a whirlwind courtship, twenty-seven-year-old Lord Colin Campbell married twenty-five-year-old Georgie Ziadie, the exotic Jamaican-born daughter of a wealthy Lebanese. Then she told him a bit about herself: she had had a very unusual and difficult childhood, having been born with a 'genital deformity'. Appearing to all intents and purposes sexless, she was registered, and brought up, as a boy. A horrific 'treatment' involving hormone injections to turn her into a boy when she was thirteen was fortunately dropped, and it was not until she was twenty-one that Georgie had had an operation that made it possible for her to lead a normal sex life as a woman (though she could never have children). Lord Colin Campbell, however, understood the sorry tale to mean that she had been born a boy and had had a sex-change operation, something he found profoundly repellent. Any attraction they had felt towards each other, any love or liking, turned to an abiding dislike. Fourteen months after they married they were divorced in a case full of bitter accusations – she was after his title, he said; he was after her father's money, she retorted; he beat her up, she said; she was an embarrassment to him, said he.

Decades after the divorce, Lady Colin Campbell has hung on determinedly to the title (she is, says her ex-husband, a 'crushing snob', but she counters that he is a 'crushing bore', adding that she had retained the title to annoy his, now late, brother, the Duke), and cultivates the friendship of society. Like the earlier Lady Colin Campbell, she writes, is reputedly an amusing and intelligent companion, and has many friends as well as a few enemies; Lord Colin Campbell, like his earlier namesake, left the country – in his case to start a new life in New York. Neither has remarried.

CHAPTER SIX

Sissinghurst Castle

SISSINGHURST CASTLE near Cranbrook in Kent, now a popular tourist attraction, was derelict when the novelist and poet (the Hon.) Vita Sackville-West and her husband, the diplomat, author and copious diarist Harold Nicolson, first set eyes on the Elizabethan building in 1930. The story of how they transformed this ancient feature of the central Weald, with its sturdy watchtower, and laid out one of Britain's finest gardens makes fascinating reading. As Sissinghurst and its glorious gardens are, without question, an exemplar of twentieth-century restoration, it may seem odd that, nowadays, this talented couple are remembered just as much for an infamous sexual scandal that caused consternation and disbelief in upper-class society circles in the years following the First World War.

Vita's notorious lesbian affair with Violet Trefusis, the daughter of Edward VII's favourite mistress, Alice Keppel (and thus the great-aunt of the present Duchess of Cornwall, the former Camilla

Parker Bowles), certainly threatened the Nicolson marriage, but in many respects it was an eventuality that had been virtually certain to occur. A glance at the lives of the three protagonists – Vita, Violet and the pig in the middle, Harold – reveals that their unconventional sexual behaviour and their willingness to break the vows of their respective wedding ceremonies were hardly surprising, to say the least.

Vita, who was christened Victoria Mary, was born in 1892 into an aristocratic family who lived at another famous Kent house, Knole, near Sevenoaks. Her grandmother, Pepita (born Josepha Duran), a beautiful and renowned Spanish dancer of humble descent, had a long affair with Lionel Sackville-West, the second Baron Sackville. Lord Sackville was a career diplomat, who, although a bachelor, fathered five illegitimate children by Pepita, including Vita's mother, Victoria. To complicate matters further, Vita's mother then went on to marry her first cousin, also called Lionel Sackville-West, who was the son of her father's brother, William. Vita's father, who was always known as 'young Lionel', then became the third Lord Sackville when Victoria's father, the older Lionel, died in 1908 without any legitimate male heirs.

The privately educated Vita was a precocious child who grew into a striking woman of over six foot, something quite rare among women in the early twentieth century. She also exhibited literary promise at a relatively early age. She wrote her first ballad at the age of eleven and had her first work, the dramatic poem 'Chatterton', published when she was only seventeen.

The teenage Vita had first met Violet Keppel, then only ten years old, when she was invited to tea at a mutual friend's London house in 1904. They did not speak much, but Violet must have liked the older girl, as she was soon asked to a tea party at the Keppels' home. Vita later remembered that Violet kissed her in the hall when she was waiting to leave. That innocent peck on the cheek was the start of a friendship that would eventually become an intense and passionate affair. The two girls, who were at the same school in South Audley Street, Mrs Helen Wolff's establishment, were soon inseparable companions, holidaying in Scotland together and visiting Florence with another close friend of Vita's, Rosamund Grosvenor, in 1908.

But after her lover, King Edward, died in 1910, Alice Keppel (see pages 247–9) decided that it was best that she should leave England and take Violet and her younger sister, Sonia, on an extended tour of the East. Violet, now sixteen, was miserable that she and Vita would be parted for so long, so the two girls went for a walk in Hyde Park, where they kissed again. Although their relationship was still almost certainly platonic, a distraught Violet swore that she would kill her best friend if she did not remain faithful while she was away. She would have been devastated if she had been able to see what was to follow in Vita's life.

Vita first met Harold Nicolson at a dinner party that summer. He came to Knole in June, but Vita did not pay him much attention until the autumn, when she wrote asking him to take her to a dance. He was twenty-four and she was eighteen. Their friendship was slow to blossom, and it was not until September 1911, when Harold returned from the British Embassy in Madrid, where he was then working, that he spent another weekend at Knole. He stayed there again at Christmas and in the New Year of 1912; by then, he had fallen in love with Vita. Her mother, Lady Sackville, noted in her diary that he was very keen on her daughter, but was worried about his lack of funds. Harold's father, Sir Arthur Nicolson, a former ambassador to St Petersburg (at that time, before the Revolution of 1917, the capital of Russia) and then a Permanent Under-Secretary at the Foreign Office, had no family money, he and his wife existing solely on his salary.

By 24 January 1912, when Harold left for a new diplomatic posting in Constantinople (Istanbul), the state of his relationship with Vita was not entirely clear. He thought they were as good as engaged; Vita was not sure what she had said. Her mother and father were adamant that they were not. At the root of her parents' lukewarm response was disappointment that their daughter seemed to wish to marry beneath herself. Lord and Lady Sackville did not view Harold's parents as their social equals, despite the fact that Sir Arthur had reached the peak of the diplomatic profession and was the holder of a baronetcy dating back to the reign of Charles I. So no engagement was announced, and Harold, over the seas in Turkey for six months, began to have serious doubts that he could maintain his somewhat tenuous hold on Vita's affections.

For Vita was already having second thoughts about Harold. On the day he left for the East, she wrote in her diary: 'I don't remember ever being so unhappy. Only today have I begun to understand that I do not love him. He went to Constantinople this morning. I was in bed all day and have had time to think.' He would have been surprised and disappointed to learn – and so, of course, would Violet Keppel – that his rival was the girl who had accompanied Vita and Violet to Florence four years earlier: Rosamund Grosvenor.

In April Vita again travelled to Florence with Rosamund. From their cottage at the Villa Pestellini, she wrote to Harold, telling him that she loved Rosamund but that there was also a place in her heart for him. He did not read anything sexual into the reference to Rosamund, nor was he supposed to. Vita, however, was frightened by her feelings. She had come to realize that she could love a man and a woman at the same time. This situation continued when Harold, who had finished a short leave in England, travelled back as far as Bologna with Vita and Rosamund. When he left them to continue his journey to Constantinople, Vita wrote to her mother: 'I want Harold back so much.' Yet she also made an entry in her diary at the same moment, stating that she 'had never been so much in love with Rosamund'.

It was therefore a relief to Vita when the Balkan Wars (1912–13) briefly stopped letters from Turkey to England. When communications resumed, her notes to Harold still gave no clue to her dilemma. There was, however, a slight hiatus after Vita returned from a trip to Spain in May, when she wrote a letter suggesting that it was time to call a halt to their liaison. If it was meant to be an ultimatum to spur Harold into action, it certainly worked. He telegraphed back immediately: 'Your last letter incomprehensible and disturbing. Am I to take it seriously? Telegraph yes or no. Am very anxious.' She wired back: 'No. Forgive me. Don't believe a word of it.' This gave Harold the signal that he craved. From that moment it was a certainty that they would become engaged.

Had Vita been brutally honest, she would have admitted that it was not pure love that caused her to cast in her lot with Harold. Her relationship with Rosamund, who was by then courting a naval officer from Dartmouth, was not so intense. Although Violet was back in England, she had not yet taken Rosamund's place. Vita had other suitors, among them Lords Granby and Lascelles, either of whom she knew her father and mother would rather have welcomed as a son-in-law, but it is probable that she felt safer and more confident with Harold. She had set him a test when she wrote that letter to him after coming back from Spain. He had passed with flying colours.

Harold returned from Constantinople on 3 July 1913, and their engagement was officially announced on 5 August. Lady Sackville produced a generous and much needed marriage settlement. She gave her daughter an allowance of £2,500 per annum and decreed that the capital from which it emanated was to go to Vita on her, Lady Sackville's, death. The wedding was a grandiose, if small, affair – the chapel at Knole could hold only twenty-six people. Vita wore the magnificent gown that her mother had sported at the Tsar of Russia's coronation in May 1896. The cynic might say that it was a portent that Vita's former lover, Rosamund, was a bridesmaid, but the whole event went off without hitch. The same was true of the honeymoon. The newlyweds had an idyllic time, first at Coker, a pretty Elizabethan house in Somerset, and then at Vita's old favourite, the cottage at the Villa Pestellini.

When it was time for Harold to resume his diplomatic work, the young couple took off for Constantinople. Vita was deliriously happy there and designed her first garden at the charming house they rented at Cospoli, above the Golden Horn. Her father visited them there. So did Rosamund, but by now Vita was bored by her, and showed no interest in her former lover. Laden with oriental artefacts from the Turkish bazaars, they returned to England in June 1914. Their first son, Ben, was born two days after war broke out on 4 August. Flush with Lady Sackville's wedding money, they bought a London house in Ebury Street, where their second and last child, Nigel, was born in January 1917. A country retreat – an old cottage, Long Barn, near Knole, which had fallen into disrepair – soon followed. Vita busied herself writing poetry and creating another country garden, while Harold, who, as a diplomat, was exempt from military service, worked hard in London. It seemed that the once wayward Vita had finally settled down.

It was a situation that was to last only until Violet Keppel invited herself to stay at Long Barn for two weeks in April 1918. Since, according to Lady Sackville's diary, her daughter had complained in 1917 that Harold was 'so physically cold', it is likely that sexual relations between the couple had ceased by the time of Violet's visit. But there is also no evidence to indicate that Vita had been anything but the dutiful and faithful wife before that tranquil spring day in the last year of the Great War. It is safe to assume, therefore, that what occurred on 18 April took Vita very much by surprise.

Vita wrote two years later: 'We were both bored. My serenity got on her nerves, and her restlessness got on mine. She went up to London as often as she could, but she came back in the evenings because the air raids frightened her. She had been here I think a week when everything changed suddenly – changed far more than I foresaw at the time; changed my life.' According to Vita, the momentous chain of events started when she dressed, like a Land Girl,[1] in a pair of breeches and gaiters that she had just acquired. She felt so carefree in her new, somewhat mannish, outfit, running, shouting and leaping over gates. Violet followed her meekly through fields and woods, saying little but never taking her eyes off her spirited companion. Vita knew immediately that the old domination she had always exerted over the younger woman was still there.

As Harold was absent in London that night, what happened later was surely inevitable. The two women dined together alone. When they had finished the meal, they adjourned to Vita's sitting room and, for four hours, talked frankly about their feelings for each other. Later, after Violet had declared her feelings for Vita, the two women made love, probably for the first time.

Vita joyously described the moment when she finally gave in to the girl she had, by her own account, always previously refused whenever things had seemed to be going too far. The passage in her autobiography, which her son, Nigel, found after her death, locked in a Gladstone bag in a little turret room next to her study in Sissinghurst's tower, is both moving and poignant:

> She lay on the sofa, I sat plunged in the armchair: she took my hands, and parted my fingers to count the points as she told me why she loved me. I hadn't dreamed of such an art of love. Such things had been direct for me always; I had known no love possessed of that Latin artistry (whether instinctive or acquired). I was infinitely troubled by the softness of her touch and her lovely voice. She appealed to my unawakened senses; she wore, I remember, a dress of red velvet, that was exactly the colour of a red rose, and that made of her, with her white skin and tawny hair, the most seductive being. She pulled me down until I kissed her – I had not done so for many years. Then she was wise enough to get up and go to bed; but I kissed her again in the dark after I had blown out our solitary lamp. She let herself go limp and entirely passive in my arms. (I shudder to think of the experiences that lay behind her abandonment.) I can't think I slept all that night – not that much of the night was left.

Violet stayed for about five more days, and the pair arranged to go for a short holiday in Cornwall. They met in London and took the train to Exeter. On the journey there they decided to travel on to Plymouth, but on their arrival found that their luggage had been taken off the train at Exeter. They went to the nearest hotel and were told that there was only one room available. 'It seemed like fate,' Vita wrote breathlessly.

On the following day Violet and Vita travelled on to Cornwall, where they stayed for five days in a cottage at Polperro belonging to the novelist Hugh Walpole. Lady Sackville thought the relationship was wholly innocent, noting without irony in her diary: 'They have gone to see the spring flowers.' Not everyone was as sanguine, however. As Vita later wrote: 'It was the first time I had ever been away from Harold, and he obviously minded me going.' Her husband was clearly becoming suspicious and was worried that he was losing his wife to Violet. Vita later remembered that 'the whole of that summer she was mine', but this blissful state of affairs was destined not to last.

When a young officer, Denys Trefusis, returned from the war on ten days' leave at the beginning of the autumn of 1918, there was bound to be trouble. The chief problem was that both Vita and Denys were in love with Violet. Trefusis was a glamorous and adventurous figure. He had run away to Russia after leaving school, only to return at the outbreak of war in 1914. He had shown great bravery to win the Military Cross and was now a company commander on the Western Front. He was also an acknowledged suitor of Violet, and, more important, the ambitious Mrs Keppel thought that he was the perfect marriage partner for her elder daughter. True, Violet had undoubtedly set out to capture Denys's heart, but not for the reasons her mother would have liked. She did not love the dashing soldier, but, cruelly, was prepared to use him to tease and cajole Vita, to whom she was utterly committed at the time.

The two young women arranged to go abroad for a month that winter, but there was tension before they departed. Vita rowed with her lover when she heard that Denys had proposed to Violet before he went back to fight. She also had a dreadful scene with her mother. Lady Sackville was appalled that she was contemplating leaving her husband and two young sons for a month, and was further worried about the gossip that such a trip might create. Nevertheless, Vita and Violet left in November 1918 and headed for Paris.

In Paris they lived like a married couple in a flat they had been lent in the Palais-Royal. Vita browned her face and dressed as a man, wearing, like a kind of narrow turban, a khaki bandage around her head, while Violet acted out the role of the dutiful and loving wife. They went to the theatre and dined together in restaurants as if they were man and wife. Violet called her handsome companion by the name Julian, the character on whom Vita modelled herself in the novel she was writing at the time, *Challenge*, which was based on her affair with Violet (Eve in the novel). They moved down to Monte Carlo after a week, where the idyll continued. Vita wrote: 'The weather was perfect, Monte Carlo was perfect, Violet was perfect.' Vita took Violet to a dance there, and they also deceived a friendly French family, who asked Vita to play bridge, viewing her as a prospective husband for their plain daughter. She even exchanged war reminiscences with their son, an officer of the French army.[2]

To the despair of their respective families, Vita and Violet did not return to England until mid-March 1919. By then, tongues were wagging furiously in London and Paris. Nothing appeared in the papers, but Lady Sackville told all her friends that 'that sexual pervert' had bewitched her daughter. Lord Sackville pleaded with Vita to give Violet up and return to Harold and her family. Denys was back in London, too, and, with Mrs Keppel's blessing, wanted to announce his engagement to Violet as soon as possible. The latter's mother understandably thought that the unwelcome gossip would cease if she could get her daughter safely married off. As a result, Mrs Keppel told all London – or all London that mattered – that they were engaged.

Vita calculated that she could have prevented the wedding with a few words, but felt that to do so would be selfish, whatever her own unhappiness. Besides, the two women believed that it would be easier to continue their liaison under the guise of respectability, which a marriage between Violet and Denys would help to create. It seems extraordinary that Denys was prepared to wed on the strict terms imposed by Violet, under which he was required to forgo his conjugal rights entirely. There was, therefore, probably some truth in the rumour that he was happy not to have his virility tested because a war wound had left him impotent.

On 26 March, a week after the lovers had returned to England, Alice Keppel had her way and the engagement between Violet and Denys was officially announced. Vita, by now, in a desperate state, rushed to Paris to join Harold, who was working at the Peace Conference there until June and now knew the real extent of his wife's affair. As she was parted from Violet, Vita was most unhappy in France. She soon came back to England and re-established contact with the younger woman. For her part, Violet declared to her lover that she could never go through with the sham of her marriage, and asked Vita to take her away to escape the ordeal. Vita later wrote that she believed that Violet was cynically using Denys as a lever to persuade her to leave Harold, but whatever Violet's motives were, the two women anyhow hatched a desperate plot that seemed almost designed to have maximum impact: they would elope the day before Violet's wedding, which was planned for 16 June.

Five days before the ceremony, Vita got cold feet. She had received from Paris three sad and pleading letters from Harold, who, besides knowing about his wife's lesbian affair, must also have sensed that something was dreadfully wrong. She realized she could not forsake him because he was so dependent on her. She told Violet, who implored her to reconsider. Vita refused her lover's entreaties with great difficulty and, to avoid further temptation, decided to put distance between herself and Violet. As a result, on Saturday, 14 June, two days before the wedding, she took the train to Folkestone and crossed the Channel to join Harold in Paris. When he met her at the station, however, she said she wanted to go back to England immediately. He persuaded her to change her mind and took her to Versailles in his car. They spent the whole of Sunday together. On Monday he went back to Paris to the Peace Conference. Vita stayed in her room, waiting for the clock to tell her when Violet was married in London.

On Tuesday night Denys and Violet reached Paris for the start of their honeymoon. The next day Vita, unable to contain herself any longer, visited Violet, who was not wearing a wedding ring, in the Ritz. She brought her back to a small hotel room she had taken and, just two days after her wedding, took Violet to her bed. 'It was dreadful, dreadful,' Vita wrote with brutal honesty. 'By then I had left Versailles and was living alone in a small hotel. I took her there, I treated her savagely, I made love to her, I had her, I didn't care, I only wanted to hurt Denys, even though he didn't know of it. I make no excuse, except that I had suffered too much during the past week and was really scarcely responsible.'

On the following day Violet, with Vita in tow, confronted Denys at the Ritz, telling her new husband that she had meant to run away with Vita and that she did not care for him. He went white, and looked as if he was going to faint. Vita said little and soon left the miserable couple to dine on her own in the hotel restaurant downstairs. Violet watched her lover eat from a window high above, while a desolate Denys wept in the bedroom behind her. Yet he and Violet left to continue their honeymoon at St-Jean-de-Luz. Vita and the long-suffering Harold went for a break to Switzerland, after which Vita returned to England alone. Three weeks later Violet came back, and the two women resumed their affair.

Since Denys worked in London and returned home only at weekends, Vita was able to spend the week with Violet at the Trefusis house, near Uckfield in Sussex. On one occasion Denys came home unexpectedly early, just as Vita was about to leave. The heartless and unsympathetic Violet quickly packed a bag and went with her. Vita later described the harrowing scene: 'I never saw anyone look so angry as he did. He was dead white and his lips were shaking. I tried to make Violet go back, because I thought it was really humiliating the man too much, but she wouldn't.'

Violet again implored Vita to go away with her. She talked of divorcing Denys, and gave him all her letters from Vita so that he should be under no illusion as to the strength of their love. In desperation, he burned them in the grate. In the end, Violet's persistence paid off and Vita agreed to go abroad. Greece was to be their destination so that Vita, who had never set foot in the country, could gather some background material for her novel *Challenge*, which was set there. Harold, amazingly, swallowing this rather lame excuse for another extended tryst between his wife and her lover, gave this holiday his blessing.

The two women left England on 19 October 1919. They travelled slowly, making their first stop in Paris. They took up there where they had left off a year earlier. Vita pulled out her old khaki bandage and once more dressed as a man. They dined in cafés and went to the theatre. They also danced, Violet, as she had before, addressing her partner as Julian.

They moved south to Carcassonne, and then to St-Raphael on the Mediterranean coast. They did not go to Greece, however, because there was rioting there. When he heard that they had ended up in Monte Carlo, Harold began to wish he had not sanctioned the journey. Just as they had in Paris, Vita and Violet tried to re-create the atmosphere of the year before. They visited the casino and played tennis, maintaining the pretence of being man and wife. When Denys arrived in Cannes for a prearranged meeting with Violet, she said she did not want to see him. But Vita, fearing he might behave irrationally if his wife reneged, took her to meet him and then travelled on to Paris to see Harold, who was laid up with a knee injury.

Both women had agreed before they said goodbye that they would tell their respective husbands that they could not bear to be apart. Their feelings for each other were every bit as intense as they had been the year before. Harold described Vita's infatuation with Violet expertly when he wrote to her: 'When you fall into Violet's hands, you become like a jellyfish addicted to cocaine.' The observation in his letter could hardly have been more perceptive. When Violet returned to London in early January 1920, the two women began to hatch a plan to elope. This time they decided to burn their boats and go for good.

Things now began to move fast. Vita told Harold of their scheme and on 1 February 1920 he, having finished his leave, returned miserably to Paris to his new job on the League of Nations staff, not quite sure whether he would ever see his wife again. Violet spent one last evening with Denys, ostensibly to discuss business but actually to accompany him to a play. On 3 February the lovers left for Lincoln, where Vita wanted to do research for *The Dragon in Shallow Waters*, a book she was writing set in the fen country. In the Saracen's Head Hotel, where they stayed for a week, they agreed impulsively that they would leave England in a few days and never return.

They came back to London and stayed in a hotel in Liverpool Street for the night, so as to break the journey between Lincoln and Dover. Violet telephoned Denys, who came to the hotel. She told him they were going. He pleaded with her to reconsider, but to no avail. As she and Vita were waiting in the lobby the next morning, he came again and gave her a long letter, which she read in the taxi on the way to Victoria and the boat train for France. It made no difference either, although Vita told Violet she would give her up if she would go back to Denys. Once more the younger woman refused, but made the strange concession that she would cross to France alone, believing that Denys would somehow mind that less. On 9 February, therefore, Violet crossed the Channel while Vita, who was to take the ferry the day after, booked into a lodging house in Dover for the night. They were to meet again in Amiens the next day.

Then the first of what was to turn into an almost unbelievable chain of events occurred. Vita, having lunched, walked down to the sea. Suddenly she saw a very anxious Denys striding towards her. When he asked where Violet was, Vita replied that she had gone. He said he wanted to follow her, but at first Vita would not reveal her destination. In the end, however, she relented and told him all the details. She had begun to feel sorry for him, which led her to make a pact. They would travel to Amiens together and give Violet one last chance to choose between them.

Denys and Vita had a rough crossing to Calais. But they were civil to each other, and even arranged to have lunch together when the boat reached France. While she was booking a table in the buffet after the ferry had docked, however, Vita was astonished when a hysterical Violet, who was supposed to be in Amiens, rushed up to her with a face as white as a sheet. Vita said at once that Denys was with her, at which Violet tried to run away. But it was too late to take evasive action, for at that moment Denys appeared. Realizing that Violet was sick, the trio sought out a hotel where they put her to bed and summoned a doctor. The situation took another, somewhat farcical, turn when Vita and Denys were given adjoining rooms, while Violet was allotted one further down the corridor.

Violet recovered sufficiently during the night, so the trio took a cab to Boulogne the next morning and then caught the train to Amiens. During the journey, Denys wrote Vita a note, saying that he knew that Violet had made up her mind and had chosen her instead of him. He would, he said, leave them at Amiens and return to Paris. He wept for the rest of the trip, knowing that he had lost his wife and that it was possible that he would never see her again. He looked a broken man when he caught the Paris train on their arrival at Amiens.

At last the two women were alone. There is no doubt that they were preparing to spend the rest of their lives together at this juncture. They had taken most of their personal belongings and enough money to buy a house. They were quite prepared to leave their husbands, their homes and, in Vita's case, her two young children.

Yet while Denys Trefusis may have given up hope, their mothers were not going to throw in the towel so easily. It was a formidable alliance. Lady Sackville and the Hon. Mrs Keppel were intelligent and resourceful women who were still resolutely determined to stop their daughters ruining their lives and their families' good names.

First of all, George Keppel, Violet's father, travelled to Amiens and called at the hotel where Vita and Violet were staying for a few days. He had reputedly asked Scotland Yard to watch the ports to prevent his daughter and Vita leaving the country, but if this is true, the ploy had clearly been remarkably ineffective. Unable to comprehend that his daughter could have run off with someone of the same sex, he had a storming row with Vita and Violet, which probably strengthened rather than weakened their resolve to stick to their guns.

When she heard that George Keppel's mission had failed, Lady Sackville took command. She urged her son-in-law, Harold, who had just returned from Paris, to contact Denys. She then interviewed Denys herself, and persuaded him that he and Harold must make a last-ditch attempt to persuade their wives to come back. Between them all, they then concocted an ambitious plan. Denys, who owned a two-seater aircraft, would fly to Amiens with Harold the next morning. 'Denys is very cool and collected,' Lady Sackville wrote, 'and fully determined either to bring Violet back or have done with her.'

The two desperate husbands landed at Amiens on the morning of 14 February 1920. Vita was astonished when Harold arrived in her room and told her to pack. There was an unpleasant row as she and Violet defied their respective spouses. Then Harold played his trump card. 'Are you sure,' he asked his wife, 'Violet is as faithful to you as she makes you believe? Because Denys has told your mother a quite different story.' A distraught Vita rushed downstairs and confronted Denys. 'Have you ever been really married to Violet?' she asked euphemistically. He replied: 'I refuse to tell you: that is a matter that lies entirely between Violet and myself.' Vita found Violet in the restaurant. 'Why have you not told me you have deceived me with Denys?' she screamed. A terrified Violet stammered some unintelligible reply. 'You have belonged to him,' Vita stated emphatically. 'Yes,' she admitted sheepishly. 'When?' 'The night before we went to Lincoln,' Violet replied.

Vita knew that Violet was still physically a virgin, but the latter's admission that she had slept with Denys and had some sort of sexual contact with him was too much to bear. Vita hurried to her room and packed. Harold and Denys then tried to prevent her from seeing Violet, but she managed to kiss her goodbye. The Nicolsons quickly left by car for Paris, though Harold had to tell the chauffeur to avoid the street where the hotel was situated for fear of upsetting his heartbroken wife. So they abandoned the direct route to the capital and drove through the slums of Amiens, which still bore the scars of damage from the war. The next day Violet, also now in Paris, tried her best to undo the damage and persuade Vita that nothing significant had happened between her and Denys that night in London. Denys also seems to have supported his wife's version, although he later told Harold that 'he had perjured himself' when he had said that 'he was not really married to Violet'.

The whole truth will never be known, but in the cold light of day Violet's admission in the restaurant of the Amiens hotel probably gave Vita the get-out clause she truly wanted. She had always suspected that she could never really trust the selfish and unreliable Violet. Now she knew for certain. The sexual side of her marriage to Harold was over, but he was a steadier and far better long-term proposition.

In fact, the love affair between Violet and Vita was to continue for two more years, but the threat to both their marriages was far less potent than it had been in the past. Harold, firmly believing that the great crisis was over, allowed Vita to visit Violet in Avignon in March. She stayed for about three weeks, but, as her husband had predicted, this time she came home of her own volition. In the early part of 1921, Vita and Violet had one last fling in Hyères, in the South of France, but their ardour was cooling when summer arrived. Violet's permanent return to Denys in the autumn signified that the relationship with Vita, which had horrified and embarrassed their families and appalled and enthralled London and Paris society, was well and truly over.

It may seem strange that Harold had capitulated so meekly when his wife's liaison with Violet was in its infancy, but while there is no suggestion that he had a male lover at the time, the fact that he was a latent homosexual probably helped him cope with her rejection and his cuckoldry. Indeed, his own discreet homosexual affairs would probably have remained under wraps if Vita's wilder and more scandalous lesbian relationships had been less public.

Since his schooldays at Wellington, where barbed wire was placed on the top of the dormitory cubicles to deter any boy who might harbour impure thoughts, Harold's homosexual leanings, and his promiscuity, had been reasonably well known. His diplomatic career had been put on hold when he contracted venereal disease in Madrid at the time when Vita was just starting her affair with Violet. In 1917 (the year of his son Nigel's birth), after a weekend at Knebworth in Hertfordshire, the home of the Earl of Lytton, where the guests had included the painter Sir John Lavery, the diplomats Horace Rumbold and Louis Mallet, and the writer Osbert Sitwell, he suspected he might have caught another sexually transmitted disease – but was not sure if the infection stemmed from 'one of the male guests (or servants)'.

The actor, composer, songwriter and dramatist Ivor Novello was rumoured to be one of his conquests, but his greatest male love was the critic Raymond Mortimer, with whom he lived for a time in Teheran in 1926 when he was British Counsellor there. Perhaps he was lucky that newspapers were reluctant to expose prominent homosexuals in those days, but Harold was quite open about, and unabashed by, his proclivities. He wrote to Raymond Mortimer after the latter had left Teheran: 'I fear it is only lust which keeps one's mind buoyant.' Later he described homosexuality in a letter to one of his sons: '. . . as if you liked oysters done in sherry: not a thing to be particularly ashamed of or particularly proud of.'

Vita also had other affairs, but, like Harold's dalliances, they never threatened their marriage, which was undoubtedly based on a strong mutual respect. Indeed, the current lovers of both Vita and Harold often attended the same weekend parties at the Nicolson homes of Long Barn and, later, Sissinghurst. In 1923 the art critic Clive Bell introduced Vita to his sister-in-law, the writer Virginia Woolf, one of the founders of the Bloomsbury Group. The two soon became inseparable and spent holidays together in Italy and France the following year, and Virginia used Vita as the model for the androgynous central character in her novel *Orlando*. Indeed, Virginia Woolf probably fascinated Vita more than any of her other female lovers, who included the poet Roy Campbell's wife, Mary, and Hilda Matheson, Talks Director at BBC Radio from 1926 to 1940. Vita was absolutely devastated when, in 1941, the novelist, in a fit of the depression to which she was prone, drowned herself.

Despite its problems and pitfalls, Harold and Vita's eccentric but enduring marriage lasted until Vita's death. Sadly, the union of her greatest love, Violet, and Denys Trefusis did not survive for anything like so long. After the affair with Vita drew to its close, Violet and Denys, who never had children, gradually forgave one another and eventually lived the happy life of the expatriate in Paris. Denys died young, of consumption, in 1929, but Violet, who lived until 1972, became a novelist of note, admired for her intellectual verve and brilliant wit.

She fled France during the Second World War when the Germans invaded, and came to visit Vita at Sissinghurst in 1940. The spark between them, which had lain dormant for nearly twenty years, was obviously still there. By now forty-eight, Vita was well aware that any more meetings would be fraught with danger. Soon after Violet left, she wrote an emotional letter to the woman who had nearly stolen her away from her husband and two young children. It contained the following poignant words of warning: 'We loved each other too deeply for too many years, and we must not play with fire again.'

Vita died, from cancer, in 1962, and Harold six years later. In 1973 the younger of their two sons, Nigel, published *Portrait of a Marriage: Vita Sackville-West and Harold Nicolson*, much of which was based on the autobiographical papers that he had found after his mother's death, and which detailed, with considerable honesty, both her and Harold's homosexual affairs and infidelities. The book was an immediate success, and caused a sensation, although not everyone admired it, leading to its author being accused of 'betraying his class and his family'; indeed, one satirical magazine published a savage little poem about Nicolson's treatment of his parents' memory, and his professed reasons for writing the book, which ended: 'A lesbian's offspring, begat by a queer, /And, self-made, a son of a bitch.' This was unjust. As *The Times* noted in its obituary of Nicolson, who died in 2004:

> Yet in fairness, many felt he was justified in publishing an account which placed his mother's passionate affair with Violet Trefusis, which had lasted for three years, in the context of an enduringly successful marriage which had lasted fifty. Moreover, Vita's own private account of her love for Violet . . . had, it seemed, been intended for publication.
>
> Even Nicolson's critics, such as the writer Rebecca West . . . did not attribute base motives to the book's author. His uncompromising integrity, indeed, was one of [his] most endearing characteristics.

Today, Vita is probably mainly remembered as a gardener and gardening writer (Sissinghurst is the most-visited garden in Britain), despite her poetry and novels, and her association with the Bloomsbury Group of writers and artists, among them Virginia Woolf. But she is remembered, too, for the passionate lesbian affair that almost destroyed two marriages, and for her own open, unorthodox, yet immensely strong relationship with her husband.

CHAPTER SEVEN

Cliveden

GEORGE VILLIERS, second Duke of Buckingham, statesman, wit, writer and notorious libertine, built the first house at Cliveden in 1666. He asked William Winde to design a glorious hunting lodge perched high on chalk cliffs where the Thames bends in a wide arc through pretty wooded countryside near Taplow, on the Berkshire–Buckinghamshire border. This beautiful, secluded estate was not far from London and was the perfect place for the Duke to entertain his many mistresses and friends, or plot with his political accomplices. Since then, Cliveden has been twice destroyed by fire but has risen from its ashes, each time to be more grandiose than before. Since the time of George I, almost every British sovereign has stayed there; Frederick, Prince of Wales,[1] the father of George III, actually lived at Cliveden for some years.

After Buckingham's death in 1687, the house remained in his family for a few years, but was then sold to the first Earl of Orkney in 1696. His descendants were the owners when Frederick, Prince of Wales, leased the property. Nearly a hundred years later, the widowed third Countess of Orkney was in residence when, on 20 May 1795, the house, with the exception of two wings, was destroyed by fire after a servant knocked over a candle. It remained derelict for twenty-six years. Sir George Warrender then purchased the estate, and commissioned a fellow Scot, the Edinburgh architect William Burn, to erect another dwelling on the site. When Sir George died in 1849, the second Duke of Sutherland bought the house.

Unbelievably, the Duke's new home, which was less than thirty years old, burned down the same year. The new Cliveden, designed by Charles Barry, the principal architect of the new Houses of Parliament (in 1834 the old buildings had also been destroyed by fire), took two years to construct, and is the Italianate mansion that stands on the site in more than 300 acres today. Queen Victoria stayed there in the early summer of 1866, but two years later the third Duke of Sutherland sold Cliveden, keeping things in the family by selling the house to his sister Constance's immensely rich husband, Hugh Lupus Grosvenor, third Marquess of Westminster, and soon to be created first Duke of Westminster.

Queen Victoria, no doubt thinking it unlikely that she would be invited there again, was most disappointed when she was told that William Waldorf Astor, America's richest man, had purchased the stately home from Westminster in 1893. 'It is grievous to think of it falling into these hands!' the old monarch is reputed to have remarked, most unfairly. The passionate anglophile, who was created first Viscount Astor in 1916, gave Cliveden to his son, also named Waldorf, in 1906.

The great house gradually became the hub of high society, and even came to rival the royal court for glamour. Invitations from the generous second Viscount, who inherited the title in 1919, and his outspoken, American-born wife Nancy, the first woman MP to take her seat in Parliament,[2] were treated like gold dust by the rich and famous. Over the years guests ranged from political leaders, such as Lord Curzon, Winston Churchill and President Franklin D.

Roosevelt, to giants of the literary world, stage and screen, among them Rudyard Kipling, George Bernard Shaw and Charlie Chaplin.

When George, Duke of Buckingham, who always sailed close to the wind both socially and politically, had been its owner Cliveden was never going to be distanced from scandal. It is worth remembering that it was Buckingham who wooed and married Mary, the daughter of Lord Fairfax,[3] in 1657, even though the banns for her intended wedding to the Earl of Chesterfield had already been read. He then managed to surpass such rakish behaviour when he accompanied Princess Henrietta, the sister of Buckingham's friend and confidant, Charles II, to Paris in 1661 for her marriage to the Duke of Orléans. Instead of chaperoning the Princess, he made advances to her so openly and with such lack of caution that he had to be recalled to London to avoid an embarrassing diplomatic incident.

His behaviour in the House of Lords was not much better, either. In 1666, the year in which he built Cliveden, he pulled the Marquess of Dorchester's wig off in a scuffle. (Dorchester seems to have come off better, however, as he emerged from the fracas with huge wads of the Duke's hair in his hands.) According to Buckingham's bête noire, the Earl of Clarendon,[4] the Upper House had never before been offended by such a flagrant misdemeanour. Both noblemen were sent to the Tower of London, although they were released after apologizing.

If the moral climate of the day was loose, and marital fidelity a rarity among the aristocracy at the time, Buckingham's later affair with the Countess of Shrewsbury still caused outrage in upper-class circles, from the King downwards. His illicit liaison with the famous beauty led to a duel with her cuckolded husband at Barn Elms, across the Thames from Hammersmith, on 16 January 1668. Shrewsbury was fatally injured, and society was astonished, if not outraged, when Buckingham installed the woman he had so recently widowed in his own houses, and even in those of his long-suffering but loyal wife.

[141]

After the duel, Samuel Pepys, who was as appalled as everyone else, wrote sarcastically: 'This will make the world think that the king hath good councillors about him, when the Duke of Buckingham, the greatest man about him, is a fellow of no more sobriety than to fight about a whore.' The famous diarist was right to question Lady Shrewsbury's morals. Like her ducal paramour, she too was not averse to murder. On one occasion, she issued a contract to kill a former lover, Harry Killigrew. He survived, but his servant was killed by the Countess's hired assassin.

Buckingham continued to live openly with Lady Shrewsbury for the next six years. In January 1674, however, the trustees of the young Earl of Shrewsbury complained in the House of Lords of Buckingham's very public intimacy with their ward's mother. Incredibly, they also claimed that the dissolute Duke had fathered the Countess's dead child, named as the Earl of Coventry, who had been buried in Westminster Abbey. The charge was probably not without foundation, for Buckingham apologized and, with the Countess, was required to put down a security of the then substantial sum of £10,000 to ensure that they would not cohabit again.

Cliveden witnessed more than its fair share of degeneracy in Buckingham's day, but the scandal that erupted there nearly 300 years later caused a far bigger rumpus than any the errant Duke had ever contrived to engineer. On the night of 8 July 1961, the third Viscount Astor, a Tory grandee who had been an MP before his father's death (for his accession to the title meant that he became a member of the House of Lords and so resigned his Parliamentary seat), decided to take a walk through the formal gardens of his home as darkness fell. He asked if any of the assembled company staying at Cliveden that Saturday night would like to join him for a brisk constitutional to settle the splendid dinner they had just consumed. One of his guests, a senior politician named John Profumo, accepted with alacrity. So the two men stepped outside on to the magnificent terrace and walked over the perfectly kept lawns to listen to the nearby Thames lapping peacefully against its banks.

It was a sultry summer's night, and as they strolled back by the swimming pool they heard the sound of splashing. Wondering who was taking a dip at that late hour, Bill Astor and Jack Profumo decided to investigate. To their surprise and, no doubt, delight, they discovered a beautiful young girl, swimming naked – her companion had apparently hidden her swimsuit. Seeing a towel on the pool's edge as the only means of preserving her modesty before the two strangers, she swam across to the far side to retrieve it. Wrapping it quickly round her as she climbed out of the pool, and still dripping provocatively with water, she set about finding her lost costume.

Captivated by this erotic, mermaid-like figure, Astor and Profumo, for the fun of it, tried to catch the attractive teenager though, naturally, the girl easily avoided the attentions of her much older and clumsier pursuers. Before long the other dinner guests arrived and the pool lights were switched on. In that harsh and sudden glare of artificial light, Jack Profumo, the Secretary of State for War in Harold Macmillan's Conservative government, was caught red-handed, playing cat-and-mouse with the girl who was to ruin his reputation and career. Her name was Christine Keeler.

At the time, Profumo's political career was burgeoning. Educated at Harrow and Oxford, this scion of an old aristocratic Italian family won Kettering for the Conservatives in 1940, only to lose the seat in the Labour landslide at the end of the war. He was back in the House of Commons in 1950, as the Member for Stratford-upon-Avon; two years later he became a transport minister. In 1960 the rich and clever forty-five-year-old, who was married to the accomplished actress Valerie Hobson, and clearly viewed by the Tory hierarchy as a safe pair of hands, was made Secretary of State for War. Favoured by the Prime Minister, Harold Macmillan, the word in Westminster was that he was destined for even higher office.

Christine Keeler's circumstances were very different from those of her new poolside playmate. Three years earlier, at the tender age of sixteen, she had moved from working-class Wraysbury in Berkshire to London. She soon found herself on the seamier side of the capital's nightlife. While working as a topless dancer in Murray's Club in Soho, she met Stephen Ward, an osteopath with an impressive list of rich and aristocratic clients, among them Lord Astor. In return for manipulating Astor's painful back, Ward was given the use of Spring Cottage, a small house in Cliveden's grounds. Keeler was spending the weekend there with Ward when she decided to take her invigorating late-night swim. It was the osteopath who had playfully hidden her swimsuit.

Astor introduced Ward, who had by now arrived back at the pool, to Profumo and his other guests, and invited him and his now clothed young friend to join his house party for a late-night drink. Profumo then took Keeler on a tour of Cliveden's fabulous rooms. When they reached the upper floors, Keeler, knowing how much the politician had enjoyed trying to catch her at the swimming pool, encouraged him to pursue her through the bedrooms. Profumo, with his wife safely conversing in the drawing room downstairs, joined in the chase with relish. A sexual relationship with the flirtatious teenager was now very much on the War Minister's mind.

A brief sexual affair would probably not have threatened Profumo's career, but the strange scenario that occurred the next day, once again around Cliveden's swimming pool, brought a new and far more dangerous dimension to the proceedings.

Another friend of Ward's arrived at Spring Cottage on that bright Sunday morning. The new guest was a good-looking Russian, Captain Eugene Ivanov, who was serving as a naval attaché at the Soviet Embassy in London. Before long the frolicking began again, and Keeler ended up astride Profumo's shoulders. Later, Astor, Ivanov and Profumo raced each other across the pool. The last emerged the winner, but broke the rules by walking in the shallow end; 'That will teach you to trust a Minister of the Crown,' he told the others with a wry smile. By the end of that boiling afternoon Profumo had made up his mind to cheat on his wife, and asked Keeler for her telephone number. Unfortunately for him, the object of his affections had herself taken a fancy to the rugged and muscular member of the Russian Embassy's staff.

Ivanov drove Keeler back to London, to Ward's Wimpole Mews flat, where she was staying. Once arrived, they quickly knocked back a bottle of vodka. No doubt emboldened by several shots of his powerful national tipple, Ivanov leaned forward and kissed her, with the inevitable result that they were soon in bed together. 'He was a wonderful lover, so masculine,' Keeler later revealed to the *News of the World.*

Meanwhile, Profumo, unaware of Keeler's recent tryst with the Soviet diplomat, was anxious to arrange another meeting. It was not long before he and Keeler had also consummated their brief relationship. These clandestine and usually rushed encounters took place at a variety of locations, including Ward's flat, in the cramped confines of Profumo's Mini Minor, and even at his home while his wife was away in Ireland. Sadly, these lovemaking sessions clearly meant far more to the besotted Profumo than they did to his young lover, who described them perfunctorily as 'screws of convenience'.

The minister gave Keeler money and presents, but, unknown to him, she was far more enamoured of Ivanov, who introduced her to the high life and to London's fashionable clubs, restaurants and bars. Profumo, by contrast, did the opposite. She later revealed that he never took her anywhere, except for 'drives all over London, and even then he was so anxious to be discreet that he used to borrow a big black car from John Hare, the Minister of Labour'.

His affair with Keeler had been going on for a month when events took a nasty turn for Profumo: MI5 became aware of his dalliance. It transpired that Ward had been contacted by the security service in June 1961, a month before the Cliveden weekend. The intelligence outfit thought that a love of the good life in the liberal West might make Ivanov a potential defector. A meeting between the Russian and Ward was therefore engineered, with the result that the two men met for lunch at the Garrick Club.

Ward, who was an accomplished artist, asked the embassy official if he could arrange for him to paint portraits of prominent Soviet politicians. His real purpose, however, was to cultivate a friendship, which it was hoped would enable MI5 to catch Ivanov in a honeytrap. Amazingly, the bait, whose job was to pass to Ward any secrets the Russian's injudicious pillow talk might reveal, was Keeler. When MI5 learned that Keeler was also involved with Profumo, its head, Sir Roger Hollis – later to be accused of being a Kremlin spy himself[5] – began to worry that Keeler's liaison with the War Secretary would compromise the operation against Ivanov. In addition, Hollis did not want to embarrass a government minister, and in consequence he told the Cabinet Secretary, Sir Norman Brook, who passed on the warning to Profumo.

The harassed Secretary of State, his judgement irretrievably damaged by passion, left the helpful mandarin's office and immediately wrote Keeler a letter, headed with the word 'Darling' – a letter that was later to incriminate him. Then, stupidly, instead of heeding Brook's warning he continued seeing Keeler for another four months. During that time, MI5 aborted the honeytrap operation on the grounds that Ward could not be trusted since he was now considered to be too deeply under the influence of Ivanov. But the damage was done as far as Profumo was concerned. He was not only having a reckless affair with a mistress young enough to be his daughter, but he was also now inadvertently involved in a counter-intelligence operation.

Profumo and Keeler last met in late 1961, but the scandal did not break until early 1963, when the latter decided after a strange and dangerous incident that the time had come to reveal her secrets. After her affair with Profumo ended, Keeler alternated between two West Indian lovers: Lucky Gordon, a singer and drug dealer, and Johnny Edgecombe, a violent character who lived in Brentwood. In October 1962 the two black suitors fought a duel over Keeler in an all-night club in Soho's Wardour Street. Gordon, whose face was slashed, ended up the loser.

Two months later, just before Christmas, Edgecombe, distraught that Keeler had ended their relationship, travelled to Ward's flat in an attempt to win her back. When she refused to let him in, he pulled a gun and fired several shots through the front door. Yet although rumours were beginning to surface in Fleet Street about

Profumo's affair with Keeler, the shooting in the peaceful London mews received scant coverage in the papers. The police, however, viewed the incident as more significant and arrested Edgecombe for attempted murder.

Ward, understandably flustered by the assault on his home, asked Keeler to leave. She sought out one of Ward's patients, a solicitor named Michael Eddowes. Because he suspected that Ward and Ivanov had been conspiring to compromise Profumo over his indiscretions, Eddowes was quite prepared to believe Keeler when she told him that the osteopath had asked her to persuade the War Minister to pass on state secrets.

Encouraged by Eddowes, Keeler repeated her claims to two equally responsive listeners a week later. This time she betrayed her confidences to a journalist, Paul Mann, and a Labour MP, John Lewis. Lewis secretly taped Keeler's confessions and gave the recording to George Wigg, another Labour MP, who specialized in defence matters. Unfortunately for Profumo, Wigg had a grudge against him and was happy to play a part in his downfall.

Mann, on the other hand, persuaded Keeler to take her story to the press. In January 1963 she met a journalist from the *Sunday Pictorial.* Showing the reporter a handwritten note from Profumo as proof, she asked the paper for £1,000 for her story. The *Pictorial,* however, was already in trouble with a parliamentary committee over its reporting of the Vassall spying scandal,[6] and wanted to be surer of its ground.

While the paper continued its protracted negotiations, Ward, well aware of the can of worms that would be opened if Keeler's story hit the front pages, tried to stop publication by tipping off the government. As a result, Profumo was persuaded to threaten to sue if any paper printed the allegations. On 28 January the Minister for War, now a desperate man, paid a visit to the Attorney-General, Sir John Hobson, and denied an affair with Keeler. He continued to dig his own grave by repeating this pack of lies to the Solicitor-General, Sir Peter Rawlinson, and the government Chief Whip, Martin Redmayne. All three doubted whether Profumo was telling the truth, but they accepted his account to protect the government's good name.

The *Pictorial* then came back to Keeler with another offer. They wanted her signature, attesting to the truth of her account, before they would publish. Ward, seeking another way to kill the story, persuaded her to refuse to sign and promised to compensate her generously for the loss of the newspaper's fee. Keeler was less than happy, therefore, when Ward's solicitor gave her £500 rather than the £5,000 she was expecting. Ward then contacted the *Sunday Pictorial* and persuaded the journalists involved that Keeler's story was a complete fabrication. The paper quickly dropped it. That was the last straw for Keeler, who decided to pay Ward back. This time she went to the police. The most serious allegation she made against her former landlord was that he procured call girls for his rich clients, among them Viscount Astor, the owner of Ward's Cliveden cottage.

The Prime Minister, Harold Macmillan, returned from holiday in Italy in February and was briefed by the government legal officers to whom Profumo had spoken. Macmillan had little doubt that his Secretary of State for War was lying but decided to let matters rest, hoping thereby to avert a scandal. With hindsight, that was probably a mistake, for on 8 March a newsletter, *Westminster Confidential*, published weekly during Parliamentary sessions and with a reputation for getting its facts right, printed the salacious tale. It did not name names, but it was blindingly obvious to whom the newssheet was referring. The article contained a paragraph which included the following revealing phrase: 'the allegation by this girl was that not only was this minister, who has a famous actress as a wife, a client, but also the Soviet military attaché, apparently Colonel [*sic*] Ivanov'. A letter on Ministry of War writing paper, signed 'Jack', was also reproduced.

In the event Profumo did not sue, on the grounds that the newsletter had a tiny circulation. A week later, however, a wider public became aware of the Secretary of State's worsening predicament. In its edition of 15 March, under the headline 'War

Minister Shock', the *Daily Express* claimed, erroneously in fact, that Profumo had resigned for 'personal reasons'. Directly below, the newspaper ran another article with the headline 'Vanished', showing a picture of Keeler, who the day before had failed to show up as the principal witness at the start of Johnny Edgecombe's Old Bailey trial for attempted murder. Those who knew how the press worked soon made the connection between the two articles, and the Westminster gossip grapevine went into overdrive. Before long, the whole of London was talking about the Minister and his nubile young mistress.

Since a national newspaper had now hinted at the scandal, George Wigg, who had been compiling a dossier on the Profumo/Keeler affair after he had received the tape containing the latter's confessions, decided that the time was ripe to plunge his own dagger into the Minister for War. On 19 March, during the debate on the case of the journalists who were jailed for refusing to reveal their sources to the Vassall tribunal, the MP for Dudley, protected from the libel laws by parliamentary privilege, stood up and raised the allegations against Profumo in the House of Commons.

'There is not an Hon. Member in the House,' Wigg thundered, 'not a journalist in the press gallery, who, in the last few days, has not heard rumour upon rumour involving a member of the government front bench.' He then went on to mention Keeler's name in connection with the Edgecombe shooting and her disappearance during the trial. He called on the Home Secretary, as the senior government member present, to deny that Keeler's vanishing act had been designed by influential people to protect the Minister in question. Two other Labour MPs, the frontbencher Richard Crossman and Barbara Castle, reiterated Wigg's demands.

When the Home Secretary, Sir Henry Brooke, rose to his feet, he attempted to brush the affair aside. 'I do not propose to comment on rumours which have been raised under the cloak of privilege and safe from any action at law,' was the first sentence of the Minister's brief and phlegmatic response. Yet although they did not dare to show their concern in public, the senior members of the government were actually extremely worried. That night, Macmillan insisted that Profumo should repeat the denials, which he had earlier made to the government's chief law officers and to the Tory Chief Whip, to the House of Commons the next morning. At eleven o'clock on 22 March, therefore, Profumo began to deliver the statement that was to bring his political life to a sticky end. Despite the fact that it was a Friday, which is usually the quietest day at Westminster, the Commons was packed to the seams to hear the Minister for War commit the cardinal sin of lying to his fellow Members of Parliament. His words are worth repeating here in full:

> I understand that in the debate on the Consolidated Fund Bill last night, under the protection of parliamentary privilege, the Hon. gentlemen, the Members for Dudley [Wigg] and Coventry East [Crossman], and the Hon. lady, the Member for Blackburn [Castle], opposite, spoke of rumours connecting a Minister with a Miss Keeler and a recent trial at the Central Criminal Court. It was alleged that people in high places might have been responsible for concealing information concerning the disappearance of a witness and the perversion of justice. I understand that my name has been connected with the disappearance of Miss Keeler. I would like to take this opportunity to make a personal statement about these matters. I last saw Miss Keeler in December 1961, and I have not seen her since. I have no idea where she is now. Any suggestion that I was in any way connected with her absence from the trial at the Old Bailey is wholly and completely untrue. My wife and I first met Miss Keeler at a house party in July 1961 at Cliveden. Among a number of people there was Dr Stephen Ward, who we already knew slightly, and Mr Ivanov, who was an attaché at the Russian Embassy.
>
> My wife and I had a standing invitation to visit Dr Ward. Between July and December 1961 I met Miss Keeler on about half a dozen occasions when I called to see him and his friends. Miss Keeler and I were on friendly terms. There was no impropriety whatsoever in

my acquaintanceship with Miss Keeler. Mr Speaker, I have made this personal statement because of what was said in the House last evening by the three Hon. Members, and which, of course, was protected by privilege. I shall not hesitate to issue writs for libel and slander if scandalous allegations are made or repeated outside the House.

Wigg, who now had the bit firmly between his teeth, was certain that Profumo was being dishonest. On 25 March he appeared on BBC TV's *Panorama* programme and stated that Ward and Ivanov were risks to national security. A furious Ward met the Labour MP the next day to protest his innocence, with the result that Wigg became even more convinced that Profumo was a liar. He reported his conversation with Ward to Harold Wilson. The new Labour leader,[7] scenting a damaging ministerial resignation that would almost certainly weaken the government, asked Wigg to write a detailed report. Wilson then sent an edited version to Macmillan, although, for some apparently inexplicable reason, the Prime Minister did not see it for nearly two weeks. Profumo, however, was not prepared to lie down just yet. With extraordinary bravado, he issued writs against two foreign magazines, *Il Tempo Illustrato* and *Paris Match*, which had dared to print allegations that he and Keeler had had sex together.[8]

The next day Brooke, the Home Secretary, summoned Hollis, the head of MI5, to discuss Ward's meeting with Wigg. They made a plan to silence the osteopath by telling the Metropolitan Police to dig up evidence to bring criminal charges against him. Consequently, the police started to question Ward's friends and patients. They even stopped the showgirl Mandy Rice-Davies, a friend of Ward and Keeler, from leaving for Spain to marry her boyfriend. She was charged with possessing a false driving licence and spent ten days on remand in prison; however, the police made it very clear that she would be free to go if she implicated Ward. She refused and went to court on 1 May, where she was found guilty and fined £42. She then left for Spain, but on her return was arrested again and charged with stealing a television set. This time her passport was confiscated and she was released on bail of £1,000 and on condition that she reported to a police station in July. The police were obviously prepared to resort to bullyboy tactics to obtain witnesses to testify against Ward.

Ward was now in a desperate state. His friends were no longer returning his calls and his clients were cancelling their appointments at the clinic. Even his greatest supporter, Lord Astor, had decided that enough was enough and told him to vacate his Cliveden bolthole, Spring Cottage. Ward was fairly confident that he was the victim of a political vendetta, but he wanted to make sure. So, on 7 May, he went to see Macmillan's Parliamentary Private Secretary, Tim Bligh. Ward told Bligh that Profumo's statement in the House of Commons had not contained the full facts and that the War Minister had in fact written several letters to Keeler. For his part, Bligh suspected that Ward was trying to blackmail the government into stopping the police investigation. He relayed his fears to Macmillan, and the Prime Minister decided to question Profumo again. Yet the hard-pressed Minister stuck to the story he had given the House.

Realizing that he was getting nowhere with Macmillan's office, Ward next wrote a letter to Harold Wilson, detailing his complaints about the police investigation and once more asserting that Profumo had lied. Wilson sent a copy to Macmillan and, on 29 May, the Prime Minister and the Leader of the Opposition met, with the outcome that Macmillan agreed to set up immediately an independent inquiry under the Lord Chancellor, Lord Dilhorne.

Profumo was recalled from holiday in Venice and ordered to appear before Dilhorne on 4 June. At last, he seems to have become aware that he had been drinking in the last-chance saloon for far too long; this time he decided to come clean. Feeling that he could not face the questioning at the inquiry, that same day he told Bligh and the Chief Whip, Redmayne, that he had indeed told a lie. He then resigned as a minister and as an MP, with immediate effect. As is usual in such circumstances, his letter to Macmillan and the latter's response were published in the press the following day. Profumo claimed he had lied to protect his wife and family, but the last paragraph of his resignation letter showed that the ex-Minister for War was contrite:

> I cannot tell you of my deep remorse for the embarrassment I have caused you, to my colleagues in the government, to my constituents and to the Party which I have served for the past twenty-five years.

Macmillan's reply was so scant that it was more of a note than a letter. The first sentence read: 'The contents of your letter of 4 June have been communicated to me, and I have heard them with great regret.' By suggesting that he had not even bothered to read Profumo's resignation letter, the wily Prime Minister made it abundantly clear to his former protégé how he viewed his fall from grace.

Profumo may have left the stage, but the show was far from finished. On 5 June, the day after the politician resigned, another trial involving his former mistress started. This time Keeler decided to attend, arriving ostentatiously in a chauffeur-driven Rolls-Royce to give evidence against her other West Indian boyfriend, Lucky Gordon, who was charged with assaulting her outside a friend's flat. The press could hardly believe their luck when Gordon, who conducted his own defence, accused Stephen Ward of being a crank and Keeler of giving him a painful dose of venereal disease.

Ward's dire situation deteriorated even further when, on 8 June, he was charged with living off money from prostitution from January 1961 to June 1963 at his Wimpole Mews flat. As the nation awaited the start of the osteopath's trial in early July, the scandal was hardly ever off the front pages. Bizarre and unlikely stories started to surface. The juiciest was the tale of a man in a mask who served guests at Ward's parties wearing nothing but his socks. Speculation was rife that the masked man was so famous that he had to protect his identity.

Lord Denning,[9] in his report on the Profumo affair, presented to Parliament in September and published at the end of October, indicated that there was more than a grain of truth in this rumour. The Master of the Rolls wrote:

> At some of these parties, the man who serves dinner is nearly naked except for a small lace apron round his waist such as a waitress might wear. He wears a black mask over his head with slits for eyeholes. He therefore cannot be recognized by any of the other guests.

The report went on to add tantalizingly that some parties descended into sex orgies and that the man in the mask was whipped: 'Guests undress and indulge in sexual intercourse one with the other: and indulge in other sexual activities of a revolting and vile nature.'

The public lapped up these revelations about a society vice ring, and the report, unsurprisingly, eventually became a bestseller. There were even suggestions that the masked figure was a member of either the Cabinet or the royal family. When, on 24 June, the *Daily Mirror* ran a headline reading 'Prince Philip and the Profumo Scandal' and printed beneath it a denial that the Queen's husband was linked to the affair, its readers, of course, began to wonder if there was no smoke without fire.

Understandably, Fleet Street was soon accused of muckraking. In response, newspaper editors shifted the emphasis to the security aspects of the affair. On 9 June, Mandy Rice-Davies told the *Sunday Mirror* that on more than one occasion Ivanov arrived to see Keeler as soon as Profumo had left the Wimpole Mews flat. 'In fact, it was something of a standing joke among us,' she revealed with a giggle. Then, on 13 June, Michael Eddowes issued a statement claiming that he had warned the Prime Minister that Profumo was a security risk much earlier than was generally believed. Now even Macmillan's position began to look threatened. The solicitor said he had given a report to Special Branch as early as 29 March but nothing had been done.

When Keeler confirmed in the *News of the World* on 16 June that someone other than Ivanov had asked her to extract sensitive secrets from Profumo, and then, a day later, Harold Wilson accused the Prime Minister of failing to act at the right time, the experienced statesman had to start fighting for his political life. There were even attacks from members of his own party, but Macmillan somehow managed to survive until the autumn. When he resigned that October, just before that year's Conservative Party conference, he said his going was for health reasons, but, in reality, the Profumo affair had irretrievably damaged his credibility. Neither his successor, Sir Alec Douglas-Home, nor the surviving administration were able to throw off the stigma, and the Conservatives lost the 1964 election to the Labour Party under Wilson.

Ward's trial at the Old Bailey at the beginning of July 1963 brought the world's media to London. The eight-day hearing even produced perhaps the most quoted remark in British legal history. When told that Lord Astor denied that he was friendly with her, Mandy Rice-Davies replied, to the packed court's delight: 'Well, he would, wouldn't he?' Ward, when he heard the judge, Sir Archie Pellow Marshall, point the jury towards a guilty verdict, knew that he was doomed. On the night of 3 July, with the judge's summing-up only half completed, he swallowed an overdose of sleeping pills in the Chelsea house of a friend, Noel Howard-Jones, and went into a coma. He was unconscious in St Stephen's Hospital when the jury delivered its verdict. Ward was found guilty on two charges of living off immoral earnings. The osteopath never came round, and died on 3 August.

His suicide note showed that Ward had reached the end of his tether. It also revealed, in its reference to 'them', that he went to his grave convinced that he was the innocent victim of a high-level, politically motivated conspiracy:

Dear Noel, I am sorry that I had to do this here! It is really more than I can stand – the horror, day after day, at the court and in the streets. It is not only fear, it is a wish not to let them get me. I would rather get myself. I do hope I have not let people down too much. I tried to do my stuff, but after Marshall's summing-up I've given up all hope.

The car needs oil in the gearbox, by the way. Be happy in it. Incidentally, it was surprisingly easy and required no guts. I am sorry to disappoint the vultures. I only hope this has done the job. Delay resuscitation as long as possible.

Some of the protagonists of this extraordinary and often tragic saga fared better than others. Keeler did not at first prosper by her involvement. She fell upon hard times after she was imprisoned for nine months for perjury in the Lucky Gordon trial. She wrote a number of books from 1983, and her 1989 autobiography, *Scandal*, which was then made into a film, and other books and articles have kept her name before the public. Mandy Rice-Davies fell out with her erstwhile friend, but also landed on her feet. She wrote novels, became a film actress, opened two nightclubs in Israel and took a millionaire as her second husband. George Wigg was made a peer in 1967 and became chairman of the turf's then funding source, the Horse Race Betting Levy Board, and later president of the Betting Office Licensees' Association. Ironically for one possessed of such crusading moral zeal, he was later charged with kerb crawling for prostitutes near Marble Arch. He died in 1983.

John Profumo vanished from political life and devoted himself to helping the needy at Toynbee Hall in London's East End. He was appointed CBE for his charitable work in 1975. His wife, who remained loyal to her husband after his resignation, died in 1998. Eugene Ivanov was recalled to Russia after the scandal broke, and, presumably because his face was so well known after all the press coverage, was never heard of again in diplomatic or espionage circles. It is probable, however, that his Soviet masters richly rewarded the personable naval attaché for the important role he played in discrediting a Western government at the height of the Cold War. The shy Lord Astor, whose health was never robust, did not recover from the embarrassment of being involved in such a lurid business. He died, just three years later, in 1966.

Conversely, his family home, which had been given by the second Viscount to the National Trust in 1942, survived intact, though it has since ceased to be used as a private house. When a friend informed Harold Macmillan that Cliveden had been turned into a luxury hotel, the former Prime Minister remarked with a wicked grin: 'My dear boy, it always has been!' Could Macmillan have been reminded of his Minister for War chasing a pretty young topless dancer from bedroom to bedroom when he made that observation? It may be that Macmillan, who lived long enough to be viewed, despite his flaws, as the grand old man of British politics (and a belted earl, to boot), believed that such disreputable behaviour was more suited to a commercial establishment for paying guests than an aristocrat's home.

CHAPTER EIGHT

Madresfield Court

THE PICTURESQUE VILLAGE OF MADRESFIELD nestles cosily at the foot of the rolling Malvern Hills. It can be sighted in the distance from the tops of Worcestershire's famous peaks but is hidden from tourists, sightseeing on foot or in their cars in the valleys far below. Indeed, only the tall spire of the Victorian church pinpoints the exact location of the village among the winding lanes and fertile farmland, which was once royal hunting country, on the outskirts of Great Malvern. Stowed away discreetly from the village is Madresfield Court, which may not rival Chatsworth or Blenheim in terms of grandeur but certainly holds its own with its fellow stately homes if the length of its owners' tenure is used as a criterion. Since William Lygon inherited the ancient manor from his grandmother, Isabel de Bracy, in 1456, the same family have held sway at Madresfield Court, although the family's earldom is now extinct.

The Lygons prospered over the centuries, and in 1806 another William Lygon, the Member of Parliament for Worcestershire, was rewarded for his loyalty to the Prime Minister of the day, William Pitt the Younger, and recommended to King George III for a peerage. He chose to be entitled the first Baron Beauchamp of Powyke. Thanks to a vast fortune inherited in 1798 by his Irish wife, Catherine, the Lygons had become one of the richest families in the land. As a result of William's ennoblement, they were now also among the most distinguished, causing the Lord Redesdale of the day to write to a friend: 'I believe that a union with the Beauchamp family is a sincere subject of congratulation.' Just before his death in 1816, William's barony was elevated to an earldom, and the head of the Lygon clan became the first Earl Beauchamp.

Frederick, the sixth Earl, who inherited the title after his brother Henry's death in 1866, was the next Beauchamp to have a distinguished parliamentary career. He was a close confidant of Benjamin Disraeli and became MP for Tewkesbury in 1857. Like the first Earl, he moved on to represent Worcestershire, after his elder brother succeeded to the earldom in 1863. He served as a Lord of the Admiralty in 1859 and was appointed Lord Steward of the Royal Household by Disraeli in 1874.

The Prime Minister's prospective appointee did not meet with Queen Victoria's approval at first. The monarch reputedly did not wish a prominent member of the Anglo-Catholic community to be close to her family on a daily basis. The persuasive Disraeli, however, managed to quell the Queen's fears, and Frederick's time in the royal household appears to have passed without mishap. His last important government appointment was as Paymaster-General between 1885 and 1887. He then retired from national politics and returned to Madresfield to manage his substantial estates.

It is hard to believe, standing in this tranquil rural backwater today, that Madresfield Court, with all its old-world charm and elegance, was the backdrop for a notorious scandal that shook high society to the core in the 1930s. It is also fair to say that the ultra-respectable and fervently religious Frederick would have turned in his grave if he had known that his beloved son and heir, William, was to be responsible for his distinguished family's darkest days.

The birth of William, Viscount Elmley, on 20 February 1872 was an occasion for much rejoicing at Madresfield. Other villages across Worcestershire, Gloucestershire and Herefordshire, where the Beauchamps owned property, also rang their church bells when the joyful news was announced.

William's mother, the former Lady Mary Stanhope, died when he was only three years old, and Frederick's second marriage, to Lady Emily Pierrepoint (both his wives were earls' daughters), in 1878 soon produced more children. Yet there was never any doubt that William was the apple of his father's eye. The significance of his unique position as the heir to Madresfield and to the earldom of Beauchamp was also drummed into the young Viscount from a very early age. At the tender age of five, he was taken by his father to London to sit on the steps of the throne in the the House of Lords during a debate, a privilege accorded to peers' eldest sons.

Despite his mother's untimely death, William seems to have had a happy childhood and was particularly close to his eldest sister, Mary. After school at Eton, he went up to Oxford to his father's old college, Christ Church. He settled in well and shone academically, but tragedy brought his time at the university to a temporary halt in 1891. William had travelled back to Madresfield in late February for a small dinner to celebrate his imminent nineteenth birthday. He returned to Oxford the next day and was immediately summoned by the college Dean, who informed him that his father was seriously ill and that he must return to Madresfield at once. On his train's arrival at Worcester station, he spotted a newspaper billboard carrying the headline: 'Death of Lord Beauchamp.' He later cut out the article reporting his father's demise and pasted it into a scrapbook next to a handwritten note: 'This was the first intimation I had of my father's death.'

The new seventh Earl Beauchamp returned to Oxford after his father's funeral, but his relationship with the Dean of Christ Church, whom he suspected of having wrongly withheld the information that his father was already dead, never recovered. Matters came to a head in 1894 when Beauchamp asked the Dean for permission to attend a twenty-first birthday party for a member of the Duke of Marlborough's family at Blenheim Palace, a few miles from Oxford. The Dean refused, but Beauchamp ignored the ruling and travelled to the celebrations. When the Dean heard of this he was furious, and told Beauchamp that, if he apologized, he would be sent down only for the remainder of the term. The young Earl, who had lost all respect for the college official since his father's death and the way he had learned of it, declined and was consequently expelled. His academic career therefore came to an abrupt end.

Beauchamp's failure to complete his scholastic studies meant an early return to Madresfield. After a Mediterranean cruise to recuperate from an illness brought on by the trauma of being sent down from Oxford, he embarked on what was to turn out to be a long and distinguished career in the world of public affairs. He was elected Mayor of Worcester in 1895 and served on the county council. Although he performed his municipal duties diligently, and also regularly attended the House of Lords, where his politics were viewed as radically progressive, he was surprised when, in 1898, at the age of only twenty-seven, he was appointed Governor of New South Wales on the advice of the Secretary of State for the Colonies, Joseph Chamberlain. Beauchamp received many letters and telegrams congratulating him on his new position. Even that master of humorous verse, Hilaire Belloc, felt moved to comment on the appointment in his *Cautionary Tales*. Belloc's immortal lines, addressed to the hopelessly incompetent Lord Lundy, 'But as it is! ... My language fails! / Go out and govern New South Wales!' were reputedly composed with Beauchamp in mind.

Lord Beauchamp set sail for Australia in April of the following year, taking with him much of the family silver, a good deal of antique furniture and many fine pictures from Madresfield. Being unmarried, in a post for which a wife was generally held to be desirable, he also took his eldest sister, Lady Mary Lygon, a lady-in-waiting to Queen Victoria, who was to act as hostess and accompany her brother to official functions. The old Queen was apparently unhappy at Lady Mary's unexpected resignation from her royal duties, commenting irritably: 'Well, I suppose he must take his nanny with him.'

His radical views and sometimes ill-judged pronouncements certainly upset many of the colony's more established elements. For instance, he enraged French colonists when he condemned the controversial trial in France of the Jewish army officer Alfred Dreyfus, a cause célèbre of its day, thanking God he was an Englishman rather than a Frenchman. He also raised a few eyebrows by embracing the bohemian set, which included such now renowned Australian literary figures as the poets John Le Gay Brereton, Victor Daley and Henry Lawson. All in all, however, while he may have ruffled the feathers of Sydney's conservative social elite on occasions, he fulfilled his gubernatorial duties faithfully and well, earning a commendation from the austere Chamberlain himself. When he left Australia in November 1901, he was pleased to note that the *Sydney Morning Herald* had been more than complimentary about his term of office.

Back in England, Beauchamp nailed his colours firmly to the Liberal Party's mast. He also took measures to preserve the long Lygon lineage by taking a wife within months of his return. On 26 July 1902 he married Lady Lettice Grosvenor, the sister of the immensely rich, and extremely reactionary, second Duke of Westminster. No one present at the wedding, for which no expense was spared, would have predicted the unfortunate scenario that lay ahead for the happy couple. This seemingly perfect union, which was greeted with delight by the Lygon family and all who lived and worked at Madresfield, was destined to act as the catalyst that precipitated Beauchamp's calamitous downfall and disgrace nearly thirty years later.

For, although William Beauchamp was to go on and father a large family, he was also a practising homosexual in an era when such an activity was a criminal offence. Informed gossip indicated that his preference was for the liveried footmen who waited on his family at Madresfield. Guests there reported that expensive diamond rings frequently adorned the fingers of the posse of handsome retainers who served at the dining table, and it was rumoured that these fine jewels were gifts to the young men for granting sexual favours to their aristocratic master. This 'weakness', as it was referred to by his contemporaries, was reasonably well known in the parliamentary and social circles in which the Earl moved; in those more chivalrous days, however, it was deemed improper and ungentlemanly to use such knowledge as a political weapon. As a result, Beauchamp was able to lead his strange double life, confidently believing that he would avoid being exposed by his opponents or the press and that his proclivities would remain undiscovered by his naive wife. His political career prospered and his official standing grew.

Beauchamp accepted a catalogue of official appointments and honours over the next three decades. He was elected to the Privy Council in 1906 and was Lord Steward of the Royal Household to King Edward VII (a position that had also been held by his father) from 1907 to 1910. He served in Liberal Cabinets during the period 1910 to 1918 – which included the entire span of the First World War – and even represented the government at Buckingham Palace when George V signed the declaration of war in 1914. After the war, he remained loyal to the by now ailing Liberals, supporting the party with his fortune and leading it in the House of Lords. By the 1920s Beauchamp was Lord-Lieutenant of Worcestershire, Warden of the Cinque Ports, Chancellor of London University and a Knight of the Order of the Garter, the oldest of all orders of chivalry. In fact, the future could hardly have looked rosier for Lord Beauchamp as the Roaring Twenties drew to a close.

It was, however, a false picture. In 1931 his star dimmed rapidly and his life suddenly fell apart. Why Bendor, Duke of Westminster,[1] should have decided to ruin his brother-in-law at that particular time is not entirely obvious. Perhaps he had not learned of Beauchamp's homosexual tendencies until then, although that would have been odd as they had been common knowledge in London society and its clubland for some years. It may be that the Duke was jealous of his brother-in-law's considerable achievements and his fine record of public service. Alternatively, it is possible that Westminster, who was on the extreme right wing of the Tory Party, objected to Beauchamp using his money to keep the fading Liberal Party afloat, for the reactionary Duke would far rather have seen what he viewed as the party of reform and licence sink into oblivion. Whatever his reasons – and it may simply have been that he harboured a bigoted hatred of homosexuals – destroying Beauchamp's life and career by fomenting a public scandal now became the vindictive Duke's main ambition in life.

Westminster went to work with a vengeance. He informed George V that he had conferred the high honour of Knight of the Garter on a licentious homosexual. The King, appalled, spluttered despairingly: 'I thought men like that shot themselves.' The Duke then made his sister aware of her husband's sexual preferences. This proved to be a tricky business, as the Countess, who had hitherto led a life of sheltered privilege, had never heard of homosexuality. After much explaining, she began at last to understand the gravity of her brother's information, and as a result suffered a dangerous nervous collapse. The Duke then turned his attention to the female Beauchamp children and invited the four daughters – Lady Lettice, Lady Sibell, Lady Mary and Lady Dorothy – to testify against their unfortunate father. Westminster became almost apoplectic with rage when the girls proudly rejected his suggestion out of hand, stoutly maintaining their loyalty to their father in the teeth of their uncle's fury.

The Duke may have lost the chance of humiliating his brother-in-law with a public scandal when the Lygon sisters refused to give evidence, but he did succeed in destroying Lord Beauchamp. At the request of the King, the embattled Earl resigned all his official appointments, with the exception of the Wardenship of the Cinque Ports. He then decided that suicide was the only honourable course of action (thus unconsciously echoing the King's view), but was dissuaded from falling on his sword by the desperate entreaties of his second son, Hughie. Instead, a broken and ruined Beauchamp, deserted by all but his children and a few loyal friends and servants, went into exile abroad, eventually residing in an old Venetian *palazzo*, a building which, like its new occupant, had seen rather better days.

Westminster continued to persecute Beauchamp, to whom, it is alleged, he regularly referred as 'my bugger-in-law' to raise a cheap laugh. When his wife died suddenly on 26 July 1936, the Earl, still in Venice, was determined to return to England to attend the funeral. His legal position was complex, however, as Westminster had persuaded the Home Office to issue a warrant for his brother-in-law's arrest on criminal charges of homosexuality. As this warrant was only effective in the United Kingdom, Beauchamp was not a voluntary exile and could be arrested and charged if he set foot on the shores of his native land.

Beauchamp immediately consulted a young lawyer, Richard Elwes, who was on holiday with his wife in Venice at the time, about his legal position. Elwes quickly travelled back to London and made an appointment with the great advocate Norman Birkett, who at that time held a senior position in the Attorney-General's office. Birkett informed Elwes that his office believed that, on grounds of sympathy, the warrant should not be operated, which would allow Beauchamp to return without fear of arrest. Nevertheless, he also added the caveat that the ultimate decision lay with the Home Secretary, Sir John Simon.

Beauchamp's problems were exacerbated when Bendor Westminster again entered the fray. The Duke informed Simon that it would be a terrible miscarriage of justice if the warrant was made inactive and his brother-in-law was permitted to desecrate the funeral of his, Westminster's, sister. As usual, the powerful Duke eventually had his way and, after much prevarication, the Home Secretary ignored the recommendation of the Attorney-General and ruled that the letter of the law should be strictly followed. Elwes rushed to Dover to intercept the steamer that was carrying the bereaved peer across the Channel. The young lawyer boarded the ferry when it docked at Dover and urged Beauchamp to remain on board, as it was probable that he would be arrested if he disembarked. Sorrowfully, the Earl took his lawyer's wise advice and returned disconsolately to Venice.

Unbelievably, Beauchamp's misfortunes were far from over. On 19 August, less than a month after his wife's death, he suffered another bereavement. This time it was his thirty-two-year-old son, Hughie, who, thanks mainly to alcoholic overindulgence, had been ill for some months. In the late summer, Hughie had decided to recharge his batteries by taking a motoring holiday in Germany with a friend. After travelling all day in an open-topped car under the boiling late-summer sun, Hughie stepped out of the vehicle in the early evening to ask a pedestrian for directions. He fell heavily and fractured his skull. Sadly, he never regained consciousness. Some say he was suffering from sunstroke, others that his fragile health had been failing for some time. Whatever the cause, Hughie was dead before the night was out.

Beauchamp, unsurprisingly, took his beloved son's untimely death extremely badly. He recalled how Hughie had talked him out of suicide when the scandal broke, and was racked with guilt that he had not paid off his son's debts to prevent the stigma of Hughie's recent bankruptcy (although that had, incidentally, been redeemed before his death). Grief-stricken, he contacted Richard Elwes once again and told him that he would definitely be returning to Madresfield for Hughie's funeral. Elwes warned his client that he would risk arrest if he did so, but this time Beauchamp refused to listen.

The young lawyer booked another appointment with Norman Birkett to discuss the new developments. Birkett and his colleagues were again sympathetic and renewed their request to Sir John Simon that the Beauchamp warrant should be rendered inactive if its subject entered the country. The Home Secretary, believing that the Earl had suffered enough, mercifully changed his tune. To the fury of the Duke of Westminster, the warrant was immediately suspended and later annulled. Beauchamp attended his son's funeral, and in 1937 returned to live quietly at Madresfield.

William, the seventh Earl Beauchamp, did not outlive his son by long. On 10 November 1938 he died of cancer in the Waldorf-Astoria Hotel in New York while on a visit to the United States to fulfil a long-standing speaking engagement. He was sixty-six. During his years of exile, in addition to Venice, Beauchamp had spent time on the French Riviera and in Germany, but Australia remained his favourite place. He made three return visits to Sydney, where he had served as Governor-General of New South Wales at the turn of the century, in 1932, 1934 and just before his death in 1938. A clue to what caused him to return to the Antipodes so often may be provided by something he wrote in 1931, not long after he fled England for exile in Venice: 'The men are splendid athletes, like Greek statues. Their skins are tanned by sun and wind, and I doubt whether anywhere in the world are finer specimens of manhood than in Sydney. The life-savers at the bathing beach are wonderful.'

In a curious twist, the tale of Bendor Westminster's hounding of his brother-in-law resurfaced in 2005 with the death, aged ninety-eight, of the seventh Earl Beauchamp's last surviving daughter, Lady Sibell Rowley. Her obituary in *The Times* that November, which had repeated the tale of Westminster's denouncing of Beauchamp, prompted Brigadier Robin Rhoderick-Jones, something of an expert on the Grosvenor family, to write to the paper, refuting that Bendor had 'denounced his brother-in-law as homosexual and demanded his arrest'. 'It was,' he wrote, 'King George V, two of whose sons, Princes Henry and Edward, were spending time at Madresfield, who was responsible for Beauchamp's exile.' He continued: 'The King tasked his legal adviser, Lord Buckmaster, to investigate Beauchamp's behaviour. Statements were taken from servants at Walmer Castle (where Beauchamp was Lord Warden of the Cinque Ports), Madresfield and the Beauchamp house in Belgrave Square. The evidence was overwhelming and Buckmaster went to see Beauchamp and advised him to go abroad to avoid arrest and the scandal.'

Brigadier Rhoderick-Jones also denies that Lady Beauchamp 'was unable to grasp the implications of her husband's habits', citing a letter from the Countess to her children in May 1931 which 'makes it clear that not only had she been aware of his bizarre behaviour, but she also approved of his exile . . . In short, Bendor approved wholeheartedly of the action taken against Beauchamp but was not responsible for it.'

Whatever the truth, however – and the tale may have been distorted by Lygon family history – there is no doubt that the second Duke of Westminster was capable of behaving in a thoroughly unpleasant manner, using his wealth and power (he was the richest man in Britain, and his descendant, the present Duke, is very nearly that) to get his way. Although his friends liked and admired him, there were many people who came to rue the day they had fallen foul of Bendor. He also demonstrated a certain aristocratic laxness in moral matters. Although first married in 1901, he was to have many affairs, most notably, for five years from 1925 (he divorced his second wife in 1926), with the great French couturier Coco (Gabrielle) Chanel, inventor of the 'little black dress'. He married again in 1930, divorced again in 1947 and, that year, married his fourth and last wife. He died in 1953 and, since his only son had died, aged five, in 1909, his title passed to a cousin.

The less pleasant aspects of Bendor Westminster's character were caught by that shrewd observer of society, Lady Diana Cooper (herself the daughter of a duke) in one volume of her memoirs (*The Light of Common Day*, 1959). On 1 September 1939, the day on which Germany invaded Poland, thus precipitating the Second World War, she and her husband, Duff Cooper,[2] who had resigned from the government in protest at the Munich Agreement of the year before, lunched with Westminster at the Savoy in London. According to Lady Diana, Bendor began by 'abusing the Jewish race' before going on to praise Nazi Germany and 'rejoicing that we were not yet at war'. When, she continued, 'he added that Hitler knew after all that we were his best friends, he set off the powder magazine. Duff spat "that by tomorrow he will know that we are his most implacable and remorseless enemies". Next day Bendor, telephoning to a friend, said that if there was a war it would be entirely due to the Jews and Duff Cooper.' On the following day, 3 September, Britain declared war on Germany.

The tragic tale did not die with its protagonist, however. Indeed, it was reborn just seven years later. In 1945 the publication of what is probably Evelyn Waugh's most famous novel, *Brideshead Revisited*, contrived to propel Madresfield Court, the seventh Earl Beauchamp and his long-suffering family back into the public eye. Waugh often drew heavily on his own experiences for his fiction, with the result that his friends and acquaintances and the houses where they lived can regularly be recognized in his books. *Brideshead* is no exception, and members of the Lygon family can be readily identified as models for characters in the book. By the same token, a private chapel, a memorable feature of their home at Madresfield, is clearly a model for a similar place of worship in the fictional stately home, Brideshead.

Waugh met the Lygon family in the early 1920s when he was an undergraduate in his second year at Oxford. He first encountered Lord Beauchamp's heir, Viscount Elmley, who had arrived at Oxford at the same time as him. When his younger brother, the Hon. Hughie Lygon, came up to Oxford in 1922, Elmley introduced him to Waugh and the two quickly became firm friends. It was not long before Hughie asked his fellow undergraduate to stay at Madresfield.

As a result of frequent visits to the Lygon seat in Worcestershire over the ensuing years, Waugh got to know Lord Beauchamp and his family well. Perhaps because of his own comfortably middle-class upbringing (exacerbated by a sometimes ferocious snobbery), he also acquired a taste for the rather decadent and extremely comfortable country-house existence that a Madresfield weekend, with its attentive staff, fine wines and excellent food, presented. As any aspiring novelist would, therefore, he filed the eccentric Lygons and their opulent lifestyle away in a corner of his mind for use at a later date.[3]

Waugh, who was actually abroad when the Beauchamp scandal erupted in 1931, tended to play down the connection between the Lygons and the Flytes, the fictional family who live at Brideshead, but there are certain similarities which suggest that Madresfield and its extraordinary domestic situation in the early 1930s was at the forefront of his mind when he sat down to write the novel more than ten years later.

In the novel, Lord Marchmain, the head of the Flyte family, leaves England to live as an exile in Venice, just as Beauchamp did. But Marchmain's caddish behaviour – he went to live abroad in 1914 with his Italian mistress – would at that time have been considered much tamer than his real-life counterpart's conduct. Some commentators, understandably enough, have expressed surprise that Waugh did not saddle Marchmain with the same sort of homosexual scandal that brought about Beauchamp's ostracism and his persecution at the hands of his brother-in-law. Arguably, a disguised description of Beauchamp's glittering career and subsequent fall from grace would have added a dangerous touch of illicit spice and made for a more intriguing novel.

Waugh was always cagey about the origins of his plots, but it is possible that he thought that a more-or-less accurate retelling of Beauchamp's problems would have caused great upset to Lady Mary Lygon and her sister, Lady Dorothy, who were among his greatest friends at the time. In the end, Marchmain poignantly returns to Brideshead to die. Beauchamp, on the other hand, died in New York but was buried at Madresfield, where he had been living for a year after the end of his six-year exile. So both the fictional character and his inspiration were able to come back to their family homes to exorcize their demons, and eventually to rest there in peace.

Waugh acknowledged to his biographer, Christopher Sykes, that Hughie Lygon was partly the model for Sebastian Flyte in

Brideshead Revisited, and this connection is therefore not in doubt. The appearance of the effete but attractive second son of Lord Marchmain, as well as his family circumstances, have clear parallels with Hughie, but Waugh is on record as having admitted that there was also a strong element of another Oxford undergraduate, Alastair Graham,[4] in Sebastian's make-up. The fact that the name Alastair sometimes appears in the original manuscript in place of Sebastian seems to corroborate the writer's assertion.

The writer was hugely attracted to the hedonistic Aesthetic Movement, which, in a nod to Oscar Wilde and the 'Aesthetes' of the 1890s, was launched at Oxford after the First World War by two homosexual students, the cultured Harold Acton and the flamboyant Brian Howard. There is a good deal of evidence that Waugh emulated his new role models by taking several male lovers. Indeed, Sykes concedes that his subject 'entered an extreme homosexual phase at the time'. Waugh's biographer also adds that the phase was 'unrestrained, emotionally and physically'. So it is more than likely that the novelist had affairs with both Hughie Lygon and Alastair Graham, since both were in the same set and among his closest acquaintances.

In the same way that he sanitized the memory of Beauchamp by giving Marchmain a mistress rather than a male lover, Waugh chose to omit the homosexual side of his own relationship with Hughie in his portrait of Sebastian Flyte. This is probably why he decided to make the book's narrator, Charles Ryder, who acts as the author's mouthpiece, entirely heterosexual and thus 'respectable'. Waugh simply wanted to cover up what he later saw as the less savoury side of his friendships with Hughie and Graham.

Lord Brideshead, Sebastian's eldest brother, also bears some resemblance to Hughie's sibling, Lord Elmley, who later became the eighth – and last – Earl Beauchamp. Like his brother, William Elmley was very much part of the more riotous side of university life at Oxford, and was president of The Hypocrites, a rather insignificant drinking club which had premises close to Christ Church, the college that both Lygons attended. Waugh was also a member of the club, having been introduced by an eccentric undergraduate friend, Terence Greenidge.

In the Michaelmas (autumn) term of 1922, The Hypocrites was invaded by a number of Old Etonian freshmen, including Hughie Lygon. Waugh described this group, later to style itself as the 'Aesthetic Movement', in *A Little Learning* as 'notable for their flamboyance of dress and manner, which was in some cases patently homosexual'. Waugh continues that Elmley, anxious to placate disapproving older and staider members of the club, decreed that 'Gentlemen may prance but not dance.' In later years Elmley may well have wished that he had been firmer with his former schoolfellows, such as Acton and Howard. Arguably, a close association with this bizarre clique was the principal reason for the start of his impressionable younger brother's precipitous descent into alcoholism, which was undoubtedly a contributing factor to his early death.

Christopher Sykes was probably right when he said that the rest of the Flyte family were products of Waugh's fertile imagination. Lady Marchmain in the novel certainly bears no resemblance to Lady Beauchamp, and the lives of the four Lygon sisters did not turn out remotely like those of Lord Marchmain's two daughters, Julia and Cordelia. The origins of two of the other minor characters in *Brideshead Revisited* are easy to work out, however.

Rex Mottram, Julia's ambitious husband, is a splendidly poisonous, if rather ungrateful, portrait of Brendan Bracken, the Canadian-born Tory politician who facilitated the writing of *Brideshead Revisited* by arranging for Waugh to have three months' leave from the Royal Marines. Even though he owed the then Minister of Information an enormous debt for acquiring this helpful sabbatical, Waugh detested Bracken and was delighted to savage him in print.

The inspiration for Mr Samgrass, Sebastian's oily 'minder', was the distinguished classical scholar and warden of Wadham College, Sir Maurice Bowra, who tutored Waugh at Oxford. When, after the novel was published, he heard that the eminent don had said that

[173]

he was not offended by the caricature, Waugh was reportedly extremely irritated. Bowra may well have come across Elmley and Hughie Lygon at Oxford, but there is no evidence that he or Bracken ever visited Madresfield Court.

Waugh always said that the waspish and outrageously camp Anthony Blanche was based on Brian Howard. Blanche is partly Jewish, as Howard was. He also calls his male friends 'my dear', as Howard constantly did. But Sykes argues convincingly that there was just as much of Harold Acton in the character. He claims that Waugh had heard that Acton was hurt by the portrait, and consequently tried to relieve an awkward situation by insisting that the character was a mixture of invention and Howard. As Waugh gave Blanche a cosmopolitan background – Acton was partly American, and his family home was in Florence – and allowed him to utter several genuine Acton dictums in *Brideshead,* this splendidly drawn character is surely a cocktail containing ingredients of both the co-founders of Oxford's Aesthetic Movement.

The great house in the novel has recognizable features of Castle Howard, where the television series of *Brideshead Revisited* was made in the early 1980s. The distinctive lantern at the Yorkshire house might easily have given Waugh the idea for the majestic dome that surmounts the fictional Brideshead. Additionally, the magnificent fountain facing the southern front of Castle Howard is similar in size and splendour to the fountain described in the book. But the model for the private chapel, which figures prominently and importantly in the novel, is certainly Madresfield's superb Art Nouveau example, with its ornate decorations by Henry Payne and, on its walls, paintings of the Lygon children. It is a last irony that Payne's designs for the Madresfield chapel were paid for with the Duke of Westminster's family money, for this fine example of the work of the contemporary Arts and Crafts Movement was the wedding present to Lord Beauchamp from his wife, Westminster's sister.

CHAPTER NINE

Powderham Castle

POWDERHAM CASTLE sits on the western side of the attractive Exe estuary, about four miles from where Devon's famous river meets the sea at Exmouth. The castle, which is not far from Kenton, has been the home of the Earls of Devon, who carry the family name of Courtenay, for over 600 years. Sir Philip Courtenay started constructing a fortress on the site in 1390. It took thirty years to complete the task, but the castle that stands there today is mostly a Victorian renovation, designed by Charles Fowler, the architect of London's Covent Garden.

Traces, however, remain to remind the visitor of Powderham's distant past. The chapel behind the rose terrace at the castle's rear still bears a fifteenth-century roof. Fourteenth-century arches are also visible in the passages leading to the kitchens and the buttery. It was an inspired ploy of Fowler's to recreate the exterior to resemble the turreted medieval castle that had stood there in Sir Philip's day.

The interior, on the other hand, is designed with a Georgian country house in mind and contains many elegant rooms. The magnificent staircase hall that leaps skywards the whole height of the house is an architectural masterpiece. The walls, decorated with charming birds and animals and motifs that celebrate peace and love, contribute to a romantic atmosphere. There is also a fabulous Music Room by James Wyatt, which was added to the castle in 1794 to celebrate the coming of age of William, third Viscount Courtenay of Powderham Castle and, later, ninth Earl of Devon.

The Courtenays crossed from France with William the Conqueror, and the early members of the British branch of the family seem to have been fearless knights, proficient in the arts of war and jousting. Indeed, Sir Philip's father, Hugh Courtenay, was so gallant that he was made a founder member of the Order of the Garter in 1344 at the tender age of seventeen. Later, Powderham was garrisoned twice for Charles I during the Civil War, and twice taken by the Parliamentarians. So it is clear that the brave Courtenays continued to serve king and country and to distinguish themselves in the profession of arms over the ensuing years. Yet it was against this proud, soldierly background that what was certainly the most infamous homosexual scandal of its time was played out, with, at centre stage, the young man in whose honour Powderham's famous Music Room would be built.

In June 1779 the inordinately wealthy William Beckford, who was on a tour of English country houses, came to visit Powderham. When Beckford, who was only nineteen years of age, saw William, the youngest child and only son of Lord and Lady Courtenay, he was smitten by the eleven-year-old's good looks and fair countenance and instantly fell in love. This infatuation, which appears to have become mutual quite quickly, continued for the next five years. But before turning to the affair and the incident that brought about its bitter and acrimonious end, it is worth examining the extraordinary life and circumstances of the wildly eccentric Beckford, whose reputation was to be ruined by his involvement with the aristocrat whom high society christened the most beautiful boy in England.

RIGHT: Sir Harold Nicolson and his wife, the writer Vita Sackville-West, relax at their home in Sissinghurst Castle in 1932. Each had a string of extramarital homosexual affairs, but Vita's notorious liaison with Violet Trefusis (*below*) from 1918–21 was something both more serious, and more scandalous.

RIGHT: Society osteopath Stephen Ward poses for the camera with a bevy of beauties, including Christine Keeler (*right*) in 1963. The carefree snapshot betrays nothing of the scandal and tragedy that were to follow.

William Lygon, seventh Earl Beauchamp (*above*). Viciously persecuted for his homosexuality by his brother-in-law, the second Duke of Westminster (*left*), Lord Beauchamp was forced to leave his beloved home, Madresfield Court, and live in exile for six long years.

It Had To Be You: As soon as William Beckford (*above*) laid eyes on William Courtenay, the future ninth Earl of Devon (*left*), he was smitten. Their subsequent liaison was the most infamous homosexual scandal of its time, and brought allegations of indecency to the Courtenay ancestral home, Powderham Castle.

ABOVE: Lady Caroline Lamb, in a drawing from *circa* 1820, whose passionate affair with the Romantic poet Lord Byron shocked high society. Famously, she described her lover as 'Mad, bad and dangerous to know.'

RIGHT: William Lamb, second Viscount Melbourne, the first of two prime ministers to own Brocket Hall (the sexually rapacious Viscount Palmerston was the other). Lamb's wife's infidelity wasn't the only scandal in his family: he himself was taken to court on two separate occasions by husbands who were enraged at the attention he was paying to their wives.

ABOVE: Edward VII, with his long-suffering wife Queen Alexandra, at the opening of his first Parliament in 1901.

LEFT: Prince Albert Victor, eldest son of Edward and Alexandra, who was known as Prince Eddy; he died aged twenty-eight before he could inherit the throne. As well as being involved in a notorious homosexual ring, his name has been suggested as the true identity of the infamous Victorian serial killer 'Jack the Ripper'.

RIGHT: The Jersey Lily: Lillie Langtry, mistress to Edward VII and actress extraordinaire, in the painting by Millais which launched her into the highest reaches of society.

LEFT: Alice Keppel, often said to have been Edward VII's greatest love, and the last of his many mistresses. She is a direct ancestress of the Duchess of Cornwall, the former Camilla Parker Bowles, as well as being the mother of Violet Trefusis, with whom the writer Vita Sackville-West had a scorching lesbian liaison in the 1920s.

Beckford was born on 20 September 1760. His father, also William, known universally as Alderman Beckford, was twice Lord Mayor of London. The Beckfords may have been nouveaux riches, but they were exorbitantly wealthy. The Alderman's grandfather, Peter Beckford, had been Governor of Jamaica, where he had made a fortune from his sugar plantations and the slave trade; however, since he was killed in a brawl in 1711, it seems that, even then, the family had a roguish streak. His son, also named Peter, was active in politics and became Speaker of the Jamaican Assembly, although he had a fierce temper and fatally stabbed the island's Deputy Judge Advocate. His brother, Thomas, also met a sticky end, dying by the hand of a man he had insulted. Peter, the Speaker, died in 1735; the rough-and-ready Alderman was his second son.

The Alderman, who had a strong Jamaican accent, went to school at Westminster in London and became a Whig MP, renowned for his radical views. In 1736 he bought the magnificent estate of Fonthill, near Hindon. He liked this beautiful and peaceful part of Wiltshire and soon settled down to live the life of a country gentleman. When the existing house was burned down in 1755, the Alderman used a substantial part of his vast fortune to replace his old dwelling with an enormous and opulent Palladian palace. He may have rebuked George III in a public speech when the King was present, but he had powerful friends, such as William Pitt the Elder, the Earl of Chatham, who became young William Beckford's godfather. He is also said to have had coarse manners, but was, nevertheless, a cultured man, whose huge wealth enabled him to become an important collector and patron of the arts.

When the Alderman died suddenly as a result of a chill in 1770, the young William, at the age of nine, inherited an enormous country house, an estate of 6,000 acres, capital of a massive £1.5 million, and an income from his Jamaican holdings of a breath-taking £70,000 a year. To put it bluntly, the late Alderman's only legitimate child could now rejoice in the title of Britain's richest man.

The Alderman was certainly not ashamed of his somewhat doubtful antecedents, and would often tease his young son that his paternal family were plebeian. William's mother, though, had plenty of aristocratic blood flowing through her veins. She was born Maria Hamilton, the daughter of the Hon. George Hamilton, the MP for the cathedral city of Wells in Somerset. Maria Beckford was therefore a granddaughter of the sixth Earl of Abercorn.

William was always extremely proud of his mother's ancient lineage, and less than enamoured of his father's more vulgar family history. Nevertheless, he inherited some of his paternal line's less desirable traits. His wilfulness, arrogance and bad temper certainly came from the Beckfords, although he did not possess their rugged masculinity. In fact, as his mother was too apprehensive to send him away to school, he grew into a delicate, sensitive teenager with an overactive imagination. Perhaps because he had no friends of his own age to distract him, he worked hard for the tutors[1] his mother imported, becoming extremely well read as well as fluent in several languages. Yet in reality William, who had everything, led a sad and isolated life at Fonthill.

By the time he reached his teenage years, he had already acquired some strange and exotic tastes for one so young. He became obsessed with the Orient and the occult. The famous 'Turkish Room', which his father had constructed at Fonthill, with its extravagant russet Persian carpet, orange silk curtains, ottomans and large floor cushions, was undoubtedly the origin of his love for all things Eastern. There is also no doubt that the painter Alexander Cozens, who was commissioned by his mother to teach her son drawing, fostered Beckford's passion for the occult. The Russian-born artist introduced his pupil to the work of Ossian and *The Arabian Nights* and to the principles of magic. In fact, Beckford was so far under Cozens's spell at the age of seventeen that he wrote *The Vision* (also known as *The Long Story*) for his mentor. In this strange tale, the artist is identified with the hero, the high priest, who can read the author's 'innermost soul'.

The perceptive Cozens may have understood why his pupil was reluctant to end his leisurely life in a fantasy world to pursue a career in public service, but Beckford's mother emphatically did not. 'The Begum', as her son had cheekily christened her, wanted Beckford to follow his father into the political arena and represent the pocket borough (a borough in which the election of an MP was controlled by one person or family) of Hindon in Parliament. She was also worried about his preoccupation with the East and the occult, and even wrote to his godfather, Lord Chatham, about her concerns. She did not like William's second excursion into the literary world either. When, in 1780, Beckford published his *Biographical Memoirs of Extraordinary Painters* – a skit on criticisms of certain Dutch painters he had read and disagreed with – to an indifferent reception and uncomplimentary reviews, his mother was furious, believing that her son should devote his energies to more worthwhile and more gentlemanly projects, such as politics and field sports.

In 1777, before he published *Biographical Memoirs*, the Begum had sent her wayward son to complete his education in Geneva, a long way from the temptations of Fonthill. Beckford was accompanied on his journey to Switzerland by his tutor, the Reverend John Lettice. As usual, he excelled at his studies, becoming fluent in Italian, Spanish, German and Portuguese. He even met Voltaire, who was most complimentary about his father's contribution to the cause of liberalism. But if his mother had thought that the bracing Swiss air might have made her son stronger and manlier, she was wrong. He refused to socialize with his hard-drinking, sports-loving student colleagues and instead sought out the company of European intellectuals, agnostics and philosophers. Alerted by the loyal and straitlaced Lettice that his charge was mixing in dangerous circles, Mrs Beckford lost her nerve and hurried to Geneva to bring her wayward son back to England.

On his return from Europe, Beckford continued to disappoint his mother. Although he liked riding, he refused to hunt or shoot. He hated all forms of cruelty to animals, such as bullfighting, and even referred to those who captured butterflies in nets as 'torturers'. He was also happier in the company of his dogs than in that of his fellow human beings. His deeply anxious mother determined to try once more to persuade her son to take up rural pursuits and to delight in the more conventional pleasures of the country set. It was for this reason that she hatched the plan she was later to regret – to dispatch Beckford and his long-suffering tutor, Lettice, on that ill-fated tour of England's stately homes.

Whether Beckford's love for William Courtenay was reciprocated on his first visit to Powderham is not known, but he was soon confiding to friends that he could think of nobody other than the curly-haired youth. He told Alexander Cozens of his infatuation, and even informed the boy's aunt, Charlotte Courtenay, who, bizarrely, fell for Beckford herself. He wrote revealing love letters to the object of his affections, calling Courtenay pet names, such as 'Little C' and 'the little Dove'. Unwisely, such indiscreet behaviour and a reckless flaunting of his feelings for the boy were to continue over the next few years and eventually cause Beckford's downfall.

Meanwhile, a worried Lettice, aware of his pupil's unhealthy interest in their host's son, somehow managed to drag Beckford away from Devon. He took his charge to the Lake District, but the damage had been done. Back at Fonthill, the tutor told the Begum of her son's infatuation with the Courtenay boy. She responded by inviting her husband's nephew, Peter Beckford, later to write *Thoughts Upon Hunting*, and his beautiful wife, Louisa, to Fonthill. If her intention was to provide an attractive older woman to direct her son's attentions away from Courtenay, his mother could hardly have made a bigger mistake. Instead, Louisa fell head over heels in love with William and became a willing accomplice in the pursuit of 'Kitty', as they called Courtenay. Mrs Beckford, who was now desperate to curtail her son's dangerous liaison before he came of age, sent him and Lettice on an extended Continental tour in the summer of 1780.

Absence certainly made the heart grow fonder in Beckford's case. He lusted over a handsome Italian youth in Venice but was racked with guilt that he had betrayed Courtenay. He continued to bombard his loved one with affectionate letters, telling Kitty that he could not wait to return to England. In the spring and summer of 1781, Beckford spent his time in London and at Fonthill, where he was preparing for his twenty-first birthday celebrations. In the capital, he continued his dalliance with Courtenay, who was at school at Westminster. Amazingly, the pair managed to spend weekends together in the Wimpole Street house of Beckford's mother, who presumably was not in residence at the time. Beckford even arranged for George Romney, one of the leading portraitists of his day, to paint Courtenay's portrait.

Louisa, still smitten with her cousin by marriage, was a regular visitor when Beckford moved down to Fonthill. Extraordinarily, she seems to have been quite happy to play second fiddle to Courtenay in Beckford's affections, writing gushingly: 'How my heart bounds with transport when I fancy that after Kitty I am the being you prefer to all others!' Luckily for Beckford, she was also prepared to act as a go-between, arranging secret trysts and carrying compromising letters when the boy was with his parents at Powderham during holidays from school.

Beckford carried out his duties to his mother, his family, his neighbours and his tenants at his coming-of-age celebrations on 29 September 1781 in exemplary fashion. There were magnificent feasts, endless dancing and plenty of fireworks and bonfires. However, as he had now reached the age of majority, he was able to ask whomever he liked to celebrate the following Christmas at Fonthill. Since Kitty headed the guest list, his parents, the Courtenays, unlike the Begum, must have been satisfied at this juncture that there was nothing untoward in their son's extremely close relationship with Beckford. Otherwise, they would surely never have allowed their young heir to attend the long and hedonistic party that England's richest man hosted in Wiltshire that December.

Alexander Cozens also joined Kitty at the party. So did Louisa who, unsurprisingly, contrived to come without her husband, Peter. Her brother, George Pitt, and her best friend, Sarah Musters, with whom Pitt was having a raging affair, also attended. Beckford's Hamilton cousins, Archibald and Alexander (the latter was later to become his host's son-in-law), were also there, and brought with them their tutor, the Reverend Samuel Henley, who, like Beckford, was fascinated by oriental literature and mysticism.

If Beckford's assertion in later life that he based many scenes in his Gothic novel, *Vathek*, on these bacchanalian celebrations is to be believed, this exclusive group, and he and Courtenay in particular, enjoyed a veritable orgy of music, acting, eating, drinking and lovemaking that Christmas.

In *Vathek*, which he wrote, in French, in January 1782[2] and published in 1786, Beckford characterized himself as the eponymous hero, a wicked caliph who is obsessed with sensual pleasures and builds a tower to heaven so that he can discover its forbidden secrets. Prince Gulchenrouz, who is described as 'the most delicate and lovely creature in the world', is clearly inspired by Kitty. This effeminate character exhibits transvestite tendencies, delighting in putting on the frocks and dresses of Princess Nouronihar, who is modelled on Kitty's aunt, Charlotte, who had worshipped Beckford since they had first met at Powderham. Princess Caranthis, who is a cruel parody of Beckford's mother, the Begum, is a witch who casts evil spells with magic potions made out of the powder of Egyptian mummies and frogs' warts.

Vathek gradually goes mad and, in an insane fit of jealousy, murders Gulchenrouz and Nouronihar. Gulchenrouz immediately ascends to heaven, where he never grows up and is surrounded by a harem of beautiful and alluring young boys. The caliph then sacrifices fifty handsome and graceful youths by throwing them over a cliff one by one, only for them to be rescued by a genie and transported to heaven to join Gulchenrouz and his sensual court. Vathek pays dearly for killing the one he loved and eventually ends up in hell.

This decadent, often humorous and partly autobiographical work clearly shows how besotted Beckford was with Courtenay at that time, but it was Louisa's indiscreet behaviour in the following spring and summer that obliged him to take another trip abroad. The third part of this strange *ménage à trois* had now grown to hate her boorish husband, and she told anyone who cared to listen of her all-consuming passion for his cousin. Knowing that she would never rival Kitty in the contest for Beckford's affections, she became even more desperate when she heard that her cousin by marriage might well become engaged to Lady Margaret Gordon. She wrote in anguish: 'Why must she possess lawfully and eternally what I would suffer ten thousand deaths to enjoy one instant? William, it must not be.' Her plea fell on deaf ears, and Beckford left England in May 1782.

As was usual when he was away, Beckford quickly started pining for Courtenay. He was ecstatic when, in Rome, he received a short note from Kitty, and replied in breathless fashion: 'I read your letter with a beating heart, my dearest Willy, and kissed it a thousand times. It is needless to repeat that I am miserable without you.' When he returned to England in November, he was greeted with the news that Louisa was seriously ill with tuberculosis. She pleaded for Beckford to visit her, but he callously refused.

In early 1783 the storm clouds began to gather ominously for Beckford and Courtenay. On 29 March Beckford wrote to Louisa in France, where she was convalescing, confirming his wholehearted love for Kitty. Courtenay added a resentful postscript to the note, informing her that they were together, having 'lived so long in Hell. You cannot imagine how we have been persecuted.' The persecution mentioned in the missive was perpetrated by none other than the Princess Nouronihar of *Vathek*, Kitty's aunt, Charlotte, who had been spurned by Beckford some time earlier.

Charlotte had never forgiven Beckford for his lack of interest in her, and she began to sow seeds of doubt in the minds of Kitty's parents. Lord Courtenay, especially, became very suspicious that Beckford's designs on his son and heir were not exactly platonic. When Charlotte married Britain's Lord Chief Justice, Alexander Wedderburn, Lord Loughborough, in September 1782, she had gained a valuable accomplice in her quest to make the millionaire pay for corrupting her innocent nephew. The bigoted Loughborough and the liberally minded Beckford were poles

[183]

apart, and the latter had mocked and criticized the judge's trenchant right-wing views whenever they had met. Consequently, Loughborough hated the arrogant Beckford, as he had also detested his Whig father, the Alderman, who had been a formidable political rival. The Lord Chief Justice was therefore quite happy to use his exalted position on the bench to make his enemy suffer.

As the now distraught Louisa had predicted, Lady Margaret Gordon, the attractive daughter of the Earl of Aboyne, usurped her place in the unusual threesome when she married Beckford on 4 May 1783. Although Beckford adored his young wife, who, commendably, was to stand by him when he was at his lowest ebb, Kitty was still in the forefront of his mind when he honeymooned in Switzerland. Lines from a wistful letter he wrote to Cozens at the time reveal a troubled state of mind. 'During these moments I dream of Wm and Fonthill whilst the confused murmur of leaves and water lull me to sound rest. Lady M walks about gathering flowers from the Shrubs which almost dip their boughs in the Lake. Why am I not happy – Is it not my own fault that I am miserable?' He still felt the same pangs for Courtenay when back at Fonthill with his new bride in March 1784, again corresponding with Cozens in a similar tone. 'With respect to Wm I have been this fortnight past in total darkness. How I long for the sight of his lovely countenance.'

Kitty was tugging dangerously at Beckford's heartstrings, but outwardly things were looking favourable for the newly married couple. They were presented at court, and Beckford, still only twenty-three, delighted his mother by becoming the MP for her father's old seat at Wells. The Begum understandably thought that the spectre of Courtenay was fading as the adoring Margaret catered for her husband's every whim. There was even talk in London that Beckford was in line for a peerage.

In June, however, a shadow fell across the Beckfords' life when Margaret gave birth to a stillborn son. But, by October, Beckford's star was back in the ascendant. The society gossips had been right, and he was in fact gazetted for a peerage; indeed, matters were so far advanced that the title of Lord Beckford of Fonthill had already been inscribed on the patent.

Then these rays of sunshine changed all too quickly to darkness. It may have been a vicious plan conceived by the Lord Chief Justice to lure Beckford into Lady Loughborough's nephew's arms, or Kitty may have managed to persuade his suspicious father that his lover's sexual preferences had changed since marriage, but the end result was that the Beckfords, rather surprisingly, were invited to stay at Powderham that autumn. The Loughboroughs were fellow guests.

Within a fortnight, Beckford, throwing caution to the winds, left his bedroom early one morning and entered Kitty's room. The boy's tutor, awakened by a commotion, hurried to the door. Finding it locked, he peered through the keyhole and allegedly saw Beckford and Kitty indulging in a homosexual act. The tutor, like a true voyeur, reputedly watched the operation through to its conclusion, then rushed to inform his employer. In turn, the appalled Lord Courtenay told Loughborough, who confronted Beckford and accused the millionaire of committing sodomy, then a capital offence, with his nephew. Beckford angrily retorted that the tutor was telling a pack of lies, and claimed that he had actually been thrashing Courtenay. Kitty, however, under severe cross-examination by his aunt's husband, was forced to confess and surrendered piles of incriminating letters. To all intents and purposes Beckford was finished.

Perhaps Loughborough had persuaded the tutor to fabricate the story or, at any rate, to exaggerate what had occurred, but it was manna from heaven as far as the Lord Chief Justice was concerned. He made sure that everybody who mattered knew that Beckford had been caught perpetrating an indecent act. Soon the newspapers picked up the story and printed the salacious details. The *Morning Herald* stated, in a masterly double entendre: 'The rumour concerning a Grammatical mistake of Mr B. and the Hon. Mr C. in regard to the genders, we hope for the honour of Nature originates in Calumny!' Reports in other publications, unluckily for Beckford, were less ambiguous.

A meeting of the Beckford, Courtenay and Gordon families was hastily convened. Only the Begum and Margaret seem to have believed Beckford, the two women in his life vehemently protesting that he was innocent. Bizarrely (or perhaps desperately), Mrs Beckford even suggested that her son should pick up six female prostitutes in Covent Garden and parade them around Mayfair to prove to London society that he was heterosexual. Margaret suggested a more sensible course of action, advising her husband to flee to the Continent. Beckford travelled to Dover on 29 October but then suffered a brave change of heart. With his head bowed, he decided to return to Fonthill to face the unpleasant music his enemies were playing with such relish.

No court case ever took place, so it is likely that Loughborough, who knew the law inside out, was well aware that his evidence was too thin to secure a conviction. But he had achieved what he had set out to do. His wife, Charlotte, had wanted Beckford ruined, and so he was. His good name and any political ambitions, including the peerage that he longed for and had so nearly procured, were gone for good. High society ostracized the master of Fonthill, and he was continuously snubbed for the remaining sixty years of his life. As a result, this sensitive and romantic figure retreated deeper and deeper into his shell. He became embittered, and even more distrustful of his fellow man than he had been in his childhood.

Beckford never saw again – or forgave – the disgraced Kitty, who, for his own good, was confined to Powderham by his disappointed father. In his *Portuguese Journal* of 1787, Beckford castigated Courtenay for stupidly letting their private correspondence slip into Loughborough's dangerous hands. With real vitriol, he reviled his former lover for allowing 'the most obnoxious papers to remain in Beelzebub's clutches', although how incriminating they were remains uncertain. He made his feelings even clearer by going on to describe Kitty as 'that cowardly effeminate fool, Wm Courtenay'.

In 1785 the Beckfords, unable to rid themselves of the ignominy of the Powderham scandal, moved to Switzerland. All too soon, Margaret died of puerperal fever after giving birth to their second daughter. Beckford was devastated. He had lost his rock and greatest support in an increasingly hostile world. He had no idea how to look after his two baby daughters, so he sent the girls back to London to be brought up by his ever-obliging mother. When he read the cruel and untruthful accusation in the British press that his liaison with Kitty had been the cause of his young wife's demise, his mood became even darker. He began to wallow in self-pity in his voluntary exile in an unfriendly foreign land.

It has always been a matter of debate whether Beckford was guilty of the crimes of which Loughborough accused him. The sycophantic tutor's doubtful testimony is the only shred of evidence that specific sexual acts took place in Kitty Courtenay's bedroom at Powderham early on that autumn morning. But the general charge is likely to be true. His lifestyle, letters and writings long after the Powderham debacle reveal that Beckford, despite having married and fathered two children, was predominately and actively homosexual. Indeed, if that clever and persuasive advocate, Loughborough, had had at his disposal evidence of Beckford's subsequent lifestyle, he would surely have fancied his chances of persuading a jury that Beckford was guilty of committing a homosexual act with Kitty Courtenay on that fateful day at Powderham.

When he returned to live at Fonthill permanently after spending the vast majority of the previous ten years abroad, Beckford constructed an eight-mile-long, twelve-foot-high wall, topped with sharp iron spikes, around his estate. His purpose was twofold – to keep the outside word at bay, and to provide his beloved animals with a safe haven. He also began to live in the manner of his dissolute fantasy hero, Vathek, importing a dwarf to be his doorkeeper, an abbot from France to hear confessions, and a harem of good-looking boys to act as his servants.

These servants were christened with weird and, more often than not, effeminate nicknames. Beckford clearly hoped that 'pale

Ambrose, infamous Poupée, horrid Ghoul, insipid Madame Bion, cadaverous Nicobuse', along with frigid Silence, Miss Long, Miss Butterfly, Countess Pox and the Turk, who bathed with his master, would perform duties beyond their domestic chores. His agent, Gregorio Franchi, whom he brought to England from Portugal, sometimes sent pornography down from London. Beckford delighted in viewing these obscene pictures in the company of his doorkeeper, the dwarf. He also wrote to Franchi, complaining that none of his stableboys was 'the least promising' and that his faithful valet, Richardson, was frigid. Not all his servants, however, were willing to grant sexual favours to their demanding master. 'It's not worth talking about Bijou – he's not of the right kind and never will be; we need other angels, if we go to another paradise', the lusting, if in this instance unrequited, Beckford informed his agent.

It is certain that Beckford also used Franchi to procure youths and rent boys. In 1807 he wrote to the agent: 'If it is at all possible, go to see an angel called Saunders, who is a tight-rope walker at the Circus Royal and the certain captivator of every bugger's soul. Ah!' Four years later, still fascinated by Saunders, Beckford followed the circus to York and, in addition, fell in love with a young horseman from the troupe. His letters to Franchi also indicate that he often visited homosexual haunts in London. The metaphors he uses are patently sexual when in 1812 he refers to St Giles parish in the Seven Dials area as 'the Holy Land', where he hoped to 'kiss the relics'. His meaning is even more obvious when he describes a clandestine encounter with a 'little rogue' he met on Hounslow Heath, 'a Paradise' where an army barracks was conveniently sited.

It is unfair to suggest that homosexual thoughts and practices were all that occupied Beckford's fertile brain. He may have been excluded from society, but he transformed Fonthill Abbey into a Gothic extravaganza with a tower to rival in height that of nearby Salisbury Cathedral. With a neat touch of irony, and a nod to *Vathek*, he commissioned James Wyatt, the architect who had designed the

Music Room at Powderham to celebrate Kitty Courtenay's coming of age, to raise the 300-foot tower towards the heavens.

Little remains of Beckford's fabulous dwelling today, but it drew gasps of incredulity from the few outsiders, among them the liberally minded Horatio Nelson, later to be the hero of Trafalgar, who attended Beckford's grand opening in 1800. Six years later, when Sir Richard Hoare of Stourhead could contain his curiosity no longer and asked to see the redesigned Fonthill, Beckford gave his neighbour a conducted tour. When the Wiltshire set heard of Hoare's visit, they demanded an explanation. Sir Richard, warned that he might be ostracized like Beckford, admitted his mistake, apologized and never visited Fonthill again. More than twenty years after the scandal that had blackened his name, Beckford was still being treated as a pariah.

By the 1820s Beckford had spent so much of his fortune on Fonthill that he was forced to take out a mortgage. His debts were a (for the time) massive £145,000. In 1822, he tired of his creation and put the whole estate on the market. The purchaser, John Farquhar, who had made his fortune manufacturing gunpowder, bought the property for £330,000, reputedly because he wanted to live like a gentleman. Beckford, it seems, had no regrets. 'I am rid of the Holy Sepulchre,' he wrote, 'which no longer interested me since its profanation.' Beckford certainly sold at an opportune moment. Three years later, at three o'clock in the afternoon on 21 December 1825, the tower, which had been built on insufficiently sturdy foundations, collapsed, destroying the whole of the Great Hall and the Octagon.

William Beckford, his debts settled by the Fonthill sale and now back in funds, bought another estate near Bath and built a smaller, but still spectacular, tower on a tract of land above the city, 800 feet above sea level, known as Lansdown Hill. The tower was finished by 1827, but not before the builders, after hearing of the Powderham saga, had briefly downed tools, declaring to the architect, Henry Goodridge, that they would not work for a bugger. Now in his late sixties, the still eccentric Beckford decided to settle down. He lived quietly at Lansdown, in a far less debauched manner than he had during those hedonistic early Fonthill days, until his death at the age of eighty-four in 1844.

What of William Courtenay, the beautiful boy whom Beckford was alleged to have corrupted? With the benefit of hindsight, the decadent young aristocrat was probably as much to blame as his older seducer. Kitty, who inherited the title of Viscount Courtenay of Powderham Castle and the estate on his father's death in 1788, never married and was an exclusive and extremely active homosexual. According to one of the diarists of the day, the landscape painter Joseph Farington, he was not very cautious about concealing his tastes. Farington wrote in 1810 that few gentlemen of Exeter would visit their licentious neighbour, and that Kitty's servants were so reviled in Torquay that he was forced to abandon plans to build a summer villa there.

Moreover, by 1811 the net was closing in on the careless Courtenay. On hearing that a warrant had been issued for his arrest by an Essex magistrate, who had gathered enough evidence to convict him of unnatural acts, including sodomy, the worried peer fled to France, where he lived in obscurity until his death twenty-four years later. In 1831 a distant cousin helped Kitty to revive the ancient Earldom of Devon, which had lain in abeyance for years. The new ninth Earl of Devon was taunted by the press for refusing to return to England to take up his seat in the House of Lords. But Kitty sensibly decided to remain at his house in Paris, as there was a real prospect that he would be arrested if he set foot on these shores.

A cousin, also named William Courtenay, inherited Powderham Castle and Kitty's titles on his death in 1835. He commissioned an extensive remodelling of the castle, rebuilt the West Wing entirely and created a new entrance there. Perhaps the tenth Earl of Devon thought a fresh look for Powderham would help to purge his distinguished family's ancient stronghold of its recent scandalous past.

CHAPTER TEN

Brocket Hall

BROCKET HALL, near Welwyn in Hertfordshire's commuter belt, may be only twenty-two miles from Hyde Park Corner, but it is still one of Britain's most beautiful stately homes. The handsome red-brick Georgian house, set in 543 acres of parkland which includes a delightful lake and, nowadays, two championship golf courses, is today used as an exclusive venue for conferences and 'corporate' hospitality. In days gone by, however, royalty and the cream of high society frequented this, the home of two of Queen Victoria's Prime Ministers, and invitations to Brocket's glittering house parties and gatherings were highly coveted.

There has been a dwelling on the site of Brocket Hall since 1239, but the famous architect James Paine designed the present house for Sir Matthew Lamb in 1760. Sir Matthew's son, Peniston, was made the first Viscount Melbourne in 1781, but this shy and undistinguished figure was not rewarded with an Irish peerage for talented work in the world of politics, public service, or anything as mundane as that. In fact, his ennoblement was entirely due to the sterling efforts in the bedroom of his attractive wife, the former Elizabeth Milbanke, who was the mistress of the Prince Regent, later to become George IV. The grateful Prince, who was a regular visitor to Brocket Hall, gave his accommodating lover a splendid painting by Sir Joshua Reynolds that still hangs in the ballroom, and created a set of rooms for his own use in the Chinese style, known as the Prince Regent Suite, which are still used by guests at Brocket today.

The upwardly mobile Lady Melbourne, who was one of the leading Whig society hostesses of the day, did not confine her amorous attentions to the hedonistic Prince Regent, who was widely believed to be the father of her son, George. She also had a serious liaison with the fifth Duke of Bedford as well as a long relationship with the third Earl of Egremont, which resulted in two more children. Indeed, it seems that her long-suffering husband could only be certain that he was the father of the eldest and youngest of his five offspring. To his credit, Lord Melbourne was happy to support those members of his brood who were not his own with his money, but he preferred to leave their upbringing and education entirely to his wife.

The shrewd Lady Melbourne soon recognized that her second son, William Lamb, whose biological father was almost certainly Lord Egremont, was the most talented of her children. So she encouraged his natural intelligence to burgeon during his education at Eton, Cambridge and Glasgow University, where he studied under the renowned Whig professor John Millar. As William, who was born in 1779, was a younger son and would therefore inherit little money, he embarked on a law career to earn his daily bread.

But when his elder brother, also named Peniston, died suddenly in early 1805, William's circumstances changed radically. Since he was now the heir to his father, to Brocket and its estates, and to the substantial Lamb family fortune, more interesting opportunities beckoned. The young man, who would later become the second Viscount Melbourne and Queen Victoria's first Prime

Minister, was now able to embark on a political career. Just as important, William's improved financial and social position meant that he could raise his sights in the marriage stakes and look for an aristocratic wife. Lady Melbourne's infidelities, which were well known in high places, had often been the subject of licentious gossip, but her racy past was positively tame compared with the future scandalous antics of the headstrong, blue-blooded girl her second son chose to make his wife.

William had first set eyes on his future bride, Lady Caroline Ponsonby, the daughter of the third Earl of Bessborough, as a child at the London home of her mother Harriet's glamorous sister, Georgiana, Duchess of Devonshire (see Chapter Two). Caroline's unorthodox childhood was divided between her parents, who were often on the Continent seeking a cure for her mother's almost continuous ill health, her maternal grandmother, the Countess Spencer,[1] and her famous aunt at Devonshire House. When they met again at Brocket in August 1802, Caroline was a precocious teenager of seventeen with short-cropped hair and a slight, boyish figure. She may not have been a conventional beauty, but William Lamb was captivated by her enchanting personality and intelligence. They passed three wonderful days together, playing parlour games, reading poetry and walking in Brocket's peaceful grounds.

It seemed, at first, that this mutual attraction would come to nothing. The only daughter of the noble Earl of Bessborough would certainly be required to aim a good deal higher than the second son of a recently created and parvenu Irish viscount. However, the death of his eldest brother three years later meant that William's status and prospects had altered significantly and he was now a worthwhile suitor. He soon pressed his claim, and found that Caroline was still as keen as she had been on that memorable weekend at Brocket.

It did not take long for William to ask the Bessboroughs for their daughter's hand. Lady Bessborough soon gave him the good news in the corridor of the theatre at Drury Lane, at which William embraced his future mother-in-law and thanked her from the bottom of his heart. For their part, the Melbournes were a little disappointed. They had wanted their son to marry money, although they still allowed the match to proceed. At the wedding on 3 June 1805, Caroline's delighted mother noted that her daughter, who, since childhood, had been prone to fierce rages followed by long periods of remorse, had miraculously calmed down. Lady Bessborough ascribed the happy change in her previously unstable daughter's demeanour to the security of her marriage, and hoped that it would last.

Caroline's mother's wish was granted for a time. Everyone who saw the young couple during their honeymoon at Brocket commented on how devoted William was to his young wife, and agreed that the two could hardly be more in love. The start of their married life also seems to have been idyllic. Caroline would often be seen sitting on William's knee, whispering intimately into his ear or twiddling his hair between her fingers. Life was also pleasantly relaxed. They had a set of rooms in the Melbourne house in London and were popular dinner guests around town. There were also outings to Cowes and regular shoots at Brocket. So when Caroline became pregnant, there was obviously much rejoicing, while both had plenty of time on their hands to celebrate.

But William soon became bored of living a life of leisure and decided to pursue his political ambitions. His regular absences – he was electioneering in Leominster – may have contributed in part to his young wife's late miscarriage in February 1806. William rushed back from his constituency, only to be greeted by the harrowing sight of his first child's tiny coffin being borne from the house. However, Caroline was soon pregnant again, and the couple were ecstatic when she gave birth to a boy, Augustus, in August the following year. In January 1809, however, they suffered another tragedy when a baby daughter died after only a few hours.

Sadly, further disappointment and heartache were not far around the corner. By 1810, Augustus, whose godfather was the Prince Regent, was three years old but could still barely speak and suffered from violent fits. Doctors said that the condition was due to immaturity and would right itself in time, but Caroline and William remained unconvinced. By 1812, aware that their only son was no better, they came to the terrible but inevitable conclusion that little Augustus would never lead a normal existence.

The unfortunate experiences that the Lambs suffered with their children certainly did not help their by now fraying marriage. Yet the increasing time that William spent away pursuing his political career was probably the principal reason why his neglected wife decided to seek solace and amorous excitement elsewhere.

The first two lovers Caroline took could hardly have been more different from her kind and reasonable husband, who calmly accepted her volatile temper and mood swings. Perhaps a craving for danger, as well as a desire to provoke her unflappable spouse, caused her to pick two of the most notorious rakes in England.

The first was Sir Godfrey Webster, the son by the first marriage of another renowned Whig hostess, Lady Holland. Caroline's brief but torrid affair with Webster, a debauched former soldier, lasted only a few months, but since it was conducted so publicly, everyone in London who mattered was aware of the scandal. Lady Melbourne was furious that her wayward daughter-in-law had behaved so indiscreetly, but William put up with his wife's first adulterous escapade with commendable restraint.

Caroline's next affair, however, tested William's famous patience to the limit. She was just twenty-seven when she met the handsome and artistic George Gordon, the sixth Baron Byron, in 1812. The previously impoverished peer, who was three years younger than Caroline, had recently emerged from obscurity thanks to his romantic poem, *Childe Harold's Pilgrimage*. Now the dark, broodingly handsome poet and his latest work were the toast of both high society and the literary world. Their first meeting resulted in Caroline's often quoted observation in her journal that the poet was 'Mad, bad and dangerous to know'. At their second meeting at Holland House, however, she realized that she was well and truly smitten, writing wistfully: 'that beautiful pale face is my fate.' Soon Byron and Caroline were lovers, and their tempestuous affair raged like a swollen river for four months during the summer of 1812.

Caroline became insatiable, and soon her increasingly unreasonable demands for emotional and sexual satisfaction caused Byron to attempt to cool the situation down. Matters came to a head when she was ordered by her parents-in-law to put a stop to the affair, which was now the only topic of conversation in the capital's most fashionable salons. The furious Caroline threatened to leave the house and flee into her now reluctant lover's arms. 'Go, and be damned!' said Lord Melbourne with unaccustomed fervour, and his daughter-in-law took the ineffectual old peer at his word.

She left the marital home at Melbourne House, but she ended up in the house of a friendly surgeon in Kensington. When he heard where she had taken refuge, Byron hurried there and somehow persuaded the hysterical Caroline to go home. Her mother, who had fainted in her carriage due to all the excitement, later wrote of her daughter's return to Melbourne House: 'I went in before her, and William most kindly promised to receive and forgive her . . . But how long will it last?'

Lady Bessborough was justified in wondering how long William would continue to put up with his errant wife. She must also have been as surprised as her son-in-law's friends that he reacted to Caroline's infidelity so calmly and with such magnanimity. For, amazingly, he again took her back without so much as a murmur. In fact, it was left to his redoubtable mother to intervene. Lady Melbourne, with great circumspection, sent the unhappy couple off to Ireland with Caroline's parents so that the unwelcome gossip would cease. She then attempted to prise Byron away from her daughter-in-law, cultivating a friendship with the poet and directing his attentions towards her niece, Annabella Milbanke, whom he eventually married.[2]

Caroline, however, did not give Byron up as easily as her mother-in-law hoped. In fact, the ending of the affair took time, and was conspicuous for a demeaning lack of dignity on Caroline's part. She made a public fool of herself at a ball in July 1813 when, overcome with jealousy after seeing Byron with his new mistress, the Countess of Oxford, she broke a glass and slashed her wrists with the pieces, in full view of all the party's guests. And as if that were not enough, she later broke into the poet's rooms and scribbled over a copy of William Beckford's *Vathek* (see Chapter Nine), which was lying open on the desk, the desperate words 'Remember me'. Byron's bitter, and now legendary, reply, which told Caroline, in no uncertain terms, that their affair was well and truly over, is worth repeating here:

> Remember thee! Remember thee!
> Till Lethe quench life's burning stream
> Remorse and shame shall cling to thee
> And haunt thee like a feverish dream!
> Remember thee! Aye, doubt it not.
> Thy husband too shall think of thee:
> By neither shalt thou be forgot,
> Thou false to him, thou fiend to me!

The Lambs' union, which had been in a parlous state before the Byron affair, was now a marriage in name only. Caroline, refusing to accept that the relationship was over, continued to bombard Byron with letters during 1814. The publication of her first novel, *Glenarvon*, in 1816 heaped further humiliation on her husband and his family. The thinly disguised autobiography, which described her amorous adventures in detail, as well as her husband's acquiescence, could hardly have been more embarrassing for the placid William.

Extraordinarily, the couple did not formally separate for another nine years. When they did, in 1825, Caroline received a generous deal from William's family. She was to receive £2,500 a year, which amounted to £500 more than her marriage settlement; moreover, when Lord Melbourne died and William inherited, the figure would rise to £3,000. Typically, Caroline refused to sign the separation papers immediately. First she threatened suicide, then retribution. Suddenly and dramatically she changed her tune and left for France on a steamer bound for Calais, but the official termination of her marriage had taken a toll on her mental stability, which had never been her strongest suit. She wrote angry letters from the Continent to all who, she believed, had misused her, and also begged William to take her back. As it happened, she returned to London after two months, but not into her husband's arms. Instead, she was immediately confined to a house on the outskirts of the city under a Dr Goddard and two nurses, provided by the distinguished contemporary expert on madness, Sir George Tuthill.[3]

Caroline's doctors concluded that she had 'a predisposition to the high form of insanity', but her confinement could not be permanent, unless she was formally consigned to Bedlam. Her family and that of her husband agreed that she should live either at Brocket or in Brighton under the supervision of the faithful Dr Goddard. Since Caroline submitted to this regime immediately, it is clear that her once indomitable spirit, as well as her health, was already broken beyond repair. Sadly, the story that she fell from her horse in shock after seeing Byron's funeral cortège pass by Brocket Hall in 1824 almost certainly belongs in the world of folklore. It is, however, an undisputed fact that, not long afterwards, she began to show the symptoms of dropsy,[4] which eventually led to her death at the age of forty-two in 1828. Touchingly, William, who must still have loved the wife who had treated him so callously, was at her bedside when she died.

Scandal continued to plague William, who inherited the title after his father's death in February 1829, following Caroline's early demise. He never married again, but was to have the unenviable record among Prime Ministers of being taken to court on two separate occasions by husbands enraged at the attention he paid to their wives.

After he resumed the political career that had been put on hold for nearly ten years as a result of his marriage problems, William was sent to Dublin by the Prime Minister, Lord Canning, to act as

Chief Secretary for Ireland. Because he was legally separated from Caroline by her death in 1828, it was hardly surprising that he should be on the lookout for some romantic involvement. In Dublin he soon met Lady Branden, the beautiful wife of a much older clergyman whose temper was never good thanks to regular attacks of gout.

As Lady Branden's unattractive husband spent much of the year away from Ireland, it was perhaps inevitable that William and his new lady friend soon embarked on a serious, though possibly unconsummated, affair. It was not long, however, before the crotchety old clergyman took umbrage and brought an action against William, alleging that the Chief Secretary had seduced his wife. Fortunately, the plaintiff's case was so full of holes that it was quickly dismissed.

The second Viscount Melbourne, as William now was, seems to have learned nothing from his close shave in Dublin. In the 1830s he started another dangerous, though again conceivably chaste, liaison, this time with Caroline, the wife of Lord Grantley's heir (although he would not live to inherit the title), the Hon. George Norton.

Caroline had produced a son by Norton, but the marriage had been on the rocks for some time. They hated each other's families and had vastly different political views. There were also regular arguments over money, for Norton was a penniless barrister who received no income whatsoever from his parsimonious brother, Grantley. In addition, George was exceedingly jealous of his wife's cleverness. The granddaughter of Richard Brinsley Sheridan, she had clearly inherited a good deal of the famous playwright's talents. Indeed, her first book, *The Sorrows of Rosalie, A Tale with Other Poems*, was well received on its publication in 1829.

Meanwhile, George, fed up with his lack of funds, asked his wife whether any of the prominent friends she had made through her recent literary success could find him a more lucrative occupation. Thinking more money might make her loveless marriage a little pleasanter, Caroline agreed to help by writing to several of her new acquaintances. In 1830 Melbourne, by now Home Secretary, curious to receive a letter from his old friend, Sheridan's grand-daughter, decided to pay Caroline a visit. It was the beginning of a friendship that would nearly ruin Melbourne's reputation and his political career.

With George's blessing, Melbourne began to visit Caroline more and more. He sometimes brought his friends and colleagues, with the result that Caroline's house became a small but influential Whig political salon. George remained content, especially when Melbourne secured him a magistrate's job at the then decent salary of £1,000 per annum. The next two years were the happiest of the Norton marriage. Thanks to Caroline's writing and George's new job, their income increased, their lifestyle improved and Caroline produced another child.

By 1832, however, with Caroline pregnant for the third time, George had resumed his bad old ways. He became increasingly violent, and Caroline's family refused to communicate with him. Then, in 1835, after a brief reconciliation, her husband beat her up so badly that she miscarried her fourth child. The final break occurred at Easter 1836, when George threw Caroline out of the house and sent their children to live with his rich cousin, Margaret Vaughan. He also took possession of the family home, her personal correspondence, clothes and manuscripts. There was nothing a desperate Caroline could do, for at the time a wife had no legal rights at all.

It seemed that matters could not get any worse, but then George dropped a bombshell. In May 1836 he brought a civil suit for 'Criminal Conversation' against Melbourne, accusing the man who was now Prime Minister of having an adulterous relationship with his wife. If George's case succeeded, it would be a vital step in the process of gaining a divorce. He was also hoping to extract the substantial sum of £10,000 in damages from Melbourne.

The forthcoming action, which had the potential to bring down Melbourne's government, quickly became the talk of London's social and political world. The Tories, knowing that William IV's health was fading fast and that the young Princess Victoria would soon succeed to the throne, scented a return to government if Melbourne lost the suit and was forced to resign. To advance their cause, therefore, they urged George Norton and his lawyers to portray the fifty-seven-year-old Prime Minister as a lecherous old roué who had deliberately seduced a young and impressionable wife. Melbourne, well aware that he was fighting for his political life, had to show that his relationship with Caroline was entirely proper.

The much-publicized trial, which took place on 23 June 1836, was a farce. The prosecution produced no convincing witnesses. Furthermore, the documentary evidence presented by George's legal team was so weak that the court greeted it with laughter. It consisted of three innocuous and innocent notes from Melbourne – words such as 'I will call about half-past four or five o'clock. Yours, Melbourne' were hardly declarations of amorous intent. Consequently, it was not surprising that the jury, without even leaving the courtroom, unanimously found in Melbourne's favour.

Again, the exonerated politician had survived by the skin of his teeth. Caroline Norton, however, was not so lucky. She was branded a scarlet woman by polite society, became a social outcast and lost the custody of her children to her disreputable husband. She later emerged as a significant campaigner for women's rights and was a major force in pushing a future infant-custody bill through Parliament. The trial itself became something of a cause célèbre and was satirized by Charles Dickens in his famous novel, *Pickwick Papers*.

A year after the Norton case, the most rewarding, and probably the happiest, period in Melbourne's life began. In 1837 William IV died and his niece, Victoria, became Queen. The eighteen-year-old sovereign, who had previously led a sheltered life, immediately took a liking to her witty and flattering Prime Minister. During the start of her reign, the unlikely pair spent as much as six hours a day together, with the worldly Melbourne acting as political adviser, secretary, tutor and mentor to the young Queen.

Victoria's solicitous Prime Minister was nearly forty years older than his sovereign, but so much time spent in each other's company made it almost inevitable that rumours would start. Sure enough, the society gossips soon went into overdrive, and there was even speculation that Melbourne's relationship with Victoria was a good deal more than avuncular. Perhaps there was a hint of romance and flirtation in the air, but even if there was not, it is possible that Melbourne actively encouraged such a belief. He was well known to be vain, and most likely relished the fact that a woman so much younger hung on his every word.

Unfortunately, his time with the monarch he adored so much was destined to be short. Victoria's marriage to Albert in 1840, and the fall of Melbourne's Whig government a year later, spelt the end of a special, if sometimes controversial, relationship. After Melbourne left office, the sovereign's new advisers discouraged the ex-Prime Minister from even writing to Victoria. To his eternal regret, his importance to the Queen quickly waned. He retired to Brocket Hall and took no further part in public life. With Victoria now no longer a part of his life, and his son Augustus having died in 1836, aged twenty-nine and still with the mind of a child, Melbourne became an increasingly sad and lonely figure. Long bouts of melancholy and illness plagued the distinguished old statesman until his death at Brocket Hall in 1848.

No concrete evidence was ever produced to prove that Melbourne committed adultery with Lady Branden or Caroline Norton, but his correspondence with those two important women in his life reveals a curious, almost fanatical, interest in flagellation. In a study of forty letters between Lady Branden and the politician, Philip Ziegler, Melbourne's biographer, made the extraordinary discovery that only four contained no mention of beating. In one note to the Irish clergyman's wife, Melbourne writes with clear delight: 'If I did not think that you were too angry to be jested with, I should say that I would certainly get a rod for you and apply it smartly the first time that I see you.' On another occasion he actually cut out from a book a print of a woman beating a naked child and wrote a detailed and lengthy account of the picture's subject matter to Lady Branden.

Many years later, Caroline Norton, who remained a close friend of Melbourne after the infamous trial, sent him a letter from Italy in which she described a decorated box she had seen in a local antique shop. She told him, with zest, that she had nearly bought the article because the design was of 'your favourite subject of a woman whipping a child'. Melbourne even dared to raise the contentious subject of wife-beating with Queen Victoria. 'Why,' he stridently lectured the young monarch, 'it is almost worthwhile for a woman to be beat, considering the exceeding pity she excites.' Is it too bizarre to suggest that Victoria's first Prime Minister could only obtain sexual satisfaction as a flagellator, or as a voyeur of the practice? Perhaps not – it may be that Lady Caroline Lamb was only looking for a more orthodox lover when she jumped headlong into the mad, bad and dangerous-to-know Lord Byron's arms.

The second of Victoria's Prime Ministers to inhabit Brocket Hall was Viscount Palmerston, who also had a propensity for attracting scandalous gossip. When he was only seventeen years old, Palmerston had inherited substantial properties in Ireland and at Broadlands,[5] near Romsey in Hampshire, but Brocket came into his life much later through a different route. His wife, Emily, who was Melbourne's sister, became the chatelaine of the Hertfordshire house and its estate after her brother's death.

Henry John Temple, third Viscount Palmerston, was born in 1784 and educated at Harrow and at the universities of Edinburgh and Cambridge. He was appointed Secretary of State for War when he was only twenty-five, having actually turned down the job of Chancellor of the Exchequer, pleading lack of experience. He stayed at the War Office for the next nineteen years, resigning in 1828 when the Duke of Wellington was Prime Minister. In 1830 Palmerston returned to government under Lord Grey (see pages 46–9) as Foreign Secretary, a position he also held with distinction in the later Whig administrations of Melbourne and Lord John Russell. So although he did not become Prime Minister for the first time until 1855, he reached great heights in the political world at a very young age.

Palmerston did not marry until 1839, when he was fifty-five, but he and his wife, who was previously wed to the fifth Earl Cowper, had been conducting an affair for the previous twenty-nine years. When Emily's husband, who had been cuckolded by Palmerston for so long, eventually died and the pair were free to marry, Melbourne was moved to proclaim, with a degree of under-statement, that his sister was 'a remarkable woman, a devoted mother, and excellent wife – but not chaste'. He might have said the same about his new brother-in-law, who had managed to maintain Emily and several other women as mistresses at the same time.

Palmerston, who, for obvious reasons, had 'Lord Cupid' as one of his nicknames, had been involved in at least two serious affairs before he took up with Lady Cowper. The famous courtesan and member of the Devonshire House set, Frances, Countess of Jersey, and the exotic Princess Lieven, the wife of the Russian Ambassador to London, were well known to be two of his mistresses. When he was put up for the exclusive gambling club Almack's, it was also rumoured that three of the lady patrons, in whose hands the final decision on membership rested, were his lovers. His election was presumably hurried through. During his affair with Lady Cowper, he also found time to woo Lady Georgiana Fane, Lady Jersey's beautiful younger sister, who reputedly turned down his proposal of marriage on three separate occasions.

His greatest indiscretion, however, took place in 1839, just a few months before his marriage to Lady Cowper. Palmerston, who was then Foreign Secretary in Melbourne's government, severely embarrassed his future brother-in-law by trying to rape one of Queen Victoria's ladies-in-waiting while he was staying at Windsor Castle. He appeared suddenly in the bedroom of Mrs Susan Brand, locked one door and blockaded the other, and then climbed on to the terrified woman's bed. Mrs Brand somehow managed to evade his lecherous advances and found protection in the nearby room of a fellow guest.

The noted diarist of the day, Charles Greville, later revealed that Mrs Brand did not conceal the attempt, and told the Queen about her ordeal. Melbourne, who would have abhorred a scandal in which his colleague and brother-in-law figured so discreditably, made it his business to pacify the indignant Victoria. Greville admirably summed up the embarrassing situation when he commented: 'Palmerston got out of the scrape with his usual luck, but the Queen has never forgotten and will never forgive it.'

Greville was right in saying that Victoria would always remember Palmerston's predatory sexual behaviour towards her innocent lady-in-waiting. When Lord John Russell was forced by popular demand to make Palmerston Foreign Secretary in his Whig administration of 1846–51, the Queen opposed the appointment on the grounds that he was uncontrollable and dangerous. Apparently, Palmerston was extremely irritated when he heard that Russell had told the monarch that, at sixty-five, the new Foreign Secretary was unlikely to cause problems among her female staff. In 1851 Victoria finally had her revenge when she persuaded Russell to remove him from office.

The Queen's satisfaction was short-lived, however. It was soon obvious that both the career and the amorous exploits of the grand old man of Victorian politics were far from over. In 1855 it was widely believed that Palmerston was the only politician who could prevent further disasters in the Crimean War, which had started in 1853. So, at the age of sixty-nine, he was made Prime Minister for the first time. His ministry, which lasted three years, was blighted by the Crimean problem and by troubles in India, culminating in the Great Mutiny of 1857, but his second term as Prime Minister, which began in 1859, was far more successful.

There was, however, a slight hiccup when, in 1863, a Mrs O'Kane claimed that she and Palmerston had committed adultery in the House of Commons. Her husband, a left-wing journalist, promptly cited the Prime Minister as a co-respondent in a divorce case and claimed £20,000 in damages. The case was dismissed, and Palmerston's popularity radically increased; indeed, he won the 1865 election with a large majority. No doubt the British electorate admired Palmerston, and even envied the fact that their sporting Prime Minister could be accused of having an illicit sexual relationship at the age of seventy-eight.

There are two very different versions of Palmerston's death at Brocket Hall on 18 October 1865. The first, which is infinitely more likely, is that he died of a fever, with government papers strewn all over his bed, after catching a chill in his carriage. It is said that the workaholic Prime Minister's last words were: 'Die, my dear doctor, that's the last thing I shall do!' The second, which some might say is more apt, is that the sprightly eighty-one-year-old peer expired while canoodling with a pretty young chambermaid on the billiard table. It is true, however, that Palmerston's demise was mourned by one and all – including Queen Victoria, who rightly gave the old profligate she had once detested a magnificent state funeral in Westminster Abbey.

Brocket Hall was in the news again in the late twentieth century, when, sensationally, its Old Etonian owner, Charles Nall-Cain, third Baron Brocket, was sent to prison for seven years for attempting to defraud an insurance company. Brocket's father had died when he was only nine years old in 1961, but his grandfather lived on until 1967. It was not until he was twenty-one that Charles Nall-Cain inherited the title, the hall and its estate from his eccentric, Nazi-sympathizer grandfather. Sadly, the second Lord Brocket, who was renowned only for having attended Hitler's fiftieth birthday and for ill-treating the crofters on his massive estate on Scotland's Knoydart peninsula, had dissipated what was once a substantial family fortune.

There was no money left for his grandson to repair Melbourne's famous old house, which had slipped into disrepair and was in danger of becoming a ruin. Brocket could not raise any funds to restore his family home to its former glory, as no British bank would touch the penniless ex-soldier with a bargepole. However, he had better luck with an American financial institution, which lent him enough to convert Brocket Hall into an exclusive conference centre and hotel.

In fact, Brocket's innovative plan worked surprisingly well. During the 1980s the hall and its beautiful grounds entertained world leaders and government ministers as delegates to various conferences. It became one of the foremost venues of its kind, and money rolled into the formerly impecunious aristocrat's pockets at the rate of £25,000 a day. As a result, he had no trouble in meeting the payments on his loan.

In 1989 Brocket's bank, which was becoming increasingly impressed by its English client's business acumen, saw that a few old Ferraris featured in the annual accounts. It also noticed that this sideline to the conference-centre business was very profitable. In fact, the classic cars that Brocket already owned had tripled in value. So the money men suggested that they should lend him a further £5 million to go out and buy some more as an investment. The happy peer, who had always had a passion for fast and exotic cars, was delighted to go shopping. Soon, Brocket Hall's magnificent showroom was home to forty-two extremely rare and very valuable Ferraris and Maseratis. It is no exaggeration to say that Charlie Brocket was in seventh heaven.

Things started to go pear-shaped from 17 January 1991, however, when the first war against Iraq started. The conflict in the Middle East and the resulting global financial shock caused Brocket's business to suffer and, even worse, the classic-car market collapsed overnight. Dealers stopped trading, and nobody was buying at any price, so Brocket's collection of vehicles was effectively worthless. When interest rates jumped to a heinous 17.5 per cent, Brocket realized that he had no way of paying off his rapidly soaring debts. Unfortunately, his bank had come to the same conclusion. It called in the loan of £5 million that it had begged Brocket to take out only two years before. Also, as its client had no cash at his disposal, the bank planned to seize the hall, which the peer had put up as a guarantee, to raise the necessary collateral.

Realizing that he was extremely close to losing his family seat, Brocket and his wife Isa, a former top model from whom he is now parted, concocted a desperate and dishonest plan to raise some much-needed cash. The hard-pressed couple conspired with two of the showroom's mechanics to dismantle four of his beloved classic cars and hide the major components. They would then pretend that they had been stolen and would put in a massive insurance claim of £4.5 million. It was hoped that the insurance company would then pay up, thereby solving their financial problems at a stroke.

It took three days of hard work to dismantle the four cars. It was vital that Brocket and his three accomplices should cover their tracks so that the insurance company's investigators would not become suspicious. First, they decided to dispose of the body parts. Damaged panels were often replaced after crashes and did not need to be original, so new ones could be bought and the cars rebuilt at a future date. They started with a Maserati Birdcage and a Ferrari 195, which had aluminium bodies and came to pieces easily. The Ferrari 250 Europa and the 340 America Cabriolet, however, were made of steel and were more difficult to dismantle. Bodywork needed to be cut up into smaller sections and flattened before the parts could be dumped.

Then the fraudsters started on the mechanical components. The engine, suspension and steering were carefully packed into wooden crates, along with irreplaceable special parts, like the unique Ferrari badges and hand-painted dashboard instruments. The aluminium body panels and the seat cushions were then burned in the showroom's enormous wood-burning boiler in order that no trace was left. Brocket then found a storage depot near Greenford, on the west side of London, where he rented a large container in which to hide the components. The inventive scam was now nearly ready to operate. All Brocket had to do was wait for a few weeks before reporting the made-up theft – and hope that the insurers did not smell a rat and unearth something incriminating.

As it turned out, Brocket need not ever have bothered to contact his insurers. His bank soon came up with a £15 million rescue package, and he immediately withdrew his claim. The insurers were not unduly surprised, as clients often run out of money or patience with the long legal process that invariably accompanies large claims. Furthermore, his crime would have remained undiscovered if his by then estranged wife had not been arrested much later for forging drug prescriptions for painkillers, and confessed to the whole ingenious plot. When the police came to Brocket to apprehend the peer, he was away at his girlfriend's house. The senior Tory politician Michael Heseltine and his fellow European trade ministers, who were attending a conference in the house, were amazed when they discovered that they were surrounded by legions of the local Hertfordshire constabulary.

Sentenced in 1996 to seven years for conspiracy to defraud, Brocket served just two and a half years in seven different prisons. His time at Her Majesty's pleasure was not easy. He was stabbed by a disgruntled inmate and only narrowly escaped with his life. The unlikely jailbird, however, emerged from his enforced confinement in some style, speeding away on a Harley-Davidson motorcycle, clad in a biker's black-leather jacket and jeans.

This extravagant departure marked an upturn in Charlie Brocket's unconventional story, which went on to have a happy ending. An official appointed by the bank eventually sold the four classic cars that had been the subject of the fraudulent claim. Brocket Hall is still owned by the extrovert aristocrat but is rented out on a long lease to a German consortium. Nowadays, Brocket lives in London and works as an architect. He has also written his autobiography, *Call Me Charlie*, and appeared on many television shows. He is best known for his 2004 appearance, as the token upper-class toff, in the popular reality-TV show *I'm a Celebrity, Get Me Out of Here!* in which contestants have to undertake a series of unpleasant tasks in the Australian bush, the winner being whoever gains the most votes from viewers for his or her behaviour under duress.

The flamboyant Brocket did not win, but appeared to revel in his new high profile. Indeed, he earned a reputation as a bit of a ladies' man by his attentions towards the model, actress and former Page 3 girl, Jordan, in full view of the cameras. His distinguished predecessors at Brocket Hall, the Viscounts Melbourne and Palmerston, who both had an eye for an attractive girl, would certainly have been intrigued by, if not envious of, the current incumbent's activities.

CHAPTER ELEVEN

Ickworth

I N 1795 THE ECCENTRIC and extravagant Frederick Augustus
Hervey, fourth Earl of Bristol, a noted collector of European fine
art, Bishop of Derry and leader of the Irish Volunteers,[1] created the
extraordinary house that stands today at Ickworth, near Bury St
Edmunds in Suffolk. Ickworth, with its magnificent rotunda and
long sweeping corridors in the curved East and West Wings, was
designed to display the wonderful hoard of Old Master paintings
by the likes of Titian and Velázquez, the eighteenth-century family
portraits by Gainsborough and Reynolds, the fine Regency
furniture and china, and that veritable treasure-trove, the largest
private collection of Georgian silver, which the Earl-Bishop, as
Frederick was known, had acquired over the years.

The outside of the Earl-Bishop's vast rotunda was virtually
completed when he died in 1803, but its interior was an empty
shell. Moreover, the foundations of the two wings, which are
attached to the central structure, were only a few feet above the

ground. So the Earl-Bishop's younger son and successor, Frederick, the fifth Earl and, later, first Marquess of Bristol, needed to find a more practical use for what was effectively a huge art gallery in the isolated Suffolk countryside. The Marquess took some years to come up with a viable plan. But eighteen years after he inherited, he instructed his architect, John Field, to construct living quarters for his family in the East Wing. Field also created a series of staterooms, used only for balls and other special occasions, in the rotunda; however, the West Wing, which was added purely to make the house symmetrical, was left empty.

In the second half of the eighteenth century, Lancelot 'Capability' Brown and other distinguished landscape architects laid out Ickworth's magnificent 1,800 acres of wooded parkland, which contains an enclosure for red and fallow deer, known as Round Hill, and a tranquil lake. Remnants of a garden created by John Hervey, the first Earl of Bristol, in the first half of the eighteenth century can still be seen beyond Ickworth's church, while his personal summerhouse and the ornamental canal he excavated also still survive.

The famous formal gardens to the south were constructed by the first Marquess in the first half of the nineteenth century to complement his father's, the Earl-Bishop's, grand design for the house. These horticultural triumphs are in the Italianate style and include the Gold and Silver Gardens, the Temple Rose Gardens and the Orangery. The Marquess also cleverly constructed a raised terrace between the south gardens and the park to provide walkers with superb views of the surrounding parkland and woodland. He also laid out the Albana Walk, to the west of the house, to enable his guests to take a pleasurable and not too strenuous constitutional after lunch.

The Marquesses of Bristol owned and lived in the house in some style until 1956, when Ickworth was gifted to the National Trust to pay the fifth Marquess's death duties. However, the head of the Hervey family continued to lease the living accommodation in the East Wing from the Trust until 1997. Nowadays, the old kitchen garden, still surrounded by tall protective brick walls, is a vineyard, the East Wing is a luxury hotel, and the West Wing will soon be developed to provide new facilities for the thousands of visitors who flock to Ickworth every year. So it may not be quite what the Earl-Bishop had in mind when he embarked on his grandiose project over two centuries ago, but the cantankerous old clergyman would probably rest easier in the knowledge that, as he intended, his fabulous house and beloved fine-art collection can now be seen by a wider public and are, with any luck, preserved for eternity.

Records reveal that Herveys owned and farmed land in Bedfordshire during the thirteenth century. Soon afterwards, they moved to Suffolk and in the fifteenth century acquired the Ickworth estate. John Hervey, the eldest son of a Sir William Hervey, held a high position in the household of Charles II's wife, Catherine of Braganza. John, who was born in 1616, seems to have been the first in a long line of Hervey courtiers and politicians who served Britain's kings and queens and their country for the next two centuries. The Herveys were well rewarded by their various sovereign masters for their loyalty and constant presence at court. Indeed, the Suffolk family steadily rose up the ranks of the peerage, culminating in the fifth Earl's creation as first Marquess of Bristol in 1826.

John Hervey left no children when he died in 1679, so Ickworth passed to his brother, Thomas. He died in 1694 and his second son,[2] named John, like his uncle, succeeded to the estate. This John, who followed his father as MP for their local seat of Bury St Edmunds, must have performed with a good deal of credit at court and in the political world. He was created Baron Hervey of Ickworth by Queen Anne in 1703 and made first Earl of Bristol in 1714 for his role in supporting the Hanoverian succession through its difficult beginning (see Chapter Three, note 17). The first Earl seems to have been a distinguished and God-fearing figure, despite siring seventeen children by two wives. He lived to the then great age of eighty-five, but during his long spell on earth the wise patriarch, who reputedly doted on his children, must have been disappointed to see the name of Hervey become a byword for scandal, a reputation which, it must be added, has tended to dog the ancient Suffolk family ever since.

The first Earl's eldest son, and the only child of his marriage to his first wife, Isabella, was named Carr after his maternal grandfather, Sir Robert Carr of Sleaford in Lincolnshire. He, like his father, was educated at Clare College, Cambridge, and he too subsequently became MP for Bury St Edmunds. Carr, who died young at thirty-two, was widely reputed to be the natural father of the great statesman Sir Robert Walpole's son, Horace Walpole, who, accused of being 'effeminate' by his detractors, is now famous as antiquarian, art historian, politician, gothic novelist[3] and avid letter writer. It is said that he had homosexual affairs with two of his Eton schoolfellows, the poet Thomas Gray and Henry Fiennes Clinton, ninth Earl of Lincoln.

Thomas Hervey, another of the first Earl's sons, but from his second marriage to Elizabeth Felton, was also the MP for Bury and, in the family tradition, held various offices at court. He gained a degree of notoriety in social circles for eloping with Elizabeth, the wife of Sir Thomas Hanmer, and for being constantly short of money during a reckless and debauched life. When Thomas, who wrote several pamphlets, died in 1775, Dr Samuel Johnson, the great essayist and lexicographer, was moved to remark of his old acquaintance: 'Tom Hervey, though a vicious man, was one of the genteelest men who ever lived.'[4]

Carr and Thomas Hervey may have been the cause of some juicy gossip during their lifetimes. Yet their rather tame adulterous liaisons, and Thomas's regular descents into debt, were trifling compared with the extraordinary sexual, literary and political exploits of their renowned brother John, who took the courtesy title of Baron Hervey of Ickworth after the death of his half-brother, Carr, in 1723.

John Hervey was born on 16 October 1696. He was educated at Westminster and, like most of the male members of his family, went on to study at Clare College, Cambridge, where he gained his MA degree in 1715. While at university, it seems he took part in the usual student pranks, drinking more than his fair share, gambling more than he could afford on dice and horses, and sleeping with the girl who did his laundry. In 1716, after John had come down from Cambridge, Lord Bristol sent his eldest son by his second marriage on a Continental tour to Paris, and then on to Hanover to pay court to the British king, George I, who preferred to spend most of his time in his native Germany.

During his time in Paris, John, who had always looked frail and rather effeminate, took to wearing white make-up to give his face a ghostly but fashionable appearance. As he also suffered from regular fainting spells, which may have been due to a form of epilepsy, and had a nervous disposition, he became, later in life, an easy satirical target for his enemies. However, his propensity for ill health and his tendency to fret did not stop him from pursuing a political career and a full social life at court and elsewhere after he returned from his travels abroad. Furthermore, his frequent swoons and ghoulish countenance did not prevent the young Suffolk dandy from chasing any girl or boy who took his fancy. It would seem that the weak and foppish John Hervey of Ickworth was a genuine bisexual with a particularly vigorous sexual appetite.

As a young man, John was in regular attendance at the court of the Prince of Wales, later George II, at Richmond. In 1720, after a secret courtship, he married one of the Princess of Wales's ladies-in-waiting, Mary Lepell, who was eventually to bear him eight children. The beautiful and agreeable Mary was the epitome of the loyal wife, but, despite producing four babies in the first six years of their marriage, she was only able to keep her husband on the straight and narrow for that span of time. In 1726, while convalescing from another bout of epilepsy in Bath, John met and immediately fell for the rustic charms of Henry Fox, a twenty-one-year-old country squire from Somerset. After Henry returned to his estate at Redlinch and John rejoined his faithful wife at

Ickworth, the pair continued to correspond through a series of extremely affectionate letters.[5]

When the two men met again in London the following year, Henry's older brother, Stephen, was also there. The elder Fox caught John's roving eye, and he at once diverted his attentions to his friend's handsome brother. The relationship between John and Stephen developed fast. Hervey visited the Fox home at Redlinch, and the two friends then moved on to Bath, ostensibly for two months of health treatment. Meanwhile, the increasingly lonely Mary remained at Ickworth, which she now, quite understandably, called 'My Hermitage'.

Sufficiently revived by Bath's invigorating waters, Hervey and Stephen Fox now decided to embark on an extended Grand Tour of the Continent, lasting fifteen months. First, they visited another spa in Ostend for the benefit of John's fragile health. After Belgium, they travelled to Paris and then on to Rome, where Stephen fell ill. Then, in hot and sultry Naples, Stephen nursed John through a series of hot flushes and dizzy spells. In Florence John had an unsightly lump removed from his chin by an incompetent surgeon, who left a noticeable and ugly scar. It was also while in the art capital of Italy that John received a letter from Mary, who must have thought she had been abandoned. Poignantly, she signed the missive 'your melancholy wife'.

It cannot be proved beyond doubt that John and Stephen conducted a homosexual relationship in Europe, but subsequent actions by John and members of his family suggest that he and Stephen definitely had something to hide. To begin with, the first twenty-six pages of John's volume of letters, which covered the period of his travels with Stephen, were torn out and destroyed by his grandson, the first Marquess of Bristol. Secondly, examination of copies of John's correspondence, including his remaining letters to Stephen, indicates that he himself erased immodest sections from the original drafts.

Some letters, however, which appear to be intact, can be interpreted as suggesting homosexual activity. In one, John writes:

'I have often thought if any very idle Body had Curiosity enough to open my Letters, they would certainly conclude they came rather from a Mistress than a Friend.' In another note, John could conceivably be revealing that Stephen's rough treatment during their lovemaking inflicted bruises on his weak and brittle body. His words can only be described as incriminating:

> You have left some such remembrance behind you that I assure you (if 'tis any satisfaction to you to know it) you are not in the least Danger of being forgotten. The favours I have received at your Honour's *Hands* are of such a Nature that tho' the impression might wear out of my Mind, yet they are written in such lasting characters on every Limb, that 'tis impossible for me to look on a Leg or an Arm without having my Memory refresh'd.

John's long time away with his male lover did not curtail his interest in his wife, though. Nine months to the day after he returned to Ickworth from his European trip, Mary gave birth to their fifth child. Even so, neither did the new addition to the Hervey brood prevent John from pursuing Stephen again. Soon, he was persuading Lord Bateman, who had separated from his wife because of his homosexual preferences, to allow Stephen to live in his house at Windsor so that visits from London would be easier to arrange.

John's amorous pursuits do not appear to have hindered in the least his progress in Westminster or at court. Nor did they stunt his prodigious literary output. He was elected for Bury St Edmunds, the parliamentary seat that was permanently occupied by the Hervey family, in 1725. At the beginning of his political career, he was not sure whether to support William Pulteney, later the first Earl of Bath, or Sir Robert Walpole, often described as Britain's first Prime Minister, who is reputed to have been cuckolded by John's late brother, Carr. In 1730, to the fury of Pulteney, who never forgave his old friend and paid him back with vitriolic satire, John sided with Walpole, and remained faithful to his fellow East Anglian for the rest of his life.

Pulteney assumed that John was the author of a 1731 pamphlet, *Sedition and Defamation*, which severely criticized his policies and supported Walpole's. So he replied with another pamphlet, *A Proper Reply to a Late Scurrilous Libel*, which portrayed John not only as a homosexual but also as a hermaphrodite. The latter was so infuriated by Pulteney's crude and libellous insinuations that he challenged him to a duel, which was fought at first light on the frosty and snowy morning of 26 January 1731 in what is now London's Green Park. John, who had Henry Fox as his second, came off much the worst. He was led away, fainting, from the field of honour with a slight wound in his side and five scratches on his hand from the rapier of the superior swordsman.

John did not take much time to recover. But when London's legions of satirists heard about his ignominious defeat in the duel, they licked their pen nibs and composed numerous essays, limericks and articles, which borrowed and embellished on the Pulteney pamphlet's insulting suggestion that Lord Bristol's heir was a hermaphrodite. These vicious attacks on John's character and sexuality went on for several years. Indeed, they culminated with Alexander Pope's famously cruel 1735 satire, *An Epistle from Mr Pope to Dr Arbuthnot*, which caricatured John as Sporus, the boy whom the Roman emperor Nero castrated and then took as his wife. Of course, Pope had his own particular axe to grind, and indeed had been satirizing John Hervey for some time. He had always been jealous of his target's aristocratic upbringing and his close friendship with their fellow poet and writer, Lady Mary Wortley Montagu, with whom Pope was infatuated.[6]

Despite his continual lampooning by the literary world and the press, John managed to hold on to the important position, which he had held since 1730, of Vice-Chamberlain in the court of George II. His duties were to oversee court functions, such as royal birthdays, marriages, funerals and official visits. It certainly helped his cause in those difficult times that he was a firm favourite of Queen Caroline, and exerted considerable influence over her. Indeed, it was due to the King's wife that he was made

Lord Privy Seal in 1740. Also, his close relationship with Caroline made governing much easier for Walpole, who knew that if John could persuade the Queen that his policies were right, the King would nearly always follow suit. Walpole rightly recognized John's contribution by making him a member of the Privy Council.

John was also very close to Caroline's son, Frederick, Prince of Wales (see also pages 79–80), who some, including Stephen Fox, speculated was his lover. Hervey himself, somewhat revealingly, compared their relationship to that of Alexander the Great and Hephaestion. They had a heated row in 1733, however – one which in fact concerned a woman, Anne Vane, a lady-in-waiting at court.

Frederick and John had both been Anne's lovers at more or less the same time, and now began to quarrel over their joint mistress, who had recently produced a child whose father's identity was, unsurprisingly, unknown. Frederick, however, quickly tired of Anne and her problems. So in 1734, which was also the year in which Mary Hervey produced a baby girl at Ickworth, Anne left the various homes that the Prince had provided and moved to a house in Wimbledon. She and Hervey continued to meet there until her death two years later. The strange *ménage à trois* of Frederick, John and Anne even spawned a cheeky ballad opera, *The Humours of Court*, which portrayed the Prince as Adonis, Anne as Vanessa and John, aptly, as Aldemar, 'a gay young Rover of Quality'. By the time of Anne's death, Frederick and John had revived their controversial friendship and spent long evenings together in the Prince's private rooms.

Somehow Hervey still managed to find the time to continue his affair with Stephen. During the less busy summer season when the royal family were based at Kew, the couple often spent two days together in London. In the end, however, Stephen's preference for rural life at Redlinch and John's need to be at court and in government in the capital caused their once ardent relationship to cool. In 1735, with John's blessing, Stephen Fox married the heiress Elizabeth Horner, with whom he had numerous offspring.

He and Hervey remained close friends until they fell out in 1742. Stephen Fox was created first Earl of Ilchester in 1756.

John celebrated the running down of his relationship with Stephen by returning to Ickworth and making his poor wife, Mary, pregnant with her eighth and last child. But by 1736 he was again involved in an extraordinary *ménage à trois*. This time, the object of his attention was Francesco Algarotti, a twenty-four-year-old Italian scholar who had, that summer, translated Isaac Newton's *Optics*, and who was visiting England.

The trouble was that Francesco, like his more senior admirer, was a promiscuous bisexual, so there was plenty of competition for his favours. This did not stop John from falling passionately in love with the Italian, as did his old friend, Lady Mary Wortley Montagu, who was even prepared to desert her husband for the glamorous Paduan, nicknamed 'the Swan of Padua' by the philosopher Voltaire for the graceful way he moved through Europe's courts. When Francesco returned to Italy from London, Mary and John were equally distraught. They bombarded the young Italian with letters, but he had no time to reply. He had found himself a new male lover in Milan.

Francesco returned to London in March 1739 and stayed briefly with John in his apartment in St James's Palace. But the nomadic Italian was soon off on his travels again. Lady Mary, now fatally smitten, deserted her husband and departed for Venice in the hope of meeting up with Francesco again. But while she was in transit, Francesco was on his way back to England. Sadly for John, who was looking forward to being reunited with his friend, Francesco stopped off for eight days at the Prussian court in Berlin, where he caught the eye of the Crown Prince Frederick, who was well known for having homosexual tastes. Francesco returned Frederick's admiring glances and the eight-day stop turned into a stay of eight months.

Francesco eventually arrived in London, but his time with John was destined to be short. After a few months, word arrived from Frederick the Great (as he would become known), now King of

Prussia after his father's death, instructing Francesco to return to Berlin. Bizarrely, Mary Hervey lent her husband's lover the money for the journey to Germany. John missed Francesco desperately, but the unfaithful 'Swan of Padua' soon forgot his mournful aristocratic British friend, slipping into Frederick's welcoming arms and replacing the furious Baron Keyserling as the King's favourite.

In 1742 John was dismissed from office after the fall of Walpole's government. In a token act of defiance against George II, he joined the Opposition. He tried to persuade Stephen Fox to follow, but he refused. Their subsequent argument signalled the end of an intimate friendship that had lasted fifteen years. John wrote a well-received political pamphlet, *Miscellaneous Thoughts on the Present Posture of Foreign and Domestic Affairs,* but became more and more prone to epileptic fits. He grew progressively weaker and died on 5 August 1743 at the age of forty-six. His old enemy, Pope, was as cruel to him after his death as he had been during his lifetime. When he was asked to comment on Hervey's demise, the creator of the ruthless *Epistle to Dr Arbuthnot,* with its spiteful portrait of Sporus, which was now in its sixth edition, employed just three sarcastic words – 'requiescat in pace' – which translates as 'rest in peace'.

John Hervey of Ickworth's last act was mean and petty. In his will, he left his long-suffering and eminently loyal wife the bare minimum required by their marriage contract, and she was forced to live in reduced circumstances until her death in 1768. Stephen Fox was appalled by John's treatment of his blameless spouse and to his credit took pity on his lover's widow, regularly visiting the poverty-stricken Mary.

John Hervey was renowned during his lifetime as the object of derisory satire from Alexander Pope, who variously caricatured him as Lord Fanny, Sporus, Adonis and Narcissus. But he is now, perhaps, just as famous for his frank and often amusing recollections of his time in royal service, *Memoirs of the Court of George II,* which was published long after his death. The detailed work contained many unflattering references to the King and to John's great friend, Frederick, Prince of Wales, but heaped praise on Queen Caroline. John's son, Augustus, the third Earl of Bristol, left instructions that the manuscript should not be published until the death of George III. In fact, the Herveys waited until 1848 before releasing the fascinating reminiscences for public consumption. The work was edited – and possibly sanitized – by the Victorian scholar J. W. Croker, but has been an important source of reference for the period of George's reign from 1730 to 1737 ever since.

John failed to outlive his much healthier father, the first Earl of Bristol, but, unusually, three of his sons were destined to inherit their grandfather's title. Two of those future Earls, it must be said, followed in their degenerate but immensely talented father's footsteps, demonstrating the Hervey family's awe-inspiring capacity for attracting scandal as often as an irritating rash recurs.

George, the eldest son of John and Mary, and second Earl of Bristol, served for some years as a soldier and then joined the diplomatic service. He was Ambassador to Spain in Madrid from 1758 to 1761 and was appointed Lord-Lieutenant of Ireland in 1766, although, strangely, he never seems to have actually visited the Emerald Isle during his short tenure. In 1769 he hired 'Capability' Brown to design Ickworth's park. He was a loyal courtier in the family tradition and, like his father, was Keeper of the Privy Seal for a short time. He was also made Keeper of the Stole to George III in 1770, although it was said that his 'inordinate pride' kept him from achieving higher office. He died, unmarried, in 1775 and was succeeded by his brother, Augustus.

Augustus, the third Earl, seems to have been a much more colourful character than his austere elder brother. He achieved rapid promotion in the navy and served with distinction under Admiral Hawke in the late 1750s, and also with Admiral Rodney in the West Indies. Augustus's life at sea effectively ended with the Peace of Paris in 1763, so he turned his attentions to the political world. Like so many other Herveys, he was MP for Bury St Edmunds from 1757 to 1763 and from 1768 to 1775, when he succeeded his brother, George, as Earl of Bristol. He was an avid debater and put his naval experience to good use, serving as a Lord of the Admiralty from 1771 to 1775. He was, too, one of the many suspected of being 'Junius' (the pseudonymous author of sixty-nine polemical letters aimed at the King, George III, and Prime Minister, the Duke of Grafton, published in the *Public Advertiser* between 1769 and 1772), and also wrote a racy account of his adventures at sea, and ashore (eventually published in 1953).

The third Earl is not, however, best remembered for his sterling work in the navy or at Westminster, but for his scandalous and extremely costly marriage. In 1744 Augustus had secretly wed the notorious Elizabeth Chudleigh, a boisterous lady-in-waiting with a reputation for granting her favours to any man at court who asked. The union – secret in order that she might retain her post at court – did not last long, and both parties agreed to separate. A child – Henry Augustus Hervey – was born in 1747, but died in infancy. In 1760 Elizabeth became the mistress of the second Duke of Kingston, who was blissfully unaware of her shady past.

Augustus had a number of affairs in the meantime, including one in 1763 with a Kitty Hunter, who the following year bore him a son, Augustus Henry. Whether it was in order to legitimize the child's birth by marrying Kitty, or because he wished to marry someone else, in 1768 he asked Elizabeth for a divorce. She refused, and instead insisted that their marriage had never taken place. She then went on to wed Kingston. But after the Duke's death in 1773, Elizabeth's contentious history emerged during a court case disputing her husband's will, and the Countess-Duchess, as Horace Walpole liked to call her, was tried for bigamy in the House of Lords in 1776 in front of 6,000 spectators. Because of her age and status, Elizabeth escaped branding on her hand, which was the usual punishment for a convicted bigamist, and was allowed to go into exile. Augustus, however, was not so lucky. He was condemned for taking part in the deception, and the Lords insisted that his marriage could never be dissolved, thus ensuring that any children born after his dead son by Elizabeth would be illegitimate. Consequently, when Augustus died in 1779, his brother Frederick became the fourth Earl of Bristol. Augustus was, however, able to bequeath his personal goods to his son Augustus Henry, including his father's manuscripts and his own memoirs – with the rider that they should not be published during George III's lifetime, and, tellingly, that his heirs should not 'give, lend, or leave them to his brother Frederic [*sic*].'

Frederick, the Earl-Bishop, had entered the Church after graduating from Cambridge in 1754. He became a royal chaplain and, while waiting to be promoted to bishop, spent some time in Italy, where he acquired his interest in art. When his brother George was Lord-Lieutenant of Ireland, he was made Bishop of Cloyne in February 1767. Having improved the see, he moved on to the much richer bishopric of Derry a year later.

He proved to be a diligent, industrious and liberal churchman who favoured religious toleration and despised the archaic system of tithes. He spent large sums of money on building roads and assisting agricultural enterprise in his see. He was, however, criticized for undue frivolity when he reportedly organized a race through a treacherous bog for some of his plumper clerics. In the event, the coveted prize of a rich living was never awarded to the disgruntled and exhausted winner. Frederick also managed to satisfy his luxurious personal tastes, notably his interest in art and architecture. He constructed huge residences at Ballyscullion and Downhill, and filled the new houses with paintings and sculptures. On his brother's death, he inherited the Ickworth estate and the then vast income of £20,000 a year, so he was certainly rich enough to fund the building of another opulent new house and to continue his hobby of collecting European fine art. He left Ireland immediately and spent a little time at Ickworth planning his building project, but he was soon on his travels to Italy again, purchasing further artefacts.

In 1782 he returned to Ireland and avidly supported the Irish Volunteer movement. He quickly rose to a prominent position in the fledgling organization, and spoke at its convention in Dublin in 1783. His speech, however, contained rebellious messages and exhortations to extreme political reform, seditious language that led the British government to contemplate his arrest. He took no further part in politics and spent his latter years on the Continent, collecting works of art.[7] In 1798, when the French occupied Rome, they confiscated his art collection and sent him to prison in Milan, where he served a custodial sentence of nine months.

The Earl-Bishop was certainly cultured, but he was also a hypocrite and, in some ways, as licentious as his father, John Hervey of Ickworth. Despite his religious calling and his marriage in 1752 to Elizabeth Davers, who subsequently bore him two sons and three daughters, he conducted a long and torrid affair with the Countess Lichtenau, the mistress of Frederick William II of Prussia. After his release from French custody in 1798 he did not return to England, but settled in Italy and continued his travels round Europe. The Irish peer Lord Charlemont, not the Earl-Bishop's greatest admirer, condemned him roundly as 'A bad father, both from caprice and avarice; a worse husband to the best and most amiable of wives; a determined deist, though a bishop, and at times so indecently impious in his conversations as to shock the most reprobate . . . His ambition and his lust can alone get the better of his avarice.' For while he was quite prepared to spend a large part of his vast fortune on Ickworth, he was also extremely mean to his family. Indeed, he often failed to pay the allowance of his most famous child, Lady Elizabeth Hervey, who, as Lady Elizabeth ('Bess') Foster, would become the long-term mistress and, later, second wife of the fifth Duke of Devonshire (see Chapter Two). Lady Bristol died at Ickworth in 1800; her husband died in 1803 on one of his journeys round Italy. His body was returned to England for burial in Ickworth churchyard, where he lies in close proximity to the extraordinary house he constructed.

✳

Since his eldest son, Augustus, predeceased him, the Earl-Bishop's younger son, Frederick, succeeded to the title. Frederick, who finished the construction of Ickworth and laid out the magnificent formal gardens, was created Marquess of Bristol in 1826 as a reward for a long and distinguished career in politics and public and royal service. Like the first Earl, he was blessed with robust health and longevity. When the first Marquess died in 1859, at the age of eighty-nine, he was succeeded by his eldest son (the second of nine children), also named Frederick, who, in the well-worn tradition of the Hervey family, served as MP for Bury St Edmunds before inheriting his father's title. The lives of the next two Marquesses,[8] who were also Members of the House of Commons while holding the courtesy title Earl Jermyn (also granted in 1826), followed an identical pattern. By the turn of the twentieth century, there had been no salacious gossip about the Herveys for a century. It might have seemed unlikely, given the family's past propensity for attracting scandal, but it appeared that Ickworth's owners had exhausted their rogue genes and turned over a new leaf.

This unusual state of respectability did not last long. The fifth Marquess, who lived to the age of ninety, was an important and successful diplomat, but his son, Victor, let the side down in a big way. As a young man, he sold guns to the Republicans during the Spanish Civil War, and then betrayed the buyers to the fascist General Franco's side. Then, in 1939, he was jailed for three years for his part in an armed jewel robbery. Since he could not have needed the money, he presumably committed the crime for the excitement or, as the Irish say, the 'craic'. He calmed down in later life and in due course became chairman of a number of companies. Married three times and twice divorced, he had three sons – all half-brothers and, confusingly, all called Frederick – and three daughters, one of whom died at birth. He moved to Monaco as a tax exile in 1978. When he died in 1985, his eldest son, Frederick John William Augustus Hervey, became the seventh Marquess and the custodian of Ickworth and its hoard of treasure.

If the sixth Marquess was a bad egg, his spoiled son John was a rotten one. When his father died, he reputedly inherited a fortune of £35 million, including a 57,000-acre sheep station in Australia and four oil wells in Louisiana. Ickworth had been gifted to the National Trust to settle his grandfather's death duties, but the Marquess, like his father, leased back sixty rooms in the East Wing.

The Earl-Bishop may have been extravagant, but the seventh Marquess brought a new meaning to the word. Like his ancestor, John, Lord Hervey of Ickworth, he was a promiscuous homosexual, although married for a time, but he will go down in history for his ability to spend. Millions (some reports suggest as much as £7 million) went on hard drugs, chiefly heroin and cocaine, for the possession or use of which the dissolute peer was imprisoned on two occasions. Indeed, his lawyer at his 1993 trial for drug possession had an impossible task to prove his innocence. He was therefore reduced to pleading that the Marquess had 'suffered from lack of love' as a child; indeed, that his parents had been so strict that he had been forced to wear long white gloves whenever he dined with them. The court must have been moved by the description of such a deprived childhood, for it gave the aristocratic defendant the exceptionally lenient term of ten months in jail.

Yachts, fast cars, helicopters, a house in the Bahamas, extravagant living and a noticeably unsuccessful career as an entrepreneur were other factors in such a remarkably rapid dissipation of wealth. Worse still, however, as the drugs took their inevitable hold the Marquess not only became more and more eccentric, but also began to develop an unpleasant vicious streak. In a drug-fuelled haze he smashed up furniture during a party at Ickworth, peppered the lock of a refrigerator door with his shotgun because he could not get a bottle of champagne out, organized a shoot of tame peacocks, which had hitherto been living peacefully in Ickworth's gardens, for his sycophantic hangers-on, and even fired on an amazed group of American tourists who, minding their own business, were walking in the grounds. To cap it all, he was also deported from Australia as an undesirable alien. Unsurprisingly, his hedonistic lifestyle destroyed the huge Hervey family fortune in only thirteen years; it also killed him. He was only forty-four when he died in January 1999, by which time he had been forced to move out of Ickworth to an estate farmhouse with a mere five bedrooms; he was also reported to be suffering from AIDS. His half-brother, Frederick, who became the eighth Marquess at the age of twenty, is worth a fraction of what his predecessors were.

There may not be a Hervey in residence in Ickworth's superb East Wing now, but the family is still in the news. The eighth Marquess's two willowy, blonde full sisters, Lady Victoria and Lady Isabella Hervey, are regulars in the gossip columns of the world's press. Lady Victoria, who was born in 1976, first hit the headlines when her mother, the sixth Marquess's third wife (and former secretary), Yvonne, cut off her allowance for failing to take up the place she had been offered at the University of Bristol. Victoria, however, was soon back in funds, finding employment as a receptionist for the film director, restaurant critic and escort of beautiful women, Michael Winner.

Soon afterwards, however, when a rather racy photograph of Victoria appeared in a tabloid, her profile soared. She quickly took over as Britain's favourite It Girl from Tara Palmer-Tomkinson, who was forced to retire due to over-abuse of recreational pharmaceuticals. She also kept the gossip writers happy by dating a string of minor celebrities, including a much older man, the restaurateur Mogens Tholstrup, whom she endearingly called 'Grandpa', as well as the lantern-jawed racing driver David Coulthard.

Apart from attending a party virtually every night, Victoria has variously been involved in a fashionable London boutique, Akademi, which closed in 2001 with debts of £350,000, appeared as a pin-up in men's magazines, written a 'Party Animal' column for *The Sunday Times*, had a small acting part in an unmemorable film, *RX*, and starred in a reality-television show, *The Farm*, with Rebecca Loos, the part-Dutch, part-English bisexual who claims to have once been the lover of the England footballer, David Beckham.

Her twenty-three-year-old sister, Lady Isabella, who missed out on a trust fund because her forgetful father, the sixth Marquess, neglected to make provisions for his younger daughter before his death, has had to make her own way in life. Like her sister, she was blessed with the looks and figure to embark on a modelling and show-business career. Reality television also appears to be her speciality. Isabella's credits include winning a gold medal in *The Games* and, in 2005, starring in the critically panned (and infinitely tacky) *Celebrity Love Island*. In the latter show, her fellow contestants included the ubiquitous Miss Loos and Abi Titmuss, the glamour girl and former lover of the disgraced *Blue Peter* host, John Leslie.

Some might say that Lady Victoria's and Lady Isabella's mode of work is demeaning and inappropriate for members of an old and aristocratic British family. Yet, recollecting the observation of their ancestor's old friend, Lady Mary Wortley Montagu, that there are 'men, women and Herveys', it is no very great surprise to find that the Herveys of Ickworth are still a law unto themselves.

CHAPTER TWELVE

Sandringham House

Sandringham, the royal family's private house and shooting estate a few miles north of King's Lynn in Norfolk, was bought in the spring of 1862 as a country home for Albert Edward, Prince of Wales, the eldest son of Queen Victoria and the Prince Consort (and later to become King Edward VII). Although Prince Albert died the year before, he had made arrangements that £220,000 should be made available to purchase Sandringham House and its 7,000-acre estate. The Prince Consort had also stipulated that a further £60,000 should be found for improvements.

So it is clear that the Prince of Wales's father had intended that no expense was to be spared for Edward's twenty-first birthday present. Victoria, who always believed that her husband would have lived far longer had he not caught a chill while lecturing their errant son at Cambridge about his involvement with the courtesan Nellie Clifden (see page 27), presumably approved of the magnificent gift on the grounds that her wayward and irresponsible heir, known as Bertie to his family, could hardly cause any trouble on the isolated north Norfolk coast. Perhaps the puritanical Queen did not realize that Sandringham was only a short train ride away from Newmarket and the irresistible temptations of its racecourse.

Sandringham appears in the Domesday Book of 1086 as 'Sant Dersingham', which means the sandy part of Dersingham, a village at the estate's northern end. The name was subsequently shortened to Sandringham, and there is evidence of a dwelling on the site of the present house as early as 1296. In the sixteenth century the land passed to the Cobb family, who were followed as owners by the Hoste family in 1686. The Sandringham House that Prince Edward first set eyes on was an unostentatious and not particularly attractive Georgian structure with a stucco exterior, which had been built in the second half of the eighteenth century by Cornish Henley, whose wife had been born a Hoste. Henley died before his new home was completed, and his son eventually sold the house and land to the owner of a large neighbouring estate, Beachemwell, in the 1830s.

As he never lived there during his ownership of a decade, the absentee landlord, John Motteux, appears to have bought Sandringham as an investment. The rich property speculator, who did nothing for his acquisition apart from planting a large number of pear trees in the grounds, is a somewhat shadowy figure. Little is known about him other than that he was the grandson of the Huguenot writer and translator Peter Anthony Motteux, and that he had once had a furious altercation with the famed Whig hostess, Lady Holland, as to whether or not prunes should be an ingredient of cock-a-leekie soup.

The property-speculator-cum-landowner was viewed as mildly eccentric and not quite 'one of us' by the traditional landed Norfolk families, and they were extremely surprised when they heard who had inherited Sandringham and Beachemwell on Motteux's death. The childless bachelor had bequeathed his two large estates, amounting to 2,000 acres of agricultural land and heath, to the youngest son of his late good friend, the fifth Earl Cowper.

The Hon. Charles Spencer Cowper may have been the stepson of one Victorian Prime Minister, Lord Palmerston, and the nephew of another, Lord Melbourne,[1] but unfortunately he had neither their inclination for hard work nor their devotion to public duty. In fact, Sandringham's new owner, who was widely reputed to be Palmerston's natural son, was a spendthrift and a gambler who was soon forced to sell Beachemwell to settle his debts. From the start, therefore, the conservative Norfolk county set viewed 'Expensive Cowper', as he was aptly known, with a degree of suspicion, but the rural backwoodsmen nearly choked on their cock-a-leekie when they learned of the chequered past of the exotic wife he married in 1852, the notorious Countess d'Orsay.

In 1827, when she was just sixteen, Harriet Gardiner, the daughter of an Irish peer, the first and last Earl of Blessington, had married the French dandy and bon vivant, Alfred, Count d'Orsay, in Italy, where her father and family had been in residence for five years. Incredibly, the twenty-one-year-old d'Orsay, who was also living with the Blessingtons, seems to have been conducting an affair at the same time with Harriet's much older, but very beautiful, stepmother, Marguerite (née Margaret), Countess of Blessington – later to become famous as the author of *A Journal of Conversations with Lord Byron* and as hostess of London's foremost literary salon of the 1840s.

When Lord Blessington died in Paris in May 1829, leaving a will that purposely deprived his extravagant wife of too much money, Harriet, d'Orsay and her stepmother came back to London and set up home together. Since residing in the same house as her husband's mistress was a certain recipe for disaster, it was inevitable that Harriet and the Count would soon be plunged into an acrimonious separation. Lady Blessington and d'Orsay, seemingly oblivious of the huge scandal that their affair had fostered, immediately started to live together and remained as a couple until her death.

[233]

Marguerite's prolific literary efforts kept the wolf from the door for nearly two decades, but early in 1849 the free-spending d'Orsay had to flee to Paris to escape his creditors. Their imposing home at Gore House in Kensington, its beautiful furniture and all its luxurious decorations had to be sold to pay off the Count's enormous debts. After an auction of thirteen days, the heartbroken Marguerite joined her lover in a modest set of rooms in Paris, where she died that summer.

Harriet, on the other hand, returned to the Continent soon after separating from d'Orsay. During the July monarchy of Louis-Philippe, she was friendly with and possibly even the mistress of the French king's son, the Duke of Orléans. After his violent death in a carriage accident in 1842, she returned to England and eventually married the spendthrift Cowper in 1852. Tragedy, however, was soon to strike the couple. In 1853 Harriet and Cowper had a daughter, Mary, who died of cholera less than a year later.

Harriet was so overcome with grief by her baby's death that she started an orphanage at Sandringham, but her time there and her good works were destined to be limited. Cowper, despite being found diplomatic work in Italy and Sweden by Palmerston, was deep in debt again in less than a decade. Some say that his shrewd old stepfather, who was Prime Minister at the time, tipped Queen Victoria and the Prince Consort the wink that Sandringham might be on the market. At any rate, the house and its estate, which had become badly run down, changed hands in 1862 for what those in the know believed was a hugely inflated price.

The Prince of Wales spent nearly a year making the old house habitable, and was able to move in with his new wife, the eighteen-year-old Princess Alexandra of Denmark, three weeks after their marriage in March 1863. As the glamorous royal couple's household increased, further accommodation was needed, so two new houses were built in the grounds: Bachelor's Cottage for guests and Park House for members of the royal household. It also soon became clear that Sandringham House itself was too cramped for the

Prince's rapidly growing family. So the old dwelling was pulled down and a new house built on the same site. Designed by the distinguished London architect A. J. Humbert, and constructed by a local building firm, Goggs Brothers of Swaffham, it was ready for occupation in 1870.

Fronted in red brick and dressed with sandstone, Edward's Sandringham House was in the neo-Jacobean style, with a gabled roof and small turrets. All that remained of the old house was the conservatory, which was retained to act as a billiard room. The interior was decorated in the latest, most fashionable style, and superb new furniture from the leading London firm of Holland and Sons adorned all the rooms.

At the same time as he was renovating the house, Edward, with the help of the acknowledged expert, his fellow Norfolk landowner the second Earl of Leicester, was developing his estate for his favourite pursuit, shooting. Sandringham, whose light sandy soil and heathland naturally favoured wild pheasants and partridges, had been neglected during the tenures of Motteux and Cowper. So the agricultural cultivation was poor, the coverts and hedges thin and the stock of game limited when Edward arrived.

Thanks to Lord Leicester's sound advice, however, shooting at Sandringham, where the clocks were always set half an hour fast to ensure an earlier start to the sport on dark winter days, was transformed within a decade. Large bags of pheasants, partridges, hares and rabbits were obtained. Invitations to the two big four-day-long shoots, which coincided with Edward and Alexandra's birthdays on 9 November and 1 December respectively, were coveted by all the best shots in England. Indeed, by the turn of the century Sandringham rivalled Lord Leicester's Holkham as the finest shoot in Britain.

If the tweedy upper-class East Anglians thought that Sandringham's intimate association with gossip and empty talk would cease after the colourful Cowpers' departure, the squires in their Norfolk jackets and their wives in their thick pleated skirts could hardly have been more wrong. They might have thought that Lady

Harriet and her rake of a husband had attracted scandal as readily as a brawl draws spectators, but they were amazed and a little disturbed to discover that it also followed Sandringham's new proprietor, Albert Edward, Prince of Wales, as closely as the most loyal shooting dog does its master.

Queen Victoria may have hoped that marriage to the lovely Princess Alix might change her son's philandering ways, but she was soon to be disappointed. It may be that Edward's young wife was sexually frigid, or perhaps too innocent for his liking. She was also pregnant on no fewer than five occasions between 1864 and 1869. But none of these tentative theories really explain why the Prince should have been playing the field again as soon as his honeymoon was over. In fact, it is doubtful if any wife would have been able to keep him happy for anything but a very short time.

During the first fifteen or so years of his marriage, Edward committed adultery on many occasions with large numbers of women. He was easily bored and he had a ravenous libido, and by nature was as polygamous and as morally lax as one of his beloved cock pheasants. He was not choosy, either. As long as he was making love to a voluptuous partner, the lustful heir to the throne did not mind if she was a Parisian whore or a countess from one of England's noblest families.

Behind its strict and God-fearing façade, Victorian London was actually a hotbed of vice. Any sexual taste or perversion was catered for in the hundreds of dark streets and dingy courts around Regent Street, Leicester Square and Piccadilly. However, a classier and more discreet type of good-time girl could be found in the capital's smarter districts, like St John's Wood and the leafy roads around Regent's Park. They may have claimed to be actresses and chorus girls, but they were also prostitutes in all but name.

These more upmarket ladies of the night were happy to accommodate the insatiable Edward with every imaginable form of sexual pleasure, and their silence was assured. So the Prince began to leave his loving wife and family at home more and more. His destination was nearly always a sleazy London nightspot, and he would often not return until the early hours of the morning. He would invariably head for the more disreputable premises, such as Cremorne Gardens, the Midnight Club and Evans's Supper Rooms, where sex, and plenty of it, always figured prominently on the menu. Nor did the Prince confine his amorous escapades to London's whores and courtesans, for he was, too, a regular at many fashionable brothels and clubs in Paris's famous red-light district during his frequent sorties to France.

Edward also pursued plenty of girls from the upper echelons of society on both sides of the Channel in the 1860s and 1870s. News of some, but not all, of these liaisons would almost certainly have reached the ears of Alix, who, Queen Victoria once rightly said, was 'very fond of Bertie, but not blind'. For instance, the Princess, according to the courtier Henry Ponsonby,[2] noticed her husband was over-attentive to the pretty 'Madame von B' at Sandringham, and how he was 'spooning with Lady Filmer' at Royal Ascot.

Alix was also aware that he had consorted with a bevy of gorgeous Russian girls in St Petersburg in 1866, and had heard tell of several intimate suppers in Paris the year after with the likes of the Princesse de Sagan and the notorious operatic soprano Hortense Schneider, who was known as *le passage des princes* because she had reputedly slept with most of the eligible males from Europe's royal families. It is reasonably certain, however, that she did not know that her husband had been asked to give money to Lady Susan Vane-Tempest,[3] who claimed to be carrying his child.

Alix, like most royal and aristocratic spouses of the time, expected her husband to conduct affairs. Because the Victorians viewed divorce as a much greater shame and embarrassment than a few harmless infidelities, she was also quite prepared to put up with Edward's conquests, provided he was discreet. Consequently, she was furious at the public humiliation she suffered when Edward appeared as a witness in the 1870 divorce suit filed by Sir Charles Mordaunt against his young wife, who had admitted adultery with several prominent society figures, including the Prince. Edward denied impropriety with Lady Mordaunt, but as he had stupidly written her letters, which were used as evidence in the trial and later appeared in the newspapers, and had visited her privately, the damage was done. The long-suffering Alix was understandably very distressed when she learned that her husband's imprudence was the talk of every club and drawing room in London.

The Princess had been consoled throughout her married life by the knowledge that Edward's many and varied sexual conquests meant so little to him that they were like ships passing in the night. Alix knew that he would soon tire of his latest flame and would return to Sandringham or their London home, Marlborough House, begging her forgiveness. But in 1877 the situation changed dramatically when, at the age of thirty-five, her husband fell seriously in love with a woman whom the British public would soon recognize as his mistress. This was Lillie Langtry, immortalized by John Everett Millais's portrait, *A Jersey Lily*, and thought by most red-blooded (and blue-blooded) males to be the most desirable woman in the land.

Emilie Charlotte Le Breton was born on the Channel Island of Jersey in 1853. She was the sixth child (of seven), and the only daughter, of the Dean of Jersey and his wife, also named Emilie. Her mother was a great beauty, with a perfect fair complexion, bright blue eyes and glorious auburn hair. Her daughter, who inherited her mother's flawless pale skin, aptly earned the nickname Lillie, which she used for the rest of her life.

If little Lillie inherited her good looks from her mother, the powerful sexual appetite she acquired in later life certainly came from her father. It might not have been in keeping with his calling, but over the years the tall and handsome Very Reverend William Corbet Le Breton reputedly enjoyed passionate adulterous relationships with several ladies of his St Saviour parish.

Lillie eventually grew into an attractive, well-educated and confident young woman with several interested suitors. In 1873 her brother, William, wed Elizabeth Price, whose sister had died from tuberculosis after only two years of marriage to a well-off Irish landowner, Edward Langtry. The twenty-year-old Lillie sparkled at her brother's wedding on Jersey, and Langtry was entranced. Soon he was taking her for trips on his smart yacht, *Red Gauntlet*, which was moored in the harbour at St Helier, the island's capital. The Dean did not approve of Langtry, who was six years older than his daughter, but Lillie was attracted by his glittering lifestyle. Within six weeks of meeting him, Lillie, following her heart rather than her head, became his second wife.

Initially, Edward and Lillie commuted between their Jersey home, Noirmont Manor, and a rented house in England. But the restless Lillie soon tired of the island's limited social scene and persuaded her husband to move permanently to England. She then became ill with typhoid and Edward, thinking the medical facilities would be better in London, rented a house in Belgravia's Eaton Square for his sick young wife's convalescence. However, invitations from London's smart set failed to drop through the Langtrys' letter box, so Lillie spent most of her time reading in bed, and Edward, who was clearly missing his sailing and fishing, took to the bottle instead. It seemed that Lillie, who craved social standing and recognition above all else, was destined to miss out on her greatest ambition.

Unexpectedly, however, her prayers were answered and the Langtry fortunes suddenly took a turn for the better. A chance encounter with an old Jersey friend led to an invitation to Sir John and Lady Sebright's London house in Lowndes Square in early 1877. As she was still in mourning for her brother, Reggie, who had recently died, Lillie decided to wear a plain black dress and no jewellery.

It was a sartorial decision she was never to regret. As the rest of the women present were bedecked in fabulous outfits and sparkling diamonds, the beautiful Lillie, in her severe attire, stood out. She soon caught the eye of John Millais, also born on Jersey, and the eminent artist took her down to dinner. During the meal, he asked if he might paint her portrait. Nor was Millais the only painter to fall for Lillie's charms that night. Before dinner was over, his fellow Pre-Raphaelite, the young Frank Miles, had

[239]

completed several sketches. Miles was a homosexual, but he recognized immediately that the girl he believed to be the belle of the ball possessed unique qualities.

Word soon spread over London about the Jersey girl's unusual beauty. In no time, invitations to the best social gatherings, hitherto noticeable for their absence, became commonplace at the Langtrys'. Miles's sketches were put on sale and prints of the artist's drawings sold in thousands in the capital's photographic shops. Lillie's pretty face had certainly reached a wider public. But when Millais's painting of Lillie was exhibited in the Royal Academy in the spring and the area around the portrait had to be roped off to prevent the huge crowds damaging the canvas, 'the Jersey Lily' became the biggest celebrity in town. It was inevitable, therefore, that the current toast of high society would soon bump into its recognized leader, Albert Edward, Prince of Wales.

Lillie's first meeting with Edward occurred on 24 May 1877 at the house of the intrepid Arctic explorer Sir Allen Young, in London's Stratford Place. Sir Allen was one of the Prince's wealthy bachelor friends who were happy to host those intimate suppers that the heir to the throne liked to attend without his wife. Ten people, including the Langtrys, were present, and Sir Allen, knowing his royal guest's penchant for an attractive girl, made sure that the twenty-three-year-old Lillie sat at the Prince's side at dinner. The dashing Sir Allen quickly knew that he had picked a winner. For the rest of the evening, a besotted Edward could not take his eyes off Lillie, who after an initial spell of shyness emerged as the life and soul of the party. When the time came to leave, the Prince, puffing on his trademark cigar, probably asked the blushing Mrs Edward Langtry if he might call on her one afternoon and Lillie, presumably even though aware of what the Prince was after, must have accepted his offer.

It is not known if Lillie succumbed to the Prince on his first visit to take tea at Eaton Square, but in no time the couple were spotted riding together in Hyde Park. Of course, the London grapevine soon knew that Edward had a new lady friend. Husbands, who were generally the last to know that they were being cuckolded, realized, not long afterwards, that Lillie and Edward were an inseparable item. The Princess of Wales, believing that acceptance was the most sensible course of action, was kind to her husband's mistress and received her and Langtry at Sandringham and Marlborough House during the next two years, when the affair was at its peak. Edward Langtry, on the other hand, thought that extended fishing trips or plenty of drink were the most suitable courses to follow.

The result of their respective partners' decisions to allow the relationship to proceed meant that the Prince and Lillie, who shared a love of racing, were entirely free to spend as much time together as they liked during 1877 and 1878. As a result, Lillie Langtry became the first of Edward's many lovers to be recognized as his official mistress. Indeed, she was the Prince's close companion at all the social season's highlights, such as the prestigious race meetings of Royal Ascot and Goodwood and the leading yachting regatta at Cowes on the Isle of Wight. In May 1878 Edward even managed to engineer the presentation of his lover to his mother at Buckingham Palace. Victoria, who always firmly disapproved of her son's frequent extramarital liaisons, was reportedly a little frosty, but Lillie did not care. Another of her great ambitions had always been to meet the Queen.

Sadly for Lillie, the Prince, as usual, began to look elsewhere. The famous French actress, Sarah Bernhardt, who had come to London in the summer of 1879, soon began to attract his straying eyes. By 1880 informed gossip suggested that the alluring thespian had returned Edward's amorous advances, with interest. Lillie, however, had other worries besides her Gallic rival.

The Langtrys' lifestyle was expensive, and Edward Langtry was rapidly running out of funds. In addition, Lillie's father's serial philandering had finally come to his superiors' attention. As a result he was sacked as the Dean of Jersey and sent across the Channel, in disgrace, to be a mere vicar in London. Then, as the public perception that Lillie was falling out of favour with the

Prince increased, the creditors, who had previously been more than happy to extend loans to the future King's mistress, closed in. In October 1880 Edward Langtry was declared bankrupt. Typically, he seized a bottle of whisky and went off fishing again, leaving his embarrassed wife to deal with the hordes of bailiffs who descended, like a pack of wolves, on their house.

Worse was still to come, however. When the Prince began to lose interest, Lillie began an affair with his young cousin, Prince Louis of Battenberg.[4] To her horror, she found that she was carrying the young naval officer's child. Anxious to keep her condition secret from her husband and the rest of London's prying eyes, she decamped to Jersey. But when Prince Edward heard of Lillie's desperate situation, he arranged for her to stay in the Paris apartment of one of his close friends. Her baby, Jeanne-Marie, was born there in March 1881. Lillie quickly placed her daughter under her mother's care in Bournemouth and hurried back to London. She may have had no money, but she was determined to make her fortune.

It was her friend, the great dramatist Oscar Wilde, who persuaded her to try her luck on the stage. She soon hit the heights as an actress. With the blessing of the Prince of Wales, who always made a point of attending her first nights, she left for a tour of the United States in 1882, having, incredibly, negotiated the highest salary ever paid to a female performer. The American public, like Edward, found her charms irresistible. Her box-office takings reached record levels, and her tour was repeated for the next five years. She also became an American citizen, and, as a result, was able to dissolve her unhappy marriage in California in 1887.

Lillie returned to England not long afterwards and purchased a string of racehorses with her newly acquired wealth. She had a brief and violent relationship with the millionaire Scottish amateur rider George Baird, who, after a drinking binge, gave her two black eyes, which led to a twelve-day stay in hospital. Then, at the age of forty-five, she married the Hon. Hugo de Bathe, nineteen years her junior, and resettled in Jersey, sometimes returning to perform in the theatres of London and New York. In 1907, now Lady de Bathe after the death of husband's father, she stylishly broke the bank at Monte Carlo. Two years later, she met for the last time, and had a long and friendly conversation with, her old lover, who was now King Edward VII, at Newmarket races. The Jersey Lily died, aged seventy-five, in Monaco in 1929 and is buried in her father's old churchyard of St Saviour, Jersey – only a stone's throw from the rectory where her extraordinary life started.

After the end of his affair with Lillie, Edward's name was linked with a number of aristocratic young women during the 1880s, although none of these dalliances was serious. During that time he continued to lavish money on improvements to Sandringham. A ballroom, designed by R. W. Edis, was added in 1881 on the east side of the house to increase the space for entertaining. The Prince also started two thoroughbred stud farms on the estate at Sandringham and Wolverton in 1886. Edward loved his racing, but shooting was his favourite outdoor sport (he was regarded as one of the best shots in England), and he was at his happiest when he was entertaining his shooting guests at Sandringham in the winter months. Sometimes these parties included the fourth Earl of Warwick's heir, Lord Brooke, who was a keen sportsman, and his pretty and well-proportioned wife, Frances, known to all as Daisy, who had once turned down a marriage proposal from Edward's youngest brother, Prince Leopold, Duke of Albany.

The Prince had attended Daisy's wedding in 1881 and had danced with her on occasions, but had never seemed to pay much attention to the bubbly blue-eyed blonde. Now the portly, but still predatory, Edward suddenly began to take an interest in the beguiling twenty-six-year-old Lady Brooke after she came to Marlborough House, one night in 1888, with a strange request.

Daisy's lover for the last two years had been the Prince's good friend, Lord Charles Beresford. When, however, Lord Charles unexpectedly fathered a child with his morally upright wife, he told Daisy that their affair was over. Furious at his rejection, she fired off a shocking letter to her former lover, telling him that one of her children was his and that he must leave his wife immediately. Unfortunately, the compromising missive was opened by Lady Charles, at which all hell was let loose. She gave it to the famous solicitor Charles Lewis, who wrote to Daisy, warning her to cease annoying his client. Daisy, now incandescent with rage, asked for her letter to be returned. Lewis refused, stating that it was the property of the addressee, Lord Charles. Terrified that her letter might fall into the wrong hands or that Lewis might publicize its scandalous contents, Daisy turned for help to the most influential person she knew, the Prince of Wales.

As the Prince stared across his study desk at his tearful and vulnerable visitor, he suddenly experienced the same sensation that had overtaken him the first time he set eyes on Lillie Langtry. It may have taken longer to ignite this particular spark, but Edward realized that he had actually fallen in love again. The perceptive Daisy, knowing that the way he looked at her was anything but avuncular, left, thinking that things would be very different in the future. She was right.

Edward went to see Lewis the next day, but the solicitor refused to release Daisy's letter. Lady Charles then informed Daisy, through Lewis, that she could have it back if she left London for the whole season. At this, Edward gave Lady Charles an ultimatum. If she did not give the letter back, she, rather than Daisy, would have to leave the capital. If she thought the Prince was bluffing, Lady Charles was wrong. She continued to hold on to the incriminating evidence, at which the Prince erased the Beresfords' names whenever they appeared on the list of a house party he was due to attend. Often he would suggest to his hosts that the Brookes should replace the Beresfords as guests. This harsh policy of social exclusion cost the Prince his friendship with Lord Charles, but it worked. Lady Charles withdrew all her threats and conditions. More important, Daisy was able to remain in London for the 1890 summer season, and thus to see a good deal more of the Prince.

Over the next nine years, Daisy played a similar role to that of her predecessor, Lillie Langtry. Indeeed, if it was possible, the Prince was more infatuated than he had been when the Jersey Lily entered his life. He even referred to his new conquest as his 'darling Daisy wife', and the pair were hardly ever apart during the early years of their relationship. They went to the races, holidayed in France (where the Prince travelled as Baron Renfrew, one of his more obscure titles), attended the same house parties, balls and social gatherings, and spent many weekends at Easton Lodge, the house in Essex which Daisy had inherited, as a child, from her grandfather, Viscount Maynard.

Daisy's husband, who became the fifth Earl of Warwick after his father's death in December 1893, did not turn to drink as had Edward Langtry. In fact, Brooke behaved immaculately and, like many other Victorian aristocrats, sought sexual satisfaction elsewhere. Princess Alexandra also handled her husband's new affair with her usual decorum. Yet, while she had tolerated Lillie and received her socially, Alix absolutely refused to entertain her husband's latest mistress (who, significantly, was seventeen years younger than the Queen) at Sandringham or Marlborough House. She had sided with Lady Charles Beresford, and was never to forgive Daisy for the very public way in which she had flaunted her relationship with Edward. The Princess had put up with the demure and respectful Lillie, but she had no time for the outspoken and self-assured Daisy, who, she believed, and with good reason, was dangerously indiscreet.

Alix's opinion that Daisy, who was justifiably known throughout society as 'the Babbling Brook', was unreliable was based on sound evidence. In the early stages of their relationship, Daisy's loose mouth had caused the Prince untold embarrassment and brought to public notice the biggest scandal of his life. Edward had been staying with the rich shipowner Arthur Wilson at his Italianate mansion, Tranby Croft, for Doncaster's St Leger meeting in September 1890. As part of the evening's entertainment, his host had organized a game of baccarat, of which the Prince was very fond; it was also illegal at the time. One of the guests, Sir William Gordon-Cumming, a most distinguished soldier, extraordinarily, had been caught cheating on two separate evenings. Without admitting guilt (some say he took the blame for the Prince, who was actually the culprit; or otherwise that he acted as he did so that the Prince's participation in illegal card games was not publicized), he signed a document stating that he would never play cards again. His fellow guests agreed to keep silent as their part of the bargain.

The sorry saga would never have seen the light of day if the Prince had not bumped into Daisy and her husband, who were travelling to Scotland to the funeral of her stepfather, the Earl of Rosslyn, at York railway station on his way home, and relayed to them the whole unfortunate tale. The Babbling Brook told all her relations about Sir William's problem and the story was soon all over London. Since the secrecy pact had been broken, Sir William, finding himself ostracized by society, instructed his solicitors to sue his accusers for libel.

The ensuing trial, which started on 1 June 1891, caused an unbelievable sensation. The Prince, as a witness, sat in the court for nine days under the gaze of huge crowds, who were appalled by the dissolute behaviour of the heir to the throne and his friends. When the Prince finally gave evidence, he was extremely unconvincing. In the end, Gordon-Cumming lost the action, but Edward was judged guilty in the people's eyes. The jury was booed, the Prince was hissed at Royal Ascot later in the month, and the newspapers had a field day, castigating Edward for his hedonistic pursuits. While the embattled Prince licked his wounds, Queen Victoria and Princess Alix were unsympathetic, and definitely not amused.

By 1897, the year of his mother's Diamond Jubilee, the Prince's ardour for Daisy was cooling. As usual, he started to sow his wild oats in other fields. In March 1898, Daisy, now thirty-six, gave birth to her third child. Her pregnancy had provided the perfect opportunity to finish her nine-year affair with the Prince. Two months before the birth, she had sat down and written two letters

– one to the Prince and the other to his wife – stressing that her relationship with Edward would now be strictly platonic. The Prince later told her that Alix had been moved to tears and was prepared to receive her in the future. Daisy could now relax, happy that Alix had, magnanimously, wiped the slate clean.

Daisy retired gracefully to pursue her interest in socialism, which had been burgeoning for some years. Sponsorship of good causes and an extravagant lifestyle meant that she and her husband were short of money after Edward's death in May 1910. On 31 July 1914, the day before war broke out in Europe,[5] an interim injunction was served on Daisy to prevent her from publishing Edward's love letters. Not long afterwards the action was stopped on condition that she destroyed all the correspondence. She was forced to hand over the letters, with which she had hoped to raise a much-needed £100,000, to George V's advisers. She eventually died on 26 July 1938 and was buried alongside her husband in Warwick Castle's family vault. Daisy, whose income had been a staggering £30,000 a year as a three-year-old child, left property worth only £37,000 to her surviving son.

The Prince and Princess of Wales, as was customary, spent Christmas 1898 and the Diamond Jubilee New Year at Sandringham. Alix seemed content, for at least the indiscreet Daisy was no longer on the scene, although the Prince was not slow in replacing her. Only a few months after he had separated from Daisy, the fifty-six-year-old Edward embarked on a passionate affair with Alice Keppel, often said to have been his greatest love.

It is not certain when Edward met Alice for the first time, but it was probably during the spring of 1898 when he was taking his annual holiday on the French Riviera. Alice, who was the youngest daughter (of eight; there was also one son) of a Scot, Sir William Edmonstone, had married the Hon. George Keppel, a son of the seventh Earl of Albemarle (see pages 78–9), in 1891. However, as the young couple were always short of money, she took a wealthy lover to ease their financial straits. His name was Ernest William

Beckett, later to become Lord Grimthorpe. Her first child, Violet, who was to gain notoriety for her lesbian relationship with the writer Vita Sackville-West (see Chapter Six), was born in 1894. Society gossip suggested that Violet was Beckett's daughter. So when the Prince first met Alice, he would have known that the twenty-nine-year-old baronet's daughter had an imperfect past.

Within a few months, Alice was established as the Prince's official mistress. She was pretty enough to interest the ageing Lothario sexually, but she was also amusing and prepared to put up with her short-tempered lover's increasingly curmudgeonly moods. In addition, she was an excellent bridge player and made a good partner for the Prince.

Alix, now well aware that her husband was incapable of fidelity, accepted his new mistress with bored resignation. The Princess reasoned that at least Alice was unlikely to attract scandal in the same way as her irresponsible predecessor, Daisy (who was by now Countess of Warwick). Indeed, Alix even saw the funny side of her portly and wheezing husband's latest amorous escapade. One day, at Sandringham, she could not contain her laughter when she saw an open carriage coming down the drive, containing Edward and Alice, who had also put on plenty of weight, sitting together like an old and very respectable married couple. The other injured party, George Keppel, strangely, almost seemed to revel in his wife's position as the future monarch's adulterous lover. Once, in the German spa of Baden-Baden, he was asked if he was related to the King's mistress. The genial George ignored the implied insult and simply laughed in reply.

When Queen Victoria died in 1901, Edward soon made it clear that, even as King, he had no intention of discarding Alice or consigning her to the background. On the contrary, she was a constant and important presence at court and at all the other big social occasions throughout his nine-year reign. Consequently, she and the Queen met on many occasions, but there was never any enmity between the two most important women in the King's life. Only when Edward, on his deathbed, summoned Alice, late at night and for the very last time, did Alix lose control of her emotions. When the King finally slipped into a coma and it was clear that the end was nigh, the Queen hissed to his doctor, Sir Frederick Laking: 'Get that woman away.' Alice Keppel, screaming hysterically, was dragged unceremoniously from the bedchamber. She never saw her royal lover alive again.

On the following day, Alice rushed to Marlborough House to sign the book of condolences, but orders had been given not to admit her. Seeing that the royal family were going to wash their hands of her, she told her friends the blatant lie that Alix had called her to the dying King's bed, wept with her and promised to look after her for the rest of her days. This ploy, however, did not change the new monarch's opinion of his father's mistress. George V, as puritanical as his father had been morally lax, let it be known that the Hon. Mrs George Keppel's time at court was well and truly over.

To avoid publicity, Alice and her family moved out of their home to stay with friends in Grafton Street. Thinking it better to leave England until the fuss subsided, she then undertook an extended tour of the Far East for two years. She and George moved to Italy in 1927, but returned to England during the Second World War. They went back to their villa near Florence in 1946, where, aged seventy-eight, Alice died just a year later. George, who never stopped loving the wife who was unfaithful to him for so long, lasted only two more months. Ironically, George V could not have been more wrong for, as we shall see, Alice Keppel's connection with the royal family turned out to be far from over.

Edward's constant womanizing, his three very public mistresses, the scandal of the Mordaunt divorce, the damaging Tranby Croft affair and a terrible fire at Sandringham in 1891, which destroyed fourteen rooms on the upper floor, were not the only problems that Alix had to endure during her long and difficult marriage. Speculation that her eldest son, Prince Albert Victor, Duke of Clarence and Avondale, was involved in an infamous homosexual ring was rife during his short life. Prince Eddy, as he was known, died suddenly, aged twenty-eight, at Sandringham on 14 January 1892 after catching a cold while out shooting, which developed into a fatal dose of influenza and pneumonia. Since that day, many more bizarre rumours have surfaced about the strange and backward young man who would have been king if he had lived.

The theory that Eddy was the notorious killer 'Jack the Ripper', who savagely murdered and disembowelled at least five prostitutes in Whitechapel in London's East End between August and November 1888, can certainly be discounted. The young Prince was provably out of London on three of the nights on which such killings occurred. Another extraordinary tale that did the rounds maintained that in 1885 Eddy secretly married, and then fathered a girl by, a London tobacco-shop worker, Annie Crook, who ended up in a lunatic asylum. This unlikely story also surely belongs in the realms of fantasy. The assertion relies entirely on the doubtful testimony of a man who claimed to be the illegitimate son of the painter Walter Sickert (also thought by some to have been the real 'Jack the Ripper') and Eddy's supposed daughter, Alice Margaret. As the so-called Joseph Sickert died in 1950 without leaving any concrete evidence to support his claim, it is safe to assume that he invented everything.

On the other hand, the rumour that Eddy was implicated in the Cleveland Street male brothel scandal of 1889 is based on altogether firmer ground. Eddy was engaged to Princess Mary of Teck, subsequently to marry his brother, George V, when he died, but various pieces of circumstantial evidence suggest that he may have had gay sexual experiences as a young man.

Homosexuality was rife on HMS *Bacchante*, the warship aboard which Eddy and his brother George spent three years from 1879 to 1882, according to the Reverend John Dalton, who had been chosen by the Prince of Wales to accompany his sons. Although he later married, Dalton was a closet homosexual and therefore presumably recognized danger signals when he requested the removal from the ship of an effeminate midshipman named Munro, who had started to take liberties with Eddy. A doctor's report that was unearthed at a later date indicates that Eddy caught venereal disease during his time at sea. He may have contracted the infection from a girl in one of their many ports of call, but a male shipmate could just as easily have been the carrier.

It may also be significant that the select group that lodged with Eddy at Bachelor's Cottage in Sandringham's grounds in the summer of 1883, for an intensive cramming session before going up to Cambridge, contained several homosexuals, including Henry Wilson, who was Eddie's best friend at Trinity, and who was later to become a prominent member of the college's secret society, The Apostles, an esoteric organization with a pronounced homosexual bias that advocated the ancient Greeks' philosophy of love.

Furthermore, the boys' tutor at Bachelor's Cottage, Virginia Woolf's cousin J. K. (Jim) Stephen, an exemplar of the Corinthian scholar-sportsman the Victorians admired so greatly, was a pronounced woman-hater. It is not known whether Eddy and Stephen, who later accompanied the Prince to Cambridge, had a physical relationship, but they were certainly extremely close. It may be a coincidence, but Stephen, who became mentally unstable, died in a lunatic asylum on 3 February 1892 after refusing to take food or drink for twenty days – that is, since he had heard of Eddy's unexpected death.

During his eighteen months at Cambridge, Eddy lived in a predominately homosexual environment. The openly gay A. C. Benson, later to find fame as a writer and as the Master of Magdalene College, was a fellow student and a regular visitor to Eddy's rooms in Nevile's Court. The young Prince also entertained the aesthete Lord Ronald Gower to dinner.[6] Gower, who was nearly twenty years older, made no secret of his sexual preference for young working-class men. Furthermore, Eddy often socialized with Oscar Browning, a flamboyant Fellow of King's College who had been sacked, when an Eton master, for his friendship with a pupil, the Hon. George Nathaniel Curzon, later to be Viceroy of India.[7] Reputedly, Browning rarely spent a night in his Cambridge rooms without a soldier, sailor or stable lad beside him.

Because he moved in homosexual circles at university, Eddy would have been well aware of the existence of establishments like the Cleveland Street brothel, and of the services such places offered. If he had visited 19 Cleveland Street himself, as the gossip at the time indicated, he must have been horrified to hear that a radical weekly, *The North London Press*, had run a story on 28 September 1889 claiming that 'the heir to a duke and the younger son of a duke' had paid for sex with young telegraph-delivery boys and other male prostitutes at the premises, near London's Tottenham Court Road.

Nearly two months later, on 16 November, the weekly's editor, Ernest Parke, published another article, naming the aristocrats as the seventh Duke of Grafton's heir, Henry FitzRoy, Earl of Euston, and Lord Arthur Somerset, the third son of the eighth Duke of Beaufort. Eddy knew Lord Arthur well. He was an equerry to his father and had charge of the Prince of Wales's stables. The piece continued that the two men had been allowed to leave the country to cover up the involvement of a person 'more distinguished and more highly placed'. Soon the whole of London knew that the prominent individual to whom Parke had referred was Prince Eddy.

Lord Arthur had certainly gone to the Continent, but Parke was wrong to suggest that Euston had also fled. On the contrary, the Earl was still in England; in fact, he had already instructed his lawyers to hire a leading barrister, Sir Charles Russell, QC, and sue the *Press*'s crusading editor for libel. Euston and the packed court had to endure graphic descriptions of the peculiar homosexual acts in which he was alleged to have indulged. But Russell quickly pulled holes in the testimony of the six unreliable defence witnesses, who swore that they had regularly seen the Earl in the brothel.

In the end, the jury chose to believe Euston's story that he had entered the premises only once, believing it to be a club where female strippers performed, and had left five minutes later when he realized his mistake. Most of his acquaintances thought that Euston – who had once been married to an actress, later found to be a bigamist, but was well known to the capital's gay community – was, at the best, being economical with the truth. The judge, however, formed a different opinion. He completely exonerated the middle-aged peer and sentenced Parke to twelve months in prison.

By the end of 1889, rumours of Eddy's involvement in the scandal were at their height. Informed gossip even suggested that he might be brought back from a trip to India to face trial. To his parents' horror, *The New York Times*'s London correspondent wrote that there was 'a general conviction that this long-necked, narrow-headed young dullard was mixed up in the scandal'. So were the revered American journal, several British papers and the London cognoscenti right to aver that Eddy was inextricably involved?

The letters that Lord Arthur Somerset sent to his friend and fellow courtier, the Hon. Reginald Brett, later the second Viscount Esher, suggest that Eddy certainly visited Cleveland Street. 'I cannot see what good I could do Prince Eddy if I went into Court,' Lord Arthur wrote incriminatingly from the safety of the Continent to Brett, who, like his friend, had homosexual inclinations. Moreover, Lord Arthur's solicitor, Arthur Newton, warned the authorities that 'a very distinguished person will be involved PAV', if his client came to trial. It is not hard to work out that the incriminating initials – PAV – very probably stand for Prince Albert Victor. Of course, none of this evidence proves that Eddy had homosexual tendencies, but it is fair to say that it is more likely than not that the ineffectual and rather stupid eldest son of the future Edward VII indulged in sexual games of one sort or another with young male prostitutes at 19 Cleveland Street.

Sandringham has clearly seen its fair share of scandal during the royal family's tenure of nearly 150 years, but one more twist remains in the Norfolk shooting lodge's rich and varied history. Park House in Sandringham's grounds was leased to Lord Fermoy between the wars, and his daughter, the Hon. Frances Roche, was born there in 1936. In 1955, by a strange quirk of fate, Frances returned to live there. She was now Viscountess Althorp, the pretty young wife of Earl Spencer's heir. Frances gave birth to five children, four of whom survived, while she was in residence at Park House. The youngest of her three daughters, Diana, was later to marry Charles, Prince of Wales, at the 'fairy-tale' wedding that captivated the world on that memorable summer afternoon of 29 July 1981.

It is now well known that this seemingly idyllic union soon ran into trouble. The Prince and his young and innocent bride quickly found that they had little in common, and gradually began to drift apart. In 1992 the sensational book by Andrew Morton, *Diana: Her True Story*, which (as was only revealed after her death in 1997) was published with the Princess of Wales's collaboration and blessing, confirmed the widely held belief that her marriage had been in desperate trouble for the past decade. But the principal reason for Diana's fury and unhappiness was Charles's categorical refusal to give up his old lover, the then Camilla Parker Bowles, who is now his second wife. It could hardly be more ironic that the woman who hastened the break-up of the marriage of the Prince and Princess of Wales is the great-granddaughter of Alice Keppel, the last mistress of Prince Charles's great-great-grandfather, Sandringham's first royal owner, King Edward VII. What is more, Alice's daughter Sonia,[8] Camilla's grandmother, was born in 1900, fairly early during Alice's time as mistress to Prince Edward, casting enough doubt on Sonia's paternity to satisfy gossip-mongers, and more recently fuelling speculation that Camilla and Prince Charles might be cousins.

Chapter Notes

CHAPTER ONE – ROYAL SCOTS

1. So nicknamed from a favourite racehorse of his; a part of the Newmarket racecourse is still called the Rowley Mile.
2. William Augustus, Duke of Cumberland (1721–65), the third son of George II and Queen Caroline. See also Chapter Four.
3. In 1536 Parliament, acting on the King's wishes, declared Elizabeth and her half-sister Mary (Henry's daughter by Catherine of Aragon) illegitimate, in favour of Henry's son by Jane Seymour, the future Edward VI. See also pages 64–5.
4. Huntley (which is also spelled Huntly) died of apoplexy after being captured; his son and others of his relations were executed.
5. At that time an independent duchy, now a part of France, to which it was ceded by Italy in the nineteenth century.
6. The document's existence is disputed, for the signed bond has never come to light.
7. Mary's complicity in plots against Elizabeth could not easily be established, but she was implicated in the Catholic 'Babington Plot' of 1586 by the English queen's Secretary of State, Sir Francis Walsingham.
8. Queen Victoria bore Prince Albert nine children, four sons and five daughters.
9. Robert Cecil, third Marquess of Salisbury (1830–1903), was Prime Minister three times between 1885 and 1902. He was the last Prime Minister to govern from the House of Lords, and the expression 'Bob's your uncle', meaning 'everything is complete', is said to derive from Salisbury's promotion of his nephew, Arthur Balfour, to the post of Chief Secretary for Ireland in 1887; Balfour also succeeded Salisbury as Prime Minister in 1902.
10. Osborne House and its estate of nearly 1,000 acres were bought privately by Queen Victoria in 1845. Edward VII, who preferred Sandringham, presented Osborne and most of its estate to the nation in 1902, the year his mother died; it is now in the stewardship of English Heritage.
11. *Regina et Imperatrix* – Queen and Empress.

CHAPTER TWO – CHATSWORTH

1. She was born Elizabeth Hardwick in 1521, and in about 1534 married a Robert Barlow, who was if anything even younger than she. He died a year later, their marriage unconsummated owing to their youth and his sickliness.
2. The Tower of London, the fortress palace begun in the eleventh century, was notorious as a state prison from the fifteenth to the mid-eighteenth centuries.
3. Younger sister of the unfortunate Lady Jane Grey, who in 1553 was briefly Queen on the death of Edward VI, but was forced to abdicate after nine days, imprisoned and later executed.
4. See page 21. In 1567 Mary had effectively been forced to abdicate the throne of Scotland in favour of her son, James VI. Escaping to England, she threw herself on Elizabeth's mercy, only to find herself kept under a kind of permanent house arrest. Apparently implicated in a plot against the English Queen, she was executed in 1587.
5. William Cecil, first Baron Burghley, was for forty years one of Elizabeth's most trusted advisers in matters of state. Immensely powerful, he was appointed Lord High Treasurer in 1572, an office he held until his death in 1598.
6. Devonshire was by no means the only nobleman to be advanced for what was, in effect, treason against his rightful king,

James II. The great military commander, John Churchill, first Duke of Marlborough, also benefited from siding with 'Dutch William' in the 'Bloodless Revolution' of 1688.

7. General Sir Charles Grey had distinguished himself in British service in the American War of Independence and in the long-running wars with France. He was created first Baron Grey in 1801, and first Earl Grey in 1806. His son Charles therefore gained the courtesy title of Viscount Howick in 1806, before inheriting his father's earldom on the latter's death in 1807.

8. In fact, this phrase is generally held to have been coined by the English radical and Quaker politician John Bright (1811–89) rather later in the nineteenth century.

9. It is extraordinary how often France figures in the history of the British aristocracy as a haven for those fleeing scandal and, sometimes, the law.

10. The ninth Duke of Devonshire had been Governor-General of Canada from 1916 to 1921; Macmillan had been his ADC from 1919 to 1920. By a curious coincidence, one of Devonshire's predecessors as Governor-General had been the fourth Earl Grey.

11. One of the very few hereditary creations since the introduction of the Life Peerages Act in 1958.

Chapter Three – Hampton Court

1. Catherine had borne Henry a daughter, Mary (later Mary I), in 1516, the only child of their marriage.

2. Percy was chided by Cardinal Wolsey for failing to tell either the King or his father of the betrothal; in the end, his father refused permission for the marriage to go ahead.

3. The secession of the English faith from Rome and the establishment of the Protestant Church of England have their origins not just in the Reformation, but in Henry's determination to be divorced from his first wife. The Pope continued to maintain that Catherine's marriage remained valid, despite Cranmer's edict to the contrary.

4. The permanent gallows west of London as the city was then defined, near the site of the present-day Marble Arch.

5. The original form of the game (lawn tennis was not invented until the nineteenth century), played with a solid ball on an indoor court. Also called royal tennis and, in the USA, court tennis. The name derives from Spanish *real*, royal.

6. London was very much smaller in the sixteenth century than it is today, when many places once outside the city now lie within its boundaries.

7. A granddaughter of the second Duke of Norfolk, and niece of the third Duke, she was also a cousin of Anne Boleyn.

8. Oatlands Palace, near Weybridge, originally a manor house which Henry took over in 1537 and developed into a large palace. It remained in royal use until 1650 when, following the end of the Civil War and the execution of Charles I, it was demolished.

9. Lascelles had a sister who was a chambermaid in the Duchess's household, and thus knew of Catherine's past. Lascelles himself was an ardent Protestant reformer, opposed to the Queen's Catholic faith, and it is said that this, rather than personal animosity, was the motive behind his visit to Cranmer.

10. Near Isleworth, and at that time an abbey which the Crown had taken over following the dissolution of the monasteries. A new house was begun on the site in 1547 and substantially remodelled in the eighteenth century; it became the property of the Earls (now Dukes) of Northumberland in 1604, and remains so. Henry VIII's body was taken to Syon House after his death in 1547; it is said that during the night the coffin burst open and that dogs 'licked up the remains', an event held by some to be God's punishment for the King's desecration of the abbey.

11. At this time the Percy family held the earldom of Northumberland, but in 1551 John Dudley, Earl of Warwick, was created first Duke of Northumberland. He was executed for treason on the accession of Mary I, and attainted; the earldom of Northumberland held by the Percys was raised to a dukedom in the eighteenth century.
12. Catherine Parr (b. 1512) became Henry VIII's sixth and last wife (and thus Elizabeth's stepmother) in 1543, and married Seymour after the King's death in 1547. She died in childbirth the following year.
13. Stuart became a powerful political influence on the young King, who richly rewarded his favourite with property and titles, including that of first Duke of Lennox.
14. Frances was a granddaughter of the first Lord Blantyre, and distantly connected to the Royal House of Stuart.
15. Charles Stuart, third Duke of Richmond and sixth Duke of Lennox, yet another kinsman of the King. He died from drowning in 1672, but 'La Belle Stuart', as she was known at court, survived him for another thirty years.
16. The term 'Orangeman' for a member of the Orange Order, a Protestant political association in Ireland, especially Northern Ireland, derives from William's Dutch title.
17. The Act of Settlement of 1701 excluded the Roman Catholic Stuarts from the succession. As a result, the Elector of Hanover, a great-grandson of James I through a Protestant line of descent, succeeded to the throne as George I on the death of Queen Anne in 1714.
18. Buckingham House (now Palace), built for the Duke of Buckingham in 1703, did not become one of the royal family's London homes until 1762, when George III bought it. Queen Victoria made it the principal royal residence in London in 1837.

Chapter Four – Fort Belvedere

1. Cumberland's eldest brother, Frederick, Prince of Wales, died, aged forty-four, supposedly as the result of being struck by a cricket ball. Frederick's son therefore succeeded his grandfather, George II, on the latter's death in 1760, reigning as George III. See also pages 79–80.
2. By a bizarre coincidence, the house was that of Ernest Simpson's sister.
3. The singer and actress Jane Birkin is a great-niece of Freda Dudley Ward.
4. They eventually divorced in 1931, and in 1937 Freda married a Spanish nobleman, the Marques de Casa Maury, from whom she was divorced in 1954. She died in 1983, aged eighty-eight.
5. She pronounced her first name in the Spanish fashion, as 'Tel-ma'.
6. Mother of the famous contemporary painter, actress, writer and designer, Gloria Vanderbilt, who was thus Thelma's niece.
7. Although American born, Channon (1897–1958) studied at Oxford and became a British citizen. Elected a Conservative MP, he held several junior ministerial posts during the Second World War, and was knighted. He is principally remembered for his diaries, which in unedited form ran to some 30 volumes and 3 million words. Initially disapproving, by 1936 he admitted he had grown to like and admire Wallis Simpson.
8. Born in 1911, son of the third Aga Khan, he eventually married, as his second wife, the film star Rita Hayworth, and became Vice-President of the General Assembly of the United Nations. He was killed in a car accident in Paris in 1960. His son by his first marriage is the present Aga Khan.
9. The fourth son (of five) and fifth child (of six) of George V and Queen Mary, Prince George, Duke of Kent, was born in 1902, and married Princess Marina of Greece and Denmark after a long string of affairs with both women and men, including Noël Coward. He was killed in a wartime flying accident in 1942 while serving with the RAF.

10 The former Lady Elizabeth Bowes-Lyon, wife of Edward's younger brother, Albert, Duke of York (later King George VI). The Duchess would become famous the world over as Queen Elizabeth, the Queen Mother. She died in 2002, aged 101.

11. The British press, fearful of the country's severe libel laws, and in any case given, in those days, to a respectful attitude towards royalty, steered clear of printing anything about the King that might be considered controversial. Many British journalists undoubtedly knew the truth about Edward and Mrs Simpson, but did not report the affair in newspapers.

12. A lawyer by training, Monckton (1891–1965) became Attorney-General to the Duchy of Cornwall (one of the Prince of Wales's titles is Duke of Cornwall) in 1932. He subsequently rose to high political office, and was created Viscount Monckton of Brenchley in 1957.

13. One American journalist, anxious to get the news back to his paper in the States and so beat his rivals, but fearful that his scoop might be leaked, announced the news of Wallis Simpson's divorce in a telegram that read 'King's Moll Renoed in Wolsey's Home Town.' People could get quick divorces in the city of Reno, Nevada (and still can); Cardinal Wolsey (see pages 58–9) was born in Ipswich.

14. Feelings ran high in the Dominions. For instance, the then Governor-General of Canada, Lord Tweedsmuir (better known as the writer John Buchan), informed the British government that the Canadian people were bitterly opposed to the King marrying the twice-divorced Mrs Simpson.

15. In fact, Edward VIII and two of his brothers, the Duke of York and the Duke of Kent, all had George as a forename; in the latter's case it was his first name.

16. It has, however, long been generally believed that both the Duke and Duchess of Windsor were, if only until the outbreak of the Second World War, admirers of Hitler, and also of the Fascist Spanish dictator General Francisco Franco.

CHAPTER FIVE – INVERARAY CASTLE

1. According to other versions of the story, the Earl of Argyll had been given the right by the King to decide whom the infant heiress was to marry and had settled on his brother, Sir John. He sent Campbell of Inverliver and his sons to fetch her from Cawdor Castle in order that he might supervise her upbringing and education, but after they had set off back with the child, her mother called for her brother and his men, who pursued them.

2. Another account has it that Inverliver's sons rode on, carrying a bundle of rags wrapped up in a child's shawls as a decoy.

3. Although Presbyterianism was the established faith in Scotland, most of the Highlands was still Catholic.

4. The full title of the current Duke of Argyll, the thirteenth and Scotland's most senior peer, who was born in 1968, is something of a mouthful: 'The most high, potent and noble prince his Grace Torquhil Ian Campbell, Duke of Argyll, Marquess of Kintyre and Lorne, Earl of Argyll, Campbell and Cowal, Viscount Lochawe and Glenyla, Lord Campbell, Lorne, Kintyre, Inveraray, Mull, Morven and Tyrie in the peerage of Scotland, Baron Sundbridge of Coombank and Baron Hamilton of Hameldon in the peerage of Great Britain, Duke of Argyll in the peerage of the United Kingdom, Baronet of Nova Scotia, Hereditary Master of the Royal Household in Scotland, Hereditary Keeper of the Great Seal of Scotland, Hereditary Keeper of the royal castles of Dunoon, Carrick, Dunstaffnage and Tarbet, Admiral of the Western coasts and isles, and Chief of the Honourable Clan Campbell, MacCailein Mor.'

5. By 2004 Campbell was the sixth most common surname listed by the General Register Office for Scotland.

CHAPTER SIX – SISSINGHURST CASTLE

1. The Women's Land Army, whose members were usually known as 'Land Girls', was formed in 1917 to help the war effort by using women to replace men who worked the land but who had gone to the front. It was re-formed when the Second World War broke out in 1939.
2. The Great War, as the First World War was commonly known then, finally ended when an armistice was declared on 11 November 1918.

CHAPTER SEVEN – CLIVEDEN

1. See also pages 79–80.
2. She succeeded her husband as Conservative MP for Plymouth in 1919, when he inherited the viscountcy and went to the Lords.
3. Fairfax was the commander-in-chief of the Parliamentary forces in the Civil War from 1645 to 1650, when he was succeeded by Cromwell. He refused to sign the order committing Charles I to execution, and later worked for the return of Charles II.
4. The influential Edward Hyde, first Earl of Clarendon (1609–74), a leading politician, lawyer and historian, held many important court and political posts; as Lord High Chancellor from 1660–7 he was effectively head of Charles II's government.
5. Director-General of MI5 from 1956–1965. According to Peter Wright in *Spycatcher* (1987), his controversial account of his time at MI5, Hollis was a Soviet double agent and the so-called 'fifth man'.
6. John Vassall was the Naval Attaché at the British Embassy in Moscow in the 1950s. A homosexual, he was compromised by the Soviets and blackmailed into spying for them, eventually providing them with thousands of classified documents. He was arrested and charged with spying in 1962, and sentenced to eighteen years in prison; however, he served only ten, and died in 1996, aged seventy-two. The failure to detect him was a cause célèbre with the press at the time, and led to a tribunal that ultimately exonerated the government.
7. Wilson had become head of the Labour Party, and thus Leader of the Opposition, following the sudden death, at the age of fifty-six, of Hugh Gaitskell.
8. As had been the case with Edward VIII's affair with Wallis Simpson (see Chapter Four), the Continental press had been less inhibited about reporting the Profumo scandal than its British counterpart.
9. At the same time, Denning was also investigating the identity of the 'headless man' in the Argyll divorce case – see pages 116–17.

CHAPTER EIGHT – MADRESFIELD COURT

1. Although christened Hugh Richard Arthur Grosvenor, the second Duke of Westminster was generally known among his circle as 'Bendor' or 'Benny', after a famous racehorse, Bend Or, owned by his father. The name comes from the 'bend or' (a broad diagonal bar, coloured gold, running across the shield from top right to bottom left) on his family coat of arms, a heraldic device or 'ordinary' which the Grosvenors were alleged to have appropriated from another aristocratic family.
2. Alfred Duff Cooper, later Sir Alfred, and later still first Viscount Norwich (1890–1954), was a diplomat, politician and writer; he served in Churchill's wartime Cabinet until becoming Ambassador to France in 1944, and among other books wrote a remarkable autobiography, *Old Men Forget*. He married the beautiful and eccentric Lady Diana Manners (1892–1986), youngest daughter of the eighth Duke of Rutland, in 1919, but had numerous affairs. His wife refused to call herself Lady Norwich after her husband was raised to the peerage in 1952, claiming that it sounded too much like 'porridge', and took an advertisement in a newspaper announcing that she would retain her previous style as Lady Diana Cooper.

3. Waugh's first novel, *Decline and Fall,* was published in 1928, three years after he left Oxford.

4. Identified by Alec Waugh as the character Hamish Lennox in his brother Evelyn's autobiographical *A Little Learning.* Alastair Graham was in a sense Waugh's first publisher, having privately printed his book, *P. R. B.: An Essay on the Pre-Raphaelite Brotherhood* in 1926.

CHAPTER NINE – POWDERHAM CASTLE

1. Legend has it that when he was five his piano teacher was none other than Wolfgang Amadeus Mozart – at the time nine years old.

2. He claimed to have written it in a single sitting of three days and two nights. It was subsequently translated into English – by whom is uncertain but the Reverend Samuel Henley has been suggested – and published under the title *An Arabian Tale from an Unpublished Manuscript.*

CHAPTER TEN – BROCKET HALL

1. Wife of the first Earl Spencer and forebear of Diana, Princess of Wales.

2. The marriage hardly lasted a year, but Annabella did give birth to his daughter, Augusta Ada, who, as Lady Lovelace, was assistant to Charles Babbage, credited with having invented the computer, and is said to have been the first computer programmer. After the break-up of his marriage, Byron went on to have, or to resume, a number of liaisons, including, it is said, one with his half-sister Augusta, and one with a Greek boy.

3. Tuthill was also medical adviser to the literary brother-and-sister couple Charles and Mary Lamb (no relation), both of whom suffered from varying degrees of mental instability (indeed, Mary killed their mother in a fit of madness and was only saved from incarceration in Bedlam by her brother, who appointed himself her

guardian). They are best known for their *Tales from Shakespeare.*

4. Oedema, probably linked to liver and/or kidney failure brought on by excessive drinking.

5. Later to become the home of Lord Mountbatten.

CHAPTER ELEVEN – ICKWORTH

1. A part-time military organization raised locally in Ireland in 1778–9 to maintain law and order and guard against invasion while regular troops were fighting the War of Independence in America; it later became involved in parliamentary reform.

2. His first son, William, died young.

3. Especially well known is his *The Castle of Otranto* (1764), said to be the first true gothic novel.

4. Johnson held the family in some affection, though far from uncritically, acknowledging the Herveys' propensity for 'vice'. Of his friend the Hon. Henry Hervey, third son of the first Earl, the good Doctor commented that he was 'a vicious man but kind to me. If you call a dog *Hervey,* I shall love him.'

5. Henry, who was created first Baron Holland of Foxley in 1763, married – indeed, eloped with – Lady Georgina Carolina Lennox (daughter of the second Duke of Richmond and Lennox), some seventeen years his junior, in 1744. The second of their three sons was the Whig statesman Charles James Fox.

6. Mary Wortley Montagu is credited with the comment, alluding to John Hervey, that 'The world consists of men, women and Herveys.' (Lord Chesterfield is supposed to have made a very similar remark – with the fourth Earl in mind.)

7. It is said that the surprising number of Hotel Bristols scattered across Europe were named in his honour.

8. Frederick William John Hervey was third Marquess of Bristol, and, because he had only daughters, his nephew, Frederick William Fane Hervey was fourth

Marquess. He too only had daughters, so
the title of fifth Marquess of Bristol went
to his youngest brother, Herbert Arthur
Robert Hervey. His only child, Victor
Frederick Cochrane Hervey, the sixth
Marquess, was born in 1915.

1. He was the son of Emily, Lady Cowper
   (later Lady Palmerston), who was Lord
   Melbourne's sister, 'remarkable . . . but not
   chaste' (see page 204).
2. Major-General Sir Henry Ponsonby,
   Private Secretary to Queen Victoria from
   1870 until his death in 1895.
3. Widow of Lieutenant-Colonel Lord
   Adolphus Vane-Tempest, a younger son of
   the third Marquess of Londonderry.
4. Later to be the father of Lord
   Mountbatten, and grandfather of Prince
   Philip, Duke of Edinburgh, Prince Louis
   changed his family's name from von
   Battenberg to Mountbatten during the
   First World War, King George V having
   changed the royal family's name from
   Saxe-Coburg and Gotha to Windsor in
   1917; later, Lord Mountbatten persuaded
   his nephew, Prince Philip, to change his
   surname, also to Mountbatten, from its
   original Schleswig-Holstein-Sonderburg-
   Glücksburg. As to Jeanne-Marie Langtry,
   Prince Louis (who became an Admiral of

the Fleet and first Marquess of Milford
Haven) paid money to support her (it
would have been profitable to have
threatened to name him, as he would have
paid for the sake of his social reputation
and naval career). Lord Mountbatten later
acknowledged Jeanne-Marie to have been
his father's daughter. If this is true, she
would have been an aunt of Prince Philip
and, by marriage, of the Queen.
5. Germany declared war on Russia on 1
   August; Britain joined the war three days
   later.
6. Benson is probably best remembered
   today as the author of the words to the
   patriotic song 'Land of Hope and Glory'.
   The homosexual aesthete Lord Ronald
   (Leveson-) Gower, a younger son of the
   Duke of Sutherland, was a sculptor, writer,
   critic and politician; his friend Oscar
   Wilde used aspects of his character in *The
   Picture of Dorian Gray* (1891). See also
   page 113.
7. Curzon was given a barony (as Lord
   Curzon of Kedleston) of the Irish peerage
   on his appointment as Viceroy in 1898; he
   was created first Marquess Curzon of
   Kedleston in 1921, the most senior of
   several titles he held by the time of his
   death in 1925.
8. Sonia Keppel's older sister, and thus
   Camilla's great-aunt, was Violet Trefusis –
   see Chapter Six.

Bibliography and Sources

ALEXANDER, BOYD *England's Wealthiest Son: A Study of William Beckford* (Centaur) 1962

AMOS, WILLIAM *The Originals: Who's Really Who in Fictions* (Jonathan Cape) 1985

ARGYLL, MARGARET, DUCHESS OF *Forget Not: Her Autobiography* (W. H. Allen) 1975

ARONSON, THEO *The King in Love: Edward VII's Mistresses: Lillie Langtry, Daisy Warwick, Alice Keppel and Others* (HarperCollins) 1988
– *Prince Eddy and the Homosexual Underworld* (John Murray) 1994

BECKFORD, WILLIAM *Vathek: An Arabian Tale from an Unpublished Manuscript* (translated, with Beckford's help, by the Rev. Samuel Henley) 1786

BRADFORD, SARAH *Elizabeth: A Biography of Her Majesty the Queen* (William Heinemann) 1996

BRANDRETH, GILES *Philip and Elizabeth: Portrait of a Marriage* (Century) 2004

BROWN, IVOR *Balmoral: The History of a Home* (Collins) 1955

BUCHAN, JOHN *The Massacre of Glencoe* (Peter Davies) 1933

CASTLE, CHARLES *The Duchess Who Dared: Margaret, Duchess of Argyll* (Sidgwick & Jackson) 1994

CHAMBERS, JAMES *Palmerston: The People's Darling* (John Murray) 2004

COWLES, VIRGINIA *Edward VII and His Circle* (Hamish Hamilton) 1956

DOUGLAS-HOME, WILLIAM (ed.) and BROWNE, JENNIFER *The Prime Ministers: Stories and Anecdotes from No. 10* (W. H. Allen) 1987

DUNN, SHEILA *Strange Tales of Hampton Court* (Lanthorn) 1985

FARINGTON, JOSEPH *The Diary of Joseph Farington* (1793 to 1821) (Yale University Press) 16 volumes, 1978–84

FOREMAN, AMANDA *Georgiana, Duchess of Devonshire* (HarperCollins) 1998

FRASER, ANTONIA *Mary Queen of Scots* (Weidenfeld & Nicolson) 1969
– *The Six Wives of Henry VIII* (Weidenfeld & Nicolson) 1992
– (ed.) *The Lives of the King and Queens of England* (Weidenfeld & Nicolson) 1988; reissued 1999

HARRIS, FRANK *My Life and Loves* (4 volumes, 1922–7) (Corgi) 1967

HIBBERT, CHRISTOPHER *Elizabeth I: A Personal History of The Virgin Queen* (Penguin) 1992

HYDE, H. MONTGOMERY *The Cleveland Street Scandal* (W. H. Allen) 1976

KEELER, CHRISTINE *Scandal* (Xanadu) 1984
– with Douglas Thompson *The Truth At Last: My Story* (Sidgwick & Jackson) 2001

KRAY, CHARLIE and FRY, COLIN *Doing the Business: Inside the Violent Empire of the Krays* (Smith Gryphon) 1994

LAMONT-BROWN, RAYMOND *John Brown: Queen Victoria's Highland Servant* (Sutton Publishing, 2000

LANGTRY, LILLIE *The Days I Knew* (Hutchinson) 1925

LAW, ERNEST *The History of Hampton Court* (3 volumes, 1885–91)

LEES-MILNE, JAMES *William Beckford* (Century) 1990

LONGFORD, ELIZABETH *Victoria, RI* (Weidenfeld & Nicolson) 1964

MORTON, ANDREW *Diana: Her True Story* (Michael O'Mara Books) 1992

NICOLSON, NIGEL *Portrait of a Marriage: Vita Sackville-West and Harold Nicolson* (Weidenfeld & Nicolson) 1973
– (ed.) *The Harold Nicolson Diaries: 1907–1963* (Phoenix) 2005

NORTON, RICHTOR (articles on website) 'William Beckford: The Fool of Fonthill', www.infopt.demon.co.uk/beckfor1.htm
– 'Homosexuality in Eighteenth-Century England: John, Lord Hervey: The Third Sex', www.infopt.demon.co.uk/hervey.htm

PARRIS, MATTHEW *Great Parliamentary Scandals: Five Centuries of Calumny, Smear and Innuendo* (Robson Books) 1995

PONSONBY, ARTHUR *Henry Ponsonby: His Life and Times* (Macmillan) 1930

RHODES-JAMES, ROBERT *Bob Boothby: A Portrait* (Hodder & Stoughton) 1991

ROSE, NORMAN *Harold Nicolson* (Cape) 2005

RUFFER, JONATHAN GARNIER *The Big Shots: Edwardian Shooting Parties* (Debrett) 1977; revised edition (Quiller Press) 1989, 2003

ST AUBYN, GILES *Edward VII: Prince and King* (Collins) 1979

SANDRINGHAM ESTATE OFFICE *Sandringham* 1996

STARKEY, DAVID *Six Wives: The Queens of Henry VIII* (Vintage) 2004

STRICKLAND, AGNES *Lives of the Queens of England* (reprint, Chivers) 1972

SYKES, CHRISTOPHER *Evelyn Waugh: A Biography* (Collins) 1975

TYRREL, REBECCA *Camilla: An Intimate Portrait* (Short Books) 2004

VICTORIA, QUEEN OF GREAT BRITAIN, ed. HELPS, SIR ARTHUR *Leaves from the Journal of Our Life in the Highlands from 1848 to 1861* (Smith Elder) 1868

WILLIAMS, DOROTHY E. *The Lygons of Madresfield Court* (Logaston Press) 2001

ZIEGLER, PHILIP *Melbourne: A Biography of William Lamb, 2nd Viscount Melbourne* (Random House) 1976
– *King Edward VIII* (Sutton Publishing) 2001

ENTRIES IN VOLUMES OF:
the *Almanach de Gotha*; *Burke's Peerage, Baronetage and Knightage*; *Debrett's Peerage and Baronetage*; *Debrett's People of Today*; *The Dictionary of National Biography*; *Who's Who*; *Who Was Who*

NEWSPAPERS, MAGAZINES:
The Daily Mail, The Daily Telegraph, The Economist, The Guardian, Hello!, The New York Times, The Sunday Telegraph, The Sunday Times, The Times, The Yorkshire Post

INTERNET SITES:
Britannia Biographies (www.britannia.com/bios); LoveToKnow Free Online Encyclopedia (www.1911encyclopedia.org); thePeerage.com (www.thepeerage.com); Wikipedia The Free Encyclopedia (en.wikipedia.org)

Index